Adult Learning in America

Eduard Lindeman and His Agenda for Lifelong Education

by

DAVID W. STEWART

with Foreword by
Malcolm Knowles

ROBERT E. KRIEGER PUBLISHING COMPANY
MALABAR, FLORIDA
1987

Original Edition 1987

Printed and Published by
ROBERT E. KRIEGER PUBLISHING COMPANY, INC.
KRIEGER DRIVE
MALABAR, FL 32950

Library of Congress Cataloging-in-Publication Data

Stewart, David Wood, 1929–
  Adult learning in America.

  Bibliography: p.
  Includes index.
  1. Adult education—United States. 2. Continuing
education—United States. 3. Lindeman, Eduard.
I. Title.
LC5251.S73 1987   374'.973   86-10465
ISBN 0-89874-936-0

10 9 8 7 6 5 4 3 2

To
CAMILLA WOOD
My Favorite Lifelong Learner

Contents

Illustrations

Foreword

Eduard C. Lindeman was my first mentor. I therefore have a very personal interest in the publication of this book, and I am grateful to David Stewart for making this fascinating and influential life available for those not fortunate enough to have known him.

I first met Lindeman when I became an administrative assistant on the state staff of the National Youth Administration of Massachusetts in the fall of 1935. My chief responsibility was to organize the "related training" program for unemployed youth between the ages of eighteen and twenty-five. I got the job, I think, because the federal policies required that a youth between those ages must be on the staff in each state. The state director was having a tough time finding someone in that age group who knew anything about training (the only job open). I was twenty-two and had several years of experience as a volunteer group leader in a settlement house while at Harvard. But my main qualification must have been my age. Incidentally, my opposite number in the Texas NYA was Lyndon Johnson, who had been trained to be a teacher.

Lindeman had just become Director of Training and Recreation Projects for the Works Progress Administration, and one of his responsibilities was supervising the training operations of the NYA in the various states. Soon after starting in this position I got a call from Lindeman inviting me to have dinner with him—an event that was repeated several times a year for the next several years; he preferred to do business in a comfortable setting. We discussed my plans for launching a program of courses to improve the employability of the youth, who worked half time and studied their "related training" the other half. The thing I remember most vividly about this first encounter was the intensity with which Lindeman listened to me; his face—particularly his eyes—was a classic study in concentration.

In subsequent meetings I experienced engaging with him in a mutual exploration of the meaning of adult education, its broad social aims, the unique characteristics of young adults as learners, and the methods of learning that were most effective with adults. What I had initially perceived to be a "holding job" (my career plan was to become a foreign service officer) gradually became a professional commitment with deep implications for the welfare of society. This was the result not of any pressure from Lindeman, but of the process of inquiry in which he engaged me. So when the State Department notified me in 1938 that there were now openings in the foreign service, I replied that I had changed my career plans: I was now an adult educator. Of course, other factors influenced this decision—the caliber of people such as Lindeman, Harry and Bonaro Overstreet, Morse Cartwright, and James Truslow Adams, whom I met at national conferences; but, most of all, the satisfaction and excitement I was experiencing in being an adult educator.

I had heard people talk about Lindeman's 1926 book *The Meaning of Adult Education*, but I was unable to get a copy; it was out of print. One day I mentioned this to Lindeman, and the next time we met he had a copy for me that he had retrieved from a friend in another part of the country. I was so excited in reading it that I couldn't put it down; I can't remember getting any sleep that night. It became my chief source of inspiration and ideas for a quarter of a century. I still reread it at least once a year for the inspiration of seeing ideas that were formulated before 1926 that have only in recent times been validated by research. I regard Lindeman as the prophet of modern adult educational theory.

My last association with Lindeman was in 1952, shortly before his death, when, as the newly appointed administrative coordinator of the Adult Education Association of the U.S.A., I spent an evening discussing my plans for the new organization with him. He supported my plans to experiment with a nonhierarchical administrative structure and open membership—which he called organizational democracy. The social philosopher in him led him to express the hope that the AEA would provide leadership in gearing the adult education movement to address societal goals and issues, and not get bogged down in organizational maintenance.

In reading the manuscript of this book I learned many new facts about Lindeman's life and contributions, and for that I am grateful. But more deeply, I experienced sharing in the life of a great human being and one of the founding fathers of the adult education movement in this country. I rejoice that this life can now be shared by many more, younger workers in our thriving field of endeavor—thriving at least in part because of the legacy of Eduard C. Lindeman.

I'd like to conclude by making a case for biography as a vehicle for conveying important knowledge. Some of the most influential works in our literature have been biographies. The *Autobiography* of Benjamin Franklin—the first great American adult educator—comes to mind. Biography provides us with a window through which we can see how great minds work—not just what they produce. As I read the manuscript of this book I found myself repeatedly saying, "Aha, that's how that idea (or insight) came into being." And I felt that I understood the idea better and appreciated it more because I saw it in the context of its life and times. It became a *living* idea, not a lifeless abstraction. What better way could there be of presenting the philosophy of a person whose maxim was "education is life"?

Malcolm S. Knowles

Preface

Eduard Lindeman: I had never heard of him or of his book *The Meaning of Adult Education*, though I had spent most of my working career in the field of adult education. It was assigned as a reading in the first course I was taking as a graduate student at the University of Wisconsin–Madison.

In reading only the first several chapters, I realized that *The Meaning of Adult Education* was not just another book. These words had power. They were also poetic and stirred deep feelings. Here was a book for these times. I turned to the frontispiece. The words which spoke so clearly to me as an adult educator—and human being—in the mid 1970s had been written in 1926.

I finished *The Meaning of Adult Education* at a single sitting. As I pondered the experience, I wondered why the book had affected me as it had. Certainly it was full of organizational and syntactic flaws. It covered far too many subjects. The progression of logic was sometimes unfathomable. Some of it was not fully understandable even on second or third reading. Still, the blurred message of this little book stuck in my mind, and I found myself frequently taking it off its place on my shelf to read once more.

As I progressed through graduate school and eventually began teaching my own graduate classes in adult education, I learned from students that my experience with Lindeman was not unique. We liked him because he made us think; he also made us feel good in some subtle way. But discussions about Lindeman in classes or conference sessions tend to founder on the rocks of fragmented statements in *The Meaning of Adult Education*. What, for example, does he really mean when he says, "Education is life"? It sounds almost nonsensical. And why should adult education aim toward *nonvocational* ideals? Aren't aspirations stemming from one's job as important as any others?

The Meaning of Adult Education was written when Lindeman's thinking about adult education was in its incipient stages. Some of its gaps stem from the haste with which the book was written. He turned it out in a few short weeks of effort; there was no rewriting. He wanted to place full trust in the intuitive stream of thinking that propelled him to the task. Content gaps were simply reflective of the incompleteness of the author's thinking about adult education. Some of the concepts he was still turning over in his own mind. Not until working them out for himself would he fully unleash them on the reading public.

The problem from a latter–day perspective is that much of Lindeman's follow-up thinking about adult education was never released through mainstream adult education channels. He wrote a number of books after *The Meaning of Adult Education*, but none of them were on adult education. He wrote many journal articles about adult education, but few of them appeared in explicitly adult educa-tion publications. He was one of America's most popular lecturers and often talked about adult education, but few of these speeches have been preserved in easily accessible records. With heavy emphasis on unpublished sources, as well as on material not expressly addressed to adult educator audiences, this is the book about adult learning that Eduard could have written at the end of his life, but didn't.

Adult Learning in America is an effort to examine Eduard Lindeman's agenda for lifelong education in the context of his life. The man who believed that education is life had a life of his own. It was a rich and tumultuous life—and one that compelled him to communicate his innermost thoughts about learning and living to other men and women. To try to understand the artistry of such a man without knowing something about his life would be the height of false economy. The patterns of Lindeman's life—as well as those of his thoughts—hold lessons that can enrich the lives of persons living today.

In searching for the sometimes elusive Eduard Lindeman, I received valuable assistance from a large group of individuals, only a few of whom can be identified in the limited space available here. The book would not exist at all were it not for the prior efforts of Betty Lindeman Leonard, Eduard Lindeman's third daughter, to collect and organize his personal papers. Eduard Lindeman had many virtues, but tidiness and organization in approaching his workday world were not among them. That fact, plus the sheer volume of papers that he generated, made the task of finding his papers and organizing them a herculean task in itself. Betty Leonard received indispensable financial aid in accomplishing this task from the Jerome Foundation (now the Northwest Foundation) of St. Paul.

It would have been easy and perhaps narrowly expedient for Betty Leonard, who is at work on her own book about her father, to deny others access to his rich store of papers until her own book is in print. She in fact received counsel to this effect from at least one advisor. Instead, she gave me every encouragement and shared extensively the results of her own work. An unexpected bonus of this six-year period of research is that I gained in Betty a new friend.

I would also like to acknowledge the cooperation of Eduard Lindeman's other living daughters, Ruth O'Neil and Barbara Sanford, and of the late Doris Lindeman Gessner's son, Stephen Gessner. It must be an uneasy feeling for a family to permit a stranger to examine and write about the inner recesses of the thought and life of a beloved parent or grandparent. This was a risk the Lindeman family was willing to take, and I am profoundly grateful to them for doing it. I hope, and believe, that I have not abused their confidence.

Librarians and archivists are of necessity the researcher's friends, but some of them become special friends when they extend courtesies that go far beyond the strict bounds of duty. To the many competent and dedicated staff members at the Library of Congress, one of the great resources of a great nation, I extend special thanks. May their budget thrive in an era of budget trimming.

One hardly expects a great archival store to be housed in a factory-like building in an industrial area of a major city, but that is exactly where the University of Minnesota's exceptional Social Welfare History Archives Center in Minneapolis is located. The Archives director, Professor Clarke A. Chambers, a distinguished historian, gave me encouragement for what was then an unfocused research effort when he spurred me on with a message that Eduard Lindeman was a 1920s figure "well worth resurrecting." Professor Chambers agreed to read the entire text of the book in draft form and provided a valuable critique. I am also grateful to the splendid Archives staff, particularly to its competent and cordial curator, David Klaassen.

A splendid collection of Lindeman papers is contained in the Rare Book and Manuscript Library at Columbia University, where a number of staff members were most helpful. At Cornell University's John M. Olin Library, the very well-organized Dorothy Whitney Straight Elmhirst Papers were made available and my many questions answered by archivist Kathleen Jacklin.

At Michigan State University's Archives and Historical Collections, archivist Dick Harms had identified and pre-sorted Lindeman-related materials even before my arrival there on a very hot day in June 1983. He also took a personal interest in my task and invented ways in which I could save time in reviewing the dusty records of Lindeman's student (and later Extension Service) days.

It was a vacation of sorts to be able to spend two days in the Archive at The Dartington Hall Trust, Totnes, Devon, where the dreams of Dorothy and Leonard Elmhirst came to fruition. Mary Bride Nicolson, curator and archivist, and Robin Johnson (who describes himself as "semiretired from the Records Office") at this handsome establishment helped me sort out strands of the Lindeman story that had resisted sorting from sources available in the New World.

I faced a major—and insurmountable—hurdle in trying to define Nikolai Grundtvig only from review of those small portions of his work that have been translated into English. It became apparent that research into previously untapped (in this country) Danish language sources was essential. I turned for help—and received it in full measure—from Professor K. E. Bugge of The Royal Danish School of Educational Studies, Copenhagen, who is one of the world's foremost scholars on the work of his famous countryman. When I visited Denmark, Professor Bugge and his cordial wife, Ilse, also took me on a guided tour which included the Grundtvig museum at Udby as well as other related sites on the Danish island of Zealand.

Important assistance also came from Uffe Himmelstrup, Counselor in charge of Cultural Relations at the Royal Danish Embassy, Washington, D.C., who read an early draft of the chapter on Danish influences and saved me from several embarrassing errors. Mr. Himmelstrup has unusual insights in that he is a member of the Vartov church in Copenhagen which Grundtvig served as minister from 1839 until his death in 1872. Professor Rose-Marie Oster of the Department of Germanic Languages at the University of Maryland, College Park, also helped me by reviewing the chapter on Denmark.

An author must hold his breath when he asks outstanding scholars to read his manuscript in draft form. Why should they say yes? The hours will be long, the compensation nil. The narrative that is presented may not be worth reading. In spite of these disincentives, some of North America's top adult education scholars agreed to read an early draft of this book. In all cases, their comments made it possible to improve the narrative immeasurably. Mistakes, if any, are of course those of the author, rather than readers of the manuscript.

Professor Malcolm Knowles, who succeeded where Lindeman did not in effecting transplant of the term "andragogy" to this country, provided information and advice that could not have been obtained from any other source. He also did me the great honor of agreeing to write a foreword for this book.

Professor Jerold Apps of the University of Wisconsin–Madison, to whom I am indebted for first introducing me to Eduard Lindeman, helped me in particular to fine tune the philosophic dimensions of Lindeman's story. Dr. Jindra Kulich of The University of British Columbia was of particular help in his critique of the Grundtvig chapter, but his advice on other aspects of the task was also sensitive and apt. Professor Alan Knox of the University of Wisconsin–Madison and Professor Harold Stubblefield of Virginia Polytechnic Institute and State University provided valuable commentary. Also a reader of the full manuscript was Professor Robert Najem of University of Wisconsin–Extension, whose capacities as a practicing adult educator are exceeded only by his capacity for friendship and caring. Elizabeth Martin was a thoughtful critic whose contribution was especially helpful in that it came from someone outside the field of adult education. Eric Rosenberg's critique on several chapters was so good that I wish I could have had it on the entire manuscript. Melanie Wisner's assistance with research was of high quality. Alexander Charters of Syracuse University was kind enough to assist me by including questions about Eduard Lindeman when he interviewed Wilbur Hallenbeck for other purposes.

Miriam Stewart was a major contributor to the research effort for this book. She was solely responsible for the sleuthing effort that resulted in the coup of finding the long lost Martha Anderson—alive and residing in Old Lyme, Connecticut. Miriam's interview with Miss Anderson, which took place just three weeks before her death in June 1984, includes information about Lindeman's work and life that could not have been obtained anywhere else.

A number of persons who knew Lindeman either as friends, colleagues, or students responded to my author's queries as published in the Book Review Section of the *New York Times* and in the *Alumni Newsletter* of the Columbia University School of Social Work. Their assistance is greatly appreciated.

I am grateful also to Mark Irwin Stewart and Ann Walsh Stewart for their interest in this project, but I am mostly grateful that they are just what they are as human beings. Lyn Stewart's support included a gift of the excellent book *Telling Lives*, edited by Marc Pachter.

This book is dedicated to Miss Camilla Wood of Kalamazoo, Michigan, for good reason. At age eighty-five, she is my favorite lifelong learner. She happens to be my aunt, but she is also an intellectual companion and one of my best friends. Her contributions to this book extend far beyond her commentary on the manuscript. Her cultivation of a life of the mind and her capacity for continuous intellectual growth have been an inspiration to me for all of my life. Camilla Wood is one of the reasons I have been able to write *Adult Learning in America* at all.

CHAPTER 1

A Fresh Hope Is Astir

> A fresh hope is astir. From many quarters comes the call to a new kind of education with its initial assumption affirming that *education is life*—not a mere preparation for an unknown kind of future living . . . This new venture is called *adult education*—not because it is confined to adults but because adulthood, maturity, defines its limits.[1]
>
> —Eduard Lindeman

These words would have been dramatic as opening sentences for the only book on adult education written during the germinal years of the 1920s that is still commonly read and prized by American adult educators of today. But the author of *The Meaning of Adult Education** placed them instead at the beginning of paragraph three, following an overlong and pedestrian paragraph one and a shorter, though still drab and rambling, paragraph two. Eduard Christian Lindeman at forty had not yet learned, as he later would, the art of writing with style and syntactic clarity.

Nonetheless, it would be Lindeman, rather than his numerous and often more eloquent contemporaries, who would set the mainstream course generally followed by American adult educators for the balance of the twentieth century. The reasons for this are to be found

---

*All citations in chapter notes are to the Harvest House (1961) edition of this volume rather than to the original New Republic (1926) edition.

in the content of *The Meaning of Adult Education*, but also in the nature and direction of Eduard Lindeman's remarkable—and uniquely American—life.

In the mid-months of 1926, Lindeman closeted himself in the third-floor study of Greystone, his High Bridge, New Jersey, home, to commence work on his first (and only) book about adult education. Ideas he had in abundance. They had been "brewing for years." As he set about the task of organizing and committing them to paper, he followed Walt Whitman's advice and "let myself go free."[2] Writing time was only a few short weeks. Nothing was rewritten, and if the result was something less than a polished narrative, then so be it.[3] And it was.

As a piece of English composition, the manuscript that Lindeman presented to his publisher was not very good if measured by conventional standards. The narrative rambled, lurched, and doubled back upon itself as it unfolded in ten often curiously titled chapters and a ramshackle "Postscript." Ideas popping up in the text often had only tenuous connections to the announced subject matter. There was not even a definition of the term "adult education."

If the quality of writing was uneven, neither did the substantive content of *The Meaning of Adult Education* break new ground in any way that was obvious at the time. The ideas were hardly original with the author. The sparse narrative is at times lucid and tantalizing. Yet, in total substance, it fails to completely satisfy.

Given the modest pretentions of, and flaws in, Eduard Lindeman's slim volume, what accounts for his massive impact upon the nature and direction of adult education in the United States? Basically, Lindeman's talents found expression—and extension—in creative synthesis. As a social philosopher he largely facilitated, rather than invented, adult education theory. His mind was fertile and quick, and he used it to popularize (in the best sense of that word) the concept of adult education.

The Meaning of Adult Education is only the barest—and earliest—major outcropping of a vast body of thought and work in adult education by its author. In years subsequent to 1926, Lindeman produced many articles (now unhappily out of general circulation) in which he largely filled in the gaps of his earliest work on adult education. Furthermore, Lindeman became one of America's most popular lecturers and never ceased educating the American public about—and advancing their consciousness of—adult education as a means for adult learning. His arresting presence as a speaker and teacher between 1926 and his death at sixty-seven in 1953—more than his writing—was perhaps the most crucial factor in impressing his ideas about adult education and related issues on the minds of Americans.

But it is with that eccentric volume called *The Meaning of Adult Education* that any account of Eduard Lindeman and his agenda for lifelong education in America must begin, for it was with this effort that his work in adult education was launched. And it is as author of this book that Lindeman is chiefly remembered by the adult educators of today.

In the ten discursive chapters that constitute *The Meaning of Adult Education* Lindeman developed the concept of adult education as shaped by the nature of "those who need to be learners."[4] By this he meant everyone, not just those persons traditionally considered educable in any real sense. And adult learners were precisely those whose intellectual aspirations were "least likely to be aroused by the rigid, uncompromising requirements of authoritative, conventionalized institutions of learning."[5]

Lindeman's adult education was to serve humanistic values. Too many Americans pursued barren pecuniary or competitive goals. So pervasive was this mindset that American service clubs such as Rotary, Kiwanis, and the like sprang up to permit "American business and professional men to behave as human beings for at least a few moments once a week."[6] But this was not enough. A wholesome society could not be fashioned out of "partially starved personalities."[7]

Of course such adult education should be voluntary. As an act of free will, it should be "wholly lacking in coercive or compulsive elements." Neither would "ordinary tests and examinations . . . suffice to determine success and failure in adult education."[8]

Adult education with respect to the use of power was examined as were its implications for intelligence, self-expression, freedom, and art or cultural appreciation. The emerging problem of specialization was analyzed in terms of its adult education implications as was the adult education contribution to collective enterprises. In a concluding chapter, Lindeman laid out ground rules that have since become cardinal principles guiding methods used within teaching-learning transactions involving adults.

The chapter headings in *The Meaning of Adult Education*, with their inexact subject-matter groupings, are not particularly serviceable in providing structure for the analysis of Lindeman's thought about adult education. More promising because of their adoption or adaptation by later theorists are four assumptions about "those who need to be learners" that are initially set forth in Chapter 1. These assumptions are: (1) that education is life, (2) that adult education revolves around nonvocational ideals, (3) that the approach to adult education will be via the route of situations, not subjects, and (4) that the resource of highest value in adult education is the learner's experience.[9]

As developed in *The Meaning of Adult Education* and amended in the full context of Lindeman's life and work, these assumptions provided the conceptual framework for Lindeman's adult education philosophy. They also led Lindeman decidedly away from the prevailing notion that adult education was a kind of educational annex in which deficiencies from prior educational efforts could be remedied.

What were the major strands from which this now-familiar synthesis of adult education philosophy was devised? Lindeman derived the bulk of his intellectual constructs from three principal sources. Bedrock philosophical underpinnings came from John Dewey (within a context earlier defined by William James and Charles Sanders Peirce). Other key roots are to be found in the philosophy and practice of the nineteenth century Danish philosopher-theologian-educator Nikolai Grundtvig. Lindeman's heavy philosophical debt to Ralph Waldo Emerson became evident in his writings that appeared after *The Meaning of Adult Education* was published.

From John Dewey, who was a colleague of Lindeman's at Columbia University and a friend, Lindeman gained his greatest aggregation of philosophical roots. It was Dewey's philosophy—pragmatism—that provided the basic foundation for Lindeman's development of the idea of adult education. At the core of this philosophy is the pragmatic view that ideas are true if they can be *experienced* as being true. Moreover, it is experience from which learning is chiefly derived by adults. Given the pragmatic mainstream of American adult education in the wake of Dewey's work, it can be seen as no accident that the term "experiential learning" has come into common use among contemporary adult educators.

As shall be seen, it is generally accurate to say that adult education, as articulated by Eduard Lindeman, is a derivative of Deweyan progressive education. Dewey spent the bulk of his "practice" time with school-age children. Lindeman focused more on pragmatism as a philosophy underlying adult education and worked primarily with adults; he is therefore a more direct ancestor of adult education in America than is Dewey.

Lindeman found his only non-American principal root in a philosopher who lived in that low and marshy country that projects like a dagger from the North European plain. Something very good happened to Denmark in 1864. That small nation lost a war to neighboring Prussia. In losing the war, Denmark lost valuable territory—the provinces of Schleswig and Holstein which it was forced to cede to Bismarck's Prussia. But Denmark, in defeat, gained something infinitely more precious than the territory it lost following the war. It gained a grassroots-based movement in community development and a system of adult education that would become a beacon to the world. As it recovered from military defeat, Denmark began building a new society that would be counted as one of the wonders of the modern world by observers in the early twentieth century.

A most remarkable human being was part of this movement and was its unquestioned philosophical leader. A great crag of a man, a bishop of the Danish State Lutheran Church, a member of Parliament, this was Nikolai Frederik Severin Grundtvig. Lindeman was familiar with Grundtvig's work and in 1920 paid his first visit to Denmark. He returned captivated—in some ways uncritically captivated—by what he believed to be the vision of a mature democratic society at its best. He was greatly influenced both by Grundtvig's philosophy of education and by the tangible expression of it in Danish society—particularly in the Danish folk high schools.

Eduard Lindeman was an avid disciple of Ralph Waldo Emerson, and his near hero worship of Emerson increased in intensity as he grew older. Lindeman read and reread all of Emerson's published books and articles. He minutely analyzed Emerson's journals. He wrote several books and articles about Emerson including an unpublished manuscript found after his death. Lindeman incorporated Emersonian ideas in nearly all of the work done in his middle and later years, and he frequently mentioned Emerson in his speeches. Beginning in the years just after Lindeman wrote *The Meaning of Adult Education*, Emerson's work became for him a crucible within which he developed and refined his own philosophy in its mature form.

In Lindeman's eyes, Emerson was the peerless spokesman for American democracy, and it was adult education that should be the principal instrument of the democratic process. Emerson's thinking about the age-old question of the intersection of means and ends particularly intrigued Lindeman. Was adult education not the ultimate *means* toward democratic ends? It was *means*, not goals or ends, that should be emphasized in any reconceptualization of education.

Emerson lived before the philosophy of pragmatism emerged, but his thinking overlapped with pragmatism to a remarkable degree. As Lindeman was quick to point out, Emerson viewed truth as possessed by those who can use it—the one condition coupled with the gift of truth being that it be put to use. The educated person was one who could apply learning to practice. This was also a good pragmatic axiom.

As he struggled toward synthesis that could facilitate adult education practice, Lindeman was remarkably adept at drawing on the great capital of ideas generated by Emerson. In an article appearing in 1942, Lindeman even cited Emerson as author of a pre–Abraham Maslow "hierarchy of human values" or needs that began with "physical or material requirements" and that progressed in four stages toward needs that were "spiritual."[10]

Important as it was to become as an ingredient of Lindeman's philosophy, the Emerson influence is largely absent in the adult education volume for which Lindeman is remembered. So it is an immature Lindeman who proceeds in *The Meaning of Adult Education* with a sporadically eloquent, though frequently digressive, discussion of far too many aspects of the announced subject matter. Rational analysis of Lindeman's philosophy of adult education tends to founder in this morass. It is small wonder that an understanding of the full force of Lindeman's work is not common currency among American adult educators.

Given its strange assortment of content and its sometimes quirky style, *The Meaning of Adult Education* seems at first to be miscast as a masterwork in adult education. Certainly it was perceived in its own time as something less than a harbinger of paradigm shift. Even now, it is on the moribund list of its publisher, having been out of print since the Harvest House edition in 1961.

Still, this miniature volume has staying power; it's a rare adult education syllabus or reading list that does not include Lindeman's modest-appearing piece of work. In a poll conducted in 1982, professors of adult education in leading graduate study programs at different universities were asked to select the most important books in the adult education field. The result was a tie between Eduard Lindeman's *The Meaning of Adult Education* and the more recent and directly practical *The Modern Practice of Adult Education* by Malcolm Knowles.[11]

Lindeman's standoff with Knowles in the context of his rating with a sample of present-day academics is in itself interesting. An acknowledged protégé of Lindeman, Knowles considers himself firmly in his mentor's philosophical tradition. Knowles's own assumptions about adult learning are tailored from Lindeman's earlier model in *The Meaning of Adult Education*.

What is the real source of this book's influence and charm? Granted, *The Meaning* is flawed. It would be a better book had the author taken the time to prune extraneous subject matter, fill in the content gaps, untangle the syntax, and strain out impurities that occasionally impair the flow of logic. Yet, strangely, the power that was always incarnate in the text of *The Meaning of Adult Education* remains. There is an odd symbiosis between content and syntax as sentences and whole paragraphs arrest attention or sing with beauty; flashes of insight ignite the imagination. The author's profoundly optimistic view of the potentials of human life is infectious; the reader senses the ring of truth and becomes emotionally engaged. Somehow the message penetrates and just *feels* right.

But are these virtues—many of them squarely in the nebulous affective domain—enough to make Lindeman's book a landmark if harder criteria are applied? Does Lindeman's philosophy, viewed in the perspective of twentieth century intellectual history, constitute one of those incipient "anomalies" that Thomas Kuhn would say heralds a paradigm shift? Is it, in this case, a reconceptualization of the way in which Americans think about learning?

It would be rash to give an unqualified yes to this question. What can unquestionably be said at this time is that Lindeman's four most basic assumptions about the adult learner undergird much of mainstream thought and practice in the America of today. Contemporary adult educators and their allies, encouraged by a body of empirical research that tends to support the essence of Lindeman's assumptions, are moving toward more direct challenge to the established educational order. Issues stemming from Lindeman's assumptions are prominent on the agendas at meetings of American educators.

But adult education, however defined, has always been considered a marginal activity within America's educational community. Night school, correspondence study, and, of course, "basketweaving" have been used pejoratively as references to allegedly inferior or trivial educational programs for adults. Life-centered study has never enjoyed the prestige that subject-centered study has.

Adult learning at the postsecondary level has been only semi-respectable in the eyes of many traditional educators. Until quite recently, the mature adult who chose to enroll in a college or university credit program was a rarity, and such courageous persons were often made to feel uncomfortable by professors discomforted by their presence.

Even with philosophical credentials of the sort Lindeman and his intellectual mentors provide, can a revolution be wrought if it originates in an often tangential sector of the educational community? The answer is yes.

Faced with declining enrollment of traditional students (the baby boom generation is now middle aged), the educational establishment is in crisis. There is demand for education as never before—but it's coming largely from adults. And it's coming from a generation that, because of its sheer numbers in American society, is accustomed to getting what it wants. The anomaly, educational programs designed to meet the needs and learning styles of adults, is becoming mainstream. And traditional educators in their traditional institutions are taking a new look at their assumptions about adults and about adult learning.

As they look to the future with high hopes for their clients, adult educators are looking for philosophical guideposts. The pathway marked by Eduard Lindeman is familiar and seems serviceable for the new age. Lindeman still touches deep chords in the hearts and minds of American adult educators. They feel in touch with their professional roots as they read and reread *The Meaning of Adult Education*. They intuitively know something else, too. They know that they have just learned something good about themselves.

CHAPTER 2

Understanding America's Adult Learning Movement at Its Roots

Adult learning. Adult education. Lifelong learning. Lifelong education. Each term is ambiguous; there is no common agreement among educators about what each of them means—a fact that becomes obvious to anyone scanning the inventory of eighteen often overlapping or conflicting comments and definitions assembled in 1983 by K. Patricia Cross.[1]

It would be convenient if Eduard Lindeman had provided usable definitions, but for reasons which shall be seen, he did not. Nevertheless, to understand Lindeman in the context of latter-day twentieth century usage, broadly generic working definitions of at least these basic terms *as used in this narrative* are necessary.

The differences in meaning between "learning" and "education" are subtle, yet real. Learning means the *acquiring* of knowledge, skills, or related learning outcomes. Education means the purposeful process of acquiring of such knowledge, skills, etc., *by means of formal schooling or systematic study*. Education therefore has institutional, as well as didactic, implications that are not necessarily implicit in learning. To educate someone is to speed up, make more efficient, or otherwise facilitate that person's learning.

The word "adult" poses definitional problems because different societies, even various groups within a society, will differ in the definitions applied. Clearly a simple age range will not suffice. One nineteen-year-old college student, for example, may still be financially and even emotionally dependent upon his parents. Another individual at exactly the same age may be married, a father, and working full time to support his family. Are both persons really adults? An adult, therefore, needs definition in terms that recognize the functional roles and responsibilities commonly associated with adulthood (e.g., parenthood, full-time employment), regardless of the individual's age.

The term "adult learning" has gradually come into general use as a function of the increasing emphasis in the middle and late twentieth century on outcomes (learning) rather than methods (teaching). Adult learning is essentially the acquisition of knowledge, skills, sensitive awareness, or insights by persons considered by a society to have adult responsibilities. Such learning is not necessarily conscious, systematic, or intended; it may be accidental. Adult learning may result from informal, as well as formal, educational arrangements.

Simon N. Patten, a professor of political economy at the University of Pennsylvania, in 1894 may have been the first American to use the term "adult education" rather than "popular education" with reference to programs for mature adults. Patten's article was an attempt to define the emerging thrust of university extension.[2] In 1895, the term was used again by William Lawton in a discussion of the newly developing university extension programs.[3] The term "adult education" was most favored by Lindeman as he developed his educational philosophy, though he used "adult learning" also.

Adult education aims at the same outcomes as adult learning, i.e., acquisition of knowledge, skills, sensitive awareness, or insights on the part of persons who have society-determined adult responsibilities, but it refers to purposeful, organized, or systematic efforts at acquisition, often but not always institutionally based.

The term "lifelong learning" has been used in the United States at least since 1919.[4] By the 1960s, the words were being used in efforts to incorporate adult learning as part of state and national education policy.[5] The term did not become common, however, until 1973, when Theodore Hesburgh, Paul A. Miller, and Clifton R. Wharton used it as they called upon colleges and universities—as well as other societal institutions—to "share responsibility for helping people to educate themselves."[6]

In broadest contemporary usage, lifelong learning refers to learning of any type by persons of whatever age, though in practice the term is ordinarily used by some adult educators to emphasize learning as a process that is ongoing during the adult years. Some twenty learning activities are enumerated in the definition of lifelong learning stated in the Higher Education Act of 1965.[7]

In an international context, the term has normative connotations stemming from the official definition adopted by the UNESCO General Assembly in 1976. The aims of lifelong learning, the UNESCO delegates said, included those of: (1) "restructuring the existing educational system," (2) "developing the entire educational potential outside the education system," and (3) enabling men and women to become "the agent of their own education."[8]

The British adult educator Basil Yeaxlee, whom Lindeman admired[9] and whose work suffers unjustified neglect in the United States, discussed "lifelong education" in a book with the same name in 1929 and refers to an earlier term, "lifetime education," which had been used by a "Professor Soddy."[10,11] (This was probably Frederick Soddy (1877–1956), the 1921 Nobel laureate in chemistry, who was much interested in the advancement of adult learning in the sciences.)[12]

Lifelong education now generally refers to organized or systematic efforts—often, though not always, institutionally based—to assist persons of whatever age to learn. The individual is seen at all times as the hub of this process.[13] A major spur to international acceptance of this term was given when UNESCO published the volume *Lifelong Education* in 1976. Editor Ravindra Dave included some twenty "concept characteristics of lifelong education" that have since been widely disseminated.[14]

These definitions may be—and frequently are—restricted by modifier words or clauses. For example, only adult learning that is voluntary or entirely learner-directed might be accepted within one such definition. Or, for other purposes, adult education might be restricted only to those activities that produce behavioral change in an individual. Such qualifiers are, however, properly stated in advance— an admonition made especially important in a nation in which the Adult Education Act covers only adult basic or literacy education and where adult education is often carelessly applied only to craft, recreational, or noncredit course work.

Eduard Lindeman probably never used either "lifelong learning" or "lifelong education" since neither term came into general usage until after his death in 1953. However, with his concept of adult education being coterminous with life, Lindeman anticipated extension of the basic adult learning and adult education reference terms.

What is adult education? About all Lindeman would say in *The Meaning of Adult Education* was that it was a "process through which learners become aware of significant experience. Recognition of significance leads to evaluation," and meanings might "accompany experience" when individuals know what is happening and what importance the event has for their personalities.[15] But this statement raises about as many questions as it answers.

The absence of a straight-out definition of adult education in a book entitled *The Meaning of Adult Education* seems at first an unforgivable omission. The reader is told much about what adult education is and about what it is not. But nowhere is there a succinct definition of the core concept itself.

What is the purpose of adult education? To "train individuals for a more fruitful participation in those smaller collective units which do so much to mold significant experience," Lindeman replies.[16] To change individuals "in continuous adjustment to changing social functions" was another way of stating the purpose of adult education.[17] But these are aims, objectives, purposes—what is adult education, really?

The absence of a definition of adult education in *The Meaning of Adult Education* was deliberate; Lindeman was not being coy. He was within a respectable tradition in postponing the task of definition to the latter stages of philosophical inquiry. Development of the concept of adult education in America was in a sensitive incipient stage; introduction of a definition would be premature. Nothing could be worse for the American adult education movement than adoption of a hardened definitional structure. Meanings would be discovered by persons while they were engaged in the process of adult education, not in advance. What Lindeman groped for was a qualitative and fresh conception of the whole process through which adults learn how to live wholesome lives.

It was undoubtedly Lindeman who was at least partially responsible, in 1926, for the refusal of the newly organized American Association for Adult Education (AAAE) to commit itself to either an inclusive or exclusive definition of adult education.[18] He was one of the organizing members.

Lindeman must have been reluctant—responding to pressure as part of a symposium on "What Is Adult Education?"—when he offered this loose, if poetic, definition to readers of the *Survey* in 1926: Adult education, he said, was:

> a cooperative venture in non-authoritarian, informal learning, the chief purpose of which is to discover the meaning of experience; a quest of the mind which digs down to the roots of the preconceptions which formulate

our conduct; a technique of learning for adults which makes education coterminous with life and hence elevates living itself to the level of adventurous experiment.[19]

A still disinclined Lindeman took on the problem of definition in an article appearing in *Progressive Education* in 1929. It remained easier for him to say what adult education is not than what it is. For example, adult education is "not pursued for ulterior rewards; entrance requirements, examinations, and academic degrees play no part in true adult education." Founded on the assumption that "adult experience has in itself some of the materials of education," it is "not a process of absorption or osmosis between students and teacher, but rather an exchange of experiences." Textbooks and "the accumulated stores of second-hand knowledge" have little to do with adult education. Neither is adult education "a process of acquiring the tools of learning (fundamental subject-matters), but rather a way of learning the relation between knowledge and living." He could offer only "generalized criteria" of definition.[20]

When he wrote the section on "Adult Education" in the 1937 edition of *Encyclopedia of the Social Sciences*, Lindeman must have been pressed by the editors to define his subject matter at the outset. This he did but with deliberate vagueness: Adult education, he told the encyclopedia's readers, "is an inclusive term which, as it is currently employed, embraces within its meaning the following varieties of activity: continuing education; corrective education; functional-group education; and folk schools or people's colleges. A term which includes so many varieties of educational endeavor must necessarily be ambiguous. There is, however, a marked trend in the direction of limiting the use of the term to projects concerned with functional-group education and folk schools or people's colleges."[21]

For all of his professional life, Lindeman was reluctant to offer a precise definition of adult education and would undoubtedly be disturbed about latter-day efforts to freeze his ideas within any of the several midstream definitions that he proffered. As late as 1947, in a memo to the Executive Committee of the Michigan Council on Adult Education, he refused to define adult education in "precise and standardized terms." Because adult education is designed to meet the changing needs of adults in a changing society, "its definition will always remain somewhat fluid."[22]

The adult learning movement that surfaced to bubble and boil in the United States in the 1920s had roots in both America and Europe. Lindeman's candidate for "father of the adult education movement in America" was Josiah Holbrook of Derby, Connecticut, who was a pioneer of the lyceum form of public lectures and concerts in the early nineteenth century. He had a "nuclear personality," Lindeman told a 1927 audience of librarians," [and] was a lively incubating centre who caused events to happen."[23] He certainly did. By the mid-1830s, less than ten years after he had rather brashly announced his intention to develop a national lyceum movement, Holbrook presided over an empire of some thirty-five hundred local lyceums and sixteen state associations.[24]

Holbrook had some distinguished company. In his scrapbook, Lindeman noted that Thoreau in 1854 included in *Walden* this sentence: "It is time we had uncommon schools, that we did not leave off our education when we begin to be men and women."[25] Lindeman borrowed some of this language (which was not Thoreau's best) to record his exclusion of vocational education and academic education from the realm of adult education.

By the early twentieth century, the descriptor "Night School" was first used in *Reader's Guide to Periodical Literature* (1900–1904 edition). The terms "Continuation Schools" and "Evening Schools" appeared in the the 1905–1909 edition. The *Reader's Guide* used the headings "Night School" or "Evening School" to characterize adult education subject matter until the 1915 edition, when its editors, reflecting what had become common practice, added "Adult Education" to the *Guide's* subject matter headings.[26] At last, in the early 1920s, the flame of America's adult education movement burst forth as a conscious national movement. It had been a long time in coming.

Among the many movers and shapers of adult education in the 1920s, Eduard Lindeman, with his slim, hastily written volume *The Meaning of Adult Education*, seems at first to be the odd candidate for gianthood in the adult education movement. But this was no ordinary man, as his contemporaries knew.

Lindeman's ideas about adult education were products of a life crammed with tumultuous events which shaped his understanding of himself and of the world in which he made his mark. This philosopher had been an adult student in and out of school settings. He knew the pain of being forced into the mold of a child for learning experiences. He knew the importance of experience as a resource for learning. Most of all, he knew that education at its best was a process that was concurrent with life.

It was a hardscrabble world that greeted Edward, the tenth child of Frederick and Frederecka Johanna Von Piper Lindemann*, when he was born on the ninth of May in 1885. The parents, immigrants to the United States, were poor folk for whom the full promise of the American dream had not been fulfilled. Frederick worked as a laborer in the great caverns of salt mines that riddled the ground in the area. Frederecka took in washing. Home for the family was a simple frame house in the eastern Michigan village of St. Clair. Rushing past the village was the St. Clair River which carried the strikingly blue waters of Lake Huron toward Lake St. Clair and Detroit. According to one account, Frederick had built the family home himself. It was made of wood which must have come from the great virgin forest then under destruction by the new Americans who were settling Michigan.**

On the day of Eduard's birth, the *New York Times* noted that Britain and Russia were at each other's throats in a dispute over the boundaries of Afghanistan. King Leopold of the Belgians had selected three officials to act as ministers in the new private domain he had carved for himself in the lower Congo. A "working man's revolutionary congress" was being held in Paris as Parliament reassembled.

Grover Cleveland, just two months before the date of Eduard's birth, had taken the oath of office as twenty-fifth President of the United States—a nation where the memory of a great civil war was still fresh. The *Washington Post* reported that Cubans—their country bankrupt—and the mother country, imperial Spain—sinking more in debt each year—were presenting a "scheme" whereby the United States would buy Cuba "next winter" for "$100 million in cash." Bestsellers in America that year would be a novel called *Huckleberry Finn* and former President Ulysses S. Grant's *Personal Memoirs*. The national budget of the United States had shown an excess of revenue over expenditures for every year since 1875.[27]

But all of this was probably of marginal interest to the Lindemanns. In common with immigrants everywhere, their first concern lay in acquiring the basics of life—food, clothing, shelter. From the little frame house in St. Clair, colonial expansion, boundary disputes, inaugurations, and other preoccupations of the middle and upper classes had little reality.

---

*Edward Lindemann did not change the spelling of his first and last names and add the middle name to become "Eduard Christian Lindeman" until he was a student in college.

**Unless otherwise indicated, information about Eduard Lindeman's childhood and youth has been provided to the author by Betty Leonard.

America in 1885 was still largely an agrarian society, though the structures and institutions of the industrial age were rapidly developing. The great river just east of the Lindemann home reached toward Lake Huron, with its Sault Ste. Marie ship canals leading into Lake Superior and Minnesota's enormously rich Mesabi iron range. This narrow water passage, which Father Louis Hennepin in 1679 had called a "fertile and pleasant strait,"[28] would become an important artery of America's developing steel industry, as it was already important for the shipping of Midwestern lumber.

The years of Eduard Lindeman's youth are largely a series of great dark ellipses. The known facts include the date he was born, the identity of his parents, and their place of residence. But with this baby's entry into the world, a great veil descends, effectively separating him from the world of public knowledge. Only occasionally, as if to tease—not to enlighten—does it lift. But the picture is still sketchy, not much more than mere conjecture.[29]

The available facts suggest that the Lindemann household was a troubled one, that in the shadows may have lurked the sinister. In later life, Eduard seldom spoke about this period except to say that the family had been poor, he had worked hard, and his parents had died when he was very young.

Such information about his childhood as was supplied by Eduard is not always reliable. Some informants were told that he had been illiterate until he was in his early twenties.[30] Another learned from Eduard that he was a voracious reader and was on that account able to be accepted at college on a higher level though he lacked formal schooling.[31] In fact, Eduard had brief spurts of education at the elementary level at a Lutheran parochial school located near the family home.

Eduard frequently mentioned in speeches, journal articles, and conversations with friends that he was the son of Danish immigrants to America. In fact, both his parents were German. Even the place of his birth was at times obfuscated by Lindeman. He told more than one friend that it had been Holland, Michigan, rather than St. Clair, where he was born.[32]

This habit of deliberately clouding the details of one's past is hardly unique to Eduard Lindeman. The mind of every man and woman possesses facts about prior experience that are so painful they must be driven deep and away from consciousness. Dostoevsky was probably correct when he observed that the more decent a man is, "the greater the number of such things in his mind."[33] The same mind that subdues portions of the past is a prism for filtering other memories so that they reinforce a newly evolving self-image.

What is clear about the youth of Eduard Lindeman is that he worked hard—perhaps beginning in the winter when he first used his sled to pick up and deliver Frederecka's parcels of laundry. He had little money, little opportunity for education, and apparently received precious little affection from his brothers and sisters. There must also have been a number of dark incidents to cloud a young mind— incidents that an older Eduard Lindeman found it necessary to repress.

At the death of someone described only as his "last brother," Lindeman wrote a friend that he was "strangely moved," in part because he was in Italy and unable to attend the funeral. A "great gulf" had separated him from all except one of his brothers and sisters. All of them, he said, had resented his "thirst for knowledge." Content as they were with their status, it was assumed that Eduard was violating a family standard. Disintegration of the family continued until "at last no real family feeling remained." Why was he "always carrying a cross as the penalty for seeking truth?" Eduard wondered.[34]

The record—or rather the absence of one—tends to confirm Eduard's account that he did not keep in touch with family members. The vast files of Lindeman papers at Columbia University and at the University of Minnesota contain not one letter from any brother or sister.

A clipped and faded obituary column from an unnamed newspaper reveals that Minnie Lindemann, a spinster sister, died at the age of seventy-eight at a Baldwin, Michigan, nursing home. Eduard Lindeman is the only blood relative mentioned as a survivor. Eduard corresponded with Minnie, with whom he had lived in the family home after the death of their mother, and was fond of her. He saw two other sisters, Rose Rano and Mollie Blankerts, infrequently.

If there was any positive outcome of his spartan childhood— beyond that of teaching sheer endurance—Eduard was hard pressed to take note of it. He did tell one friend that because there were no traditions or a family pattern that he could follow, he developed an early sense of latitude and freedom that might not otherwise have been possible.[35]

Eduard and his sister, Minnie, remained in the family home after the death of their mother. The young man labored as a stable cleaner, nurseryman, grave digger, brickyard worker, and deliverer of groceries. He also worked in a shipyard, in Detroit factories, and as riveter with the crew digging the tunnel between Detroit and Windsor, Ontario, in Canada.[36]

These years of hard manual labor imprinted themselves on the mind of the rough-hewn young man. In 1923, he wrote that the "automatic machine" was a part of his life for a period of ten years while he was "growing up in the steel [shipbuilding?] industry." Step by step, process after process was removed from the aegis of the individual worker by inventions of the new machine era. But the difficulty with modern industrial organization was not being caused by machines. Rather, it was the "non-intellectual control of it by people who do not know how to deal with human beings." It was here, Lindeman said, that he determined "this gigantic machine which seems about to consume us can be controlled consciously—effectively by the human mind."[37]

The exact circumstances surrounding young Eduard's interest in obtaining more education than would ordinarily have been acquired by a rural youth from a poverty-ridden home are unknown. He told Frank Karelsen that the impetus came from visits to the home of a farm woman who had books. He arranged to borrow some of them, and eventually this unnamed woman encouraged him to pursue educational opportunities that would release him forever from the narrow circle at St. Clair.[38]

A different version appeared in a *New York Times* article published during Lindeman's lifetime and based, presumably, on information supplied by him.[39] In this account a "sympathetic farmer in Ohio" (Lindeman thought his last name was Brokaw) encouraged him to go to college as he sat visiting with Eduard one night under a tree. College catalogs were sent for and it was learned that Eduard, in spite of his patchy education in the Lutheran parochial school, was qualified for entry under a special program at Michigan Agricultural College.[40]

Also contributing to the decision to opt for college may have been an injury sustained by Eduard. While working with a pick and shovel, he broke his leg. During the recovery period, he reflected on the incident and realized there might not always be work for those who labored with their hands.[41] Watching someone else injured while at work in a factory was also a growth experience. Within four minutes' time, as the young man watched, the injured man was replaced by another.

So this was how the world was. Any man could replace another man on a routine job, but no man could replace another man who was unique. In any case, the manual worker was vulnerable. Survival on decent terms meant getting a good education, and Eduard decided he wanted to become a person rather than a function.[42]

It was 1907; Eduard Lindeman was twenty-two years old. The road out of poverty and insecurity led toward East Lansing. It was here that Michigan Agricultural College, M.A.C. as the students called it, was located. There were few indicators in those days pointing toward development of the academic behemoth that Michigan Agricultural College, as Michigan State University, would later become.

East Lansing was a bucolic suburb of Michigan's capital city. Its sole industry was the land grant university that was beginning to show its mettle as a healthy academic enterprise—with roots planted deep in the souls of the ordinary Americans who were its natural constituency. There was an occasional sound of metal on metal as a car on the street railway made its way to or from the mother city to the west.

The oldest agricultural college in the United States[43] rested quietly on its flat, tree-shaded campus on the banks of the Red Cedar River. The only overt hint of the coming machine age was presented by the new streetcar turnabout with its overhead Maypole of electrical wires. Students and visitors to the campus could sometimes catch special Pere Marquette Railroad excursion trains that landed passengers near the college boiler house.

The grounds were spacious and there was a feeling of openness. This was in part a result of far-sighted action by Lindeman's future father-in-law, Professor of Horticulture Levi R. Taft, who had enhanced growth of some trees by supervising the removal of others just a few years before Eduard's arrival.[44]

The buildings set in these surroundings were attractive, if generally unpretentious, as was befitting in a college designed to meet the needs of America's masses. The campus architectural centerpiece was College Hall. Of mid-nineteenth century vintage, its age and honest dignity were not always appreciated by students, who made fun of "the queer architecture of those olden days" and noted how its "window frames all slant artistically and how the monotony of the brick walls is broken by large cracks." The main function of College Hall, according to the *Wolverine*, was to serve as a subject for sophomore orators who argue: "Shall Old College Hall be Torn Down—or Left to Fall of Its Own Accord?"[45]

As the land grant college for Michigan since 1863, M.A.C. had an academic focus on agriculture.[46] Its administration was headed by Jonathan L. Snyder, who had assumed the presidency in 1896 at the age of thirty-seven. Shortly after taking charge of the institution, President Snyder had put his stamp of approval on significant change by authorizing a shift of the long vacation period from the winter to the summer months, development of a course of studies (home economics) for women, and the offering of four special six-week courses during the winter.[47]

Michigan Agricultural College had an adult education arm that took its professors to nearly every corner of Michigan. "Corn Gospel Trains," an invention of M.A.C. alumnus Perry G. Holden, had been introduced in Michigan by Professor Taft in 1906. At each local stop, rural folk boarding the trains would see an exhibit calling attention to a problem known to every farmer—the planting of kernels of corn that would not grow. Using a germination box, traveling faculty members would demonstrate a method for selecting ears of corn that would produce the highest percentage of kernels that would sprout if used as seed. Other short lectures would be followed by an opportunity to view exhibits located in the train's baggage car.

These were not Cooperative Extension institutes, but they were typical of adult programs that were incorporated in Cooperative Extension programming following passage of the Smith-Lever Act in 1914. President Snyder, among others, was consulted when the Smith-Lever Bill was drafted.[48] In 1914, recent M.A.C. graduate Eduard Lindeman would become one of the nation's first Cooperative Extension Service agents.

The idea of Present Snyder's that made it possible for Eduard Lindeman to attend M.A.C. at all was the Sub-Freshman Program, a predecessor of what, in a later era, would be called programs for minority and disadvantaged students. Designed for rural youth primarily, the Sub-Freshman Program was begun in 1899. As the name implies, it was simply a pre-freshman year, in which inadequately prepared young people—generally rural youth who had been forced to interrupt or terminate secondary schooling—could acquire knowledge and learning skills needed for successful academic performance at the college level.

The sub-freshman year was a great boon for Eduard Lindeman and for many students like him. He would later cite it as the "splendid democracy of M.A.C." which had disregarded his mental and material poverty and given him "the opportunity to prove my worth."[49]

Eduard Lindeman was one of 140 students admitted to M.A.C. as sub-freshmen. Photos of most of these youths appear in the 1908 *Wolverine*, the college yearbook, but Eduard's photo is not among them. Undoubtedly, he was too poor to have one taken. According to one account, he had lost, while working on a farm, all the money he had saved for starting college—some eighty-five dollars.[50] Only after a personal appeal to President Snyder himself was the young man admitted without it.[51] To help pay expenses, he got a job cleaning out the College's cow barns, using the substance of his labors to fertilize the nursery.[52]

During the fall, winter, and spring terms in that sub-freshman year, Eduard labored to catch up academically. It was a grueling experience.

If Eduard was a latecomer to academic life, he showed no reluctance to fully enter the life of the college. He was president of the YMCA and also of the Eunomian Literary Society.[53] He managed the football team during the great winning season in 1910. He was a debater, literary editor of the Junior Annual, and a member or officer of numerous other groups and clubs.[54]

Always the organizer—a trait he would carry with him throughout life—Lindeman helped found the Ethico-Sociological Society and a club called The Penmen, whose members set for themselves the task of "materially [raising] the standard of news sent out from the college to the state papers. . . " The Penmen also organized discussion of the art of writing. Eduard kicked this program off with a paper on contemporary poets "and some of their choice selections." The energetic young man also found time to accept the first presidency of the Cosmopolitan Club, an organization devoted to fostering a "spirit of universal brotherhood."[55]

The young Eduard's creative talents also surfaced during these college years. A number of poems by Lindeman appeared in the student newspaper as did a special Thanksgiving story entitled "The Awakening" which he had earlier presented at a Eunomian Society meeting.[56] By 1910, as a sophomore, Lindeman taught a Sunday evening class on literature of the Bible.[57] Lindeman's play, "In the Hearts of the People," was awarded the Dramatic Club's $25 prize in 1911.[58]

Students at M.A.C. during Eduard's tenure there flocked to the new glamour courses in the social sciences. Lindeman shared this interest and saw to it that the student newspaper published an article by Professor W. O. Hedrick in which he presented the fundmental facts about these studies of "man's problems."[59]

Eduard's most ambitious undertaking while at M.A.C. was that of editor of the *Holcad*, the College's student newspaper. A review of its columns during Lindeman's tenure provides a number of revealing snapshots of the intellectual development of the *Holcad's* young editor. The name of Ralph Waldo Emerson, for example, first appears, with an Emerson quote (man as "metamorphosed into a thing"), on a *Holcad* editorial page.[60]

Under Lindeman's editorship, which began in 1910, the *Holcad* perked up. Coverage of news improved; articles were livelier; the format was enhanced; publication became more frequent.[61] There was also a minor explosion in the number of factual and typographical errors. Eduard did not, it seems, have a managing editor who could cover the imperfect strokes of his rather broad brush.

In light of his subsequent career, it is intriguing to see identifiable adult education concerns occasionally raised by the young man who was editor of this publication. In 1911, for example, the *Holcad* set forth some thirty-three "policies" for which it was taking a "definite stand." The bulk of these mirrored traditional undergraduate concerns of the day, e.g., "Abandon Chapel if it is dead." But others might have been aimed at a more mature audience.

The short courses in agriculture for adult farmers were cited as "one of the most beneficent features of this institution. We should help them grow and reach more people." Class standings should not be graded; marks should indicate only whether or not the student had passed a course. Also, the curriculum demanded too much "class room time" of the student.[62]

In his mid-twenties by the time he graduated, Lindeman was more mature than the average M.A.C. student. Sometimes the rougher edges of late adolescent behavior irked him. "Outside etiquette" at parties, for example, left something to be desired. Some young gentlemen without dates had the habit of standing at the Armory doors during dancing parties and making "unpleasant or embarrassing remarks" to those who came in and out of the doors.[63] Not that there weren't enough rules to discourage this sort of behavior. *In loco parentis* was explicit at M.A.C., as at other American colleges of that period.

What did students talk about? Not always about the elevated topics posed at the Eunomian Literary Society or one of the other officially high-minded groups. According to Eduard Lindeman's *Holcad*, these topics were "Conversation Starters" in 1911: reciprocity [a reference to a proposed agricultural trade agreement with Canada], rats, wigs, J-hop, the new auditorium, and street car hold-ups.[64]

From the same source sprang the news that "two striking evidences" of the approach of spring were "fussers and football." Great caution was advised, however, since fussing, after all, constituted "a germ of a breach of promise suit."[65]

Eduard was undoubtedly popular with the girls at M.A.C., as he would be for all of his life. The portrait that stares from page 39 of the

1911 *Wolverine* is that of a rather serious, but strikingly handsome, young man with penetrating eyes. He was wearing a bow tie when he had his picture taken.

The character portrait of Eduard that emerges from college days is an attractive one. He was a good student with many friends, active in a wide range of intellectual and social activities—a young man of promise. It was in any event a greatly matured Eduard Lindeman who presented himself for graduation exercises with other members of the M.A.C. class of 1911.

As shaken out since freshman days, the class consisted of 26 "young lady graduates of the cap and gown" (it did not seem necessary to mention that all were home economics majors), 58 "real engineers," 40 "near farmers," and 21 "woodsmen" (forestry majors) for a total of 145 souls. Lindeman was one of the near farmers and was numbered, too, among the 19 percent of class members who had started out as "preps" or sub-freshmen.[66]

The commencement speaker of that year was Dr. James K. Patterson, president emeritus of Kentucky University. Lindeman and his classmates received a long and exceedingly florid discourse largely focused on the Morrill Act of 1862, that piece of nineteenth century legislation that made possible the creation of Michigan Agricultural College and its sister institutions in other states.[67]

While it is tempting to speculate that Eduard Lindeman might have received a significant degree of inspiration in the direction of adult education from a speech at his commencement about a major piece of adult education legislation, it is unlikely that this is so. The Smith-Lever Act, which was essentially a projection of the Morrill Act to facilitate extension programming by land-grant universities, was not enacted until 1914. In 1911, the importance of the Morrill Act as a centerpiece of adult education history was not as evident as it would later become.

The young man who marched into his place in front of the rostrum to Brede's "King of Clubs" and who listened to Dr. Patterson's words was quite different from the raw, countrified youth who had entered Michigan Agricultural College five years before. For one thing, he didn't even have the same name.

One of the minor puzzles of Lindeman's life is the evolution of his name. He was born Edward Lindemann. He became Eduard Christian Lindeman. Why? The answer must lie in the deepest of the repressed recesses of his childhood and youth—for he seems to have revealed the full answer to no one inside or outside of his family. It is possible to trace the evolution of the new name—a process that began, but did not quite end, during his stay at Michigan Agricultural College.

The young man was admitted to M.A.C. with the name given him by his parents,[68] but when he took up residence in the college's Twaits' Hall in 1907, he had become "E. C. Lindemann," the "C" being added. The E. C. Lindemann name was retained in M.A.C.'s directories of staff and students between 1908 and 1910, but for his final year as a resident of Dormitory 8D, the name had become "E. C. Lindeman."

First use of the spelling "Eduard," along with the fully spelled-out "Christian," seems to have been in the 1910 college yearbook, where "Eduard Christian Lindemann" put in an appearance for the first time.

Consistency in matters of detail was never Eduard Lindeman's long suit, though it seems odd that even he would be so careless as he was in the use of his own name. Was it the reflection of internal turmoil that he seems to have had trouble making up his mind which form of his name to use? In his incarnation as president of the M.A.C. YMCA in 1910, he was "E. C. Lindemann," but for that same year "E. C. Lindeman" was editor for the Eunomian Literary Society.[69] The *Holcad's* editor-in-chief for 1911, according to the masthead, was "E. C. Lindemann."

Adding a certain richness of detail to an already complicated personal nomenclature, Lindeman sometimes used "Lindy," the nickname affectionately given him by his college friends, in signing articles in the *Holcad*. It was also "Lindy" to whom letters to the editor were addressed.[70]

One might think that a consistent "Eduard Christian Lindeman" would take the path of life that led away from the undergraduate world at East Lansing, but this did not happen. "Eduard C. Lindemann" returned to write his first book in 1912,[71] to edit a publication called *The Gleaner* in 1911,[72] and to write a publication for the Michigan Department of Public Instruction in 1919.[73] "Eduard Christian Lindeman" was also active during this same period. As late as 1926, Lindeman referred to himself as "Edward" in a letter to a friend.[74]

In later life, Lindeman permitted even his best friends to misspell his first name. For all of their long correspondence in the 1920s and 1930s, Dorothy Straight Elmhirst almost always wrote to "Dear Edward." Lindeman's best friend of early adult life, Herbert Croly, would often misspell his friend's first name, at one point even adding a new variation: "My dear Edouard."[75]

Why would the young Edward Lindemann want any other spelling or form of his name? It is probably safe to assume that dropping the second "n" from his last name came in response to consistent misspellings of it by others—a common annoyance for many individuals bearing names ending in a Teutonic "mann" in an anglicized society. Adding a middle name is also understandable. Like Harry Truman, Lindeman may have wanted the distinctiveness of an initial to better set off his first and last names. As a young man active in the church, the choice of the name "Christian" would be understandable.

As for "Edward" becoming "Eduard," the possible answers are less clear. Perhaps, as he worked through the identity crisis of his early adulthood, young Lindeman simply wanted a name that was more distinctive than the relatively common "Edward." But why would he change it to "Eduard," which is the spelling preferred in Germany?[76] In later life, Lindeman would do everything possible to mask his German heritage. The probable answer is that he was ignorant of the ethnic derivation of this version.

As the newly minted college graduate prepared to leave for his new job as editor of the *Gleaner* in Detroit, Lindeman had no intention of shaking all of the dust of the town of East Lansing from his feet. Some clues to what would become permanent ties to that quiet and pleasant college community can be found in what passed for society news in the columns of the *Holcad* during Eduard Lindeman's year of editorship.

On October 3, 1910, it was noted that Miss Hazel Taft "spent a few days of last week at her home, her school being closed on account of the County Fair." In the October 31 edition, it was reported that Miss Taft had visited the campus to attend a Eunomian party and see a football game with Notre Dame. Hazel's visits at home were also recorded on November 28 and on January 9, 1911. Could the *Holcad's* student readers really have been that interested in the routine activities of a young woman who had graduated the year before?

CHAPTER 3

Young Man in a Hurry

Hazel Charlotte Taft was not the sort of young woman Eduard Lindeman would have met had he remained in farm or factory work. Her father, who had a distinguished academic career, was Professor of Horticulture and Landscape Gardening at Michigan Agricultural College and also served as superintendent of farmers' institutes and state inspector of nurseries and orchards. An inventive man, Taft introduced to Michigan the system of spraying orchards to control fruit tree diseases and also developed experimental greenhouses.[1]

Levi Rawson Taft, with his full face, handlebar mustache, and reddish hair parted in the middle, bore a striking resemblance to his cousin, the twenty-seventh President of the United States. Like President Taft, Levi was also full of figure— "a veritable human beanpole"—was how the student yearbook, which had irreverent names for all the faculty, put it.[2] Hazel's mother, the former Ella Maynard, had in common with her husband a proud New England family heritage.[3]

The Tafts, who lived in a pleasant home on faculty row at M.A.C., had been Americans for generations, and Levi and Ella would undoubtedly have found it difficult to talk for long with Frederick and Frederecka Von Piper Lindemann. But it was the son of these simple immigrant folk who caught Hazel's eye.

The two met at the home of the M.A.C. Dean of Women, who had a Christmas party for Eduard and other students who had no homes for the holidays. Hazel had been one of the local students invited to the affair. Shortly afterward, the usually pacific Hazel was impressed as she heard Eduard address a rally of students called to protest the administration's dismissal of several among their number.[4]

Little is known about the college romance of this strong, active, yet reserved young woman and the assertive young man who would become her life partner. Like Eduard, Hazel was a good student, with her share of the accomplishments that were expected of a young lady of good family in that day. Her piano solo of "Minuet" by Schubert was part of a program given by students of music in the parlor of the women's building in 1909.[5] Hazel was also a crack tennis player—a game she would enjoy all her life.[6]

Graduating a year ahead of Eduard, in 1910, Hazel took one of the few options then open to women when she signed on as a teacher in the public schools of Ionia, Michigan.[7] But by the first month of the new year, it was all over with Hazel Taft and the Ionia Public Schools (which one suspects she hadn't much liked anyway). She had "resigned her position," the *Holcad* said, and was back at home where she had a new job as assistant registrar at the college.[8] Undoubtedly her developing friendship with Eduard was a contributing factor in her return to the campus.

When Eduard left M.A.C. in June 1912, he went to Detroit, where he assumed the editorship of the *Gleaner*, an agricultural journal aimed at Michigan farmers. His former peers on the *Holcad* were ecstatic at the good fortune of their departed editor-in-chief. Headlines in the *Holcad's* October 23, 1911, edition fairly screamed out the news: "*LINDY'S FIRST 'GLEANER' APPEARS.*[9] One of their own was already making good.

It is unfortunate that no copies of the *Gleaner* during Lindeman's editorship appear to survive in any public repository. Gisela Konopka reviewed a now-lost private file in her 1958 study of Lindeman's social work philosophy. She reports that Lindeman introduced adult education topics to the publication for the first time in December 1911 in an article entitled "Education for Busy Farmers," which described agriculture short courses such as were offered at M.A.C.[10] Undoubtedly a review of issues for the balance of his short tenure there would be instructive in revealing the genesis of Lindeman's interest in the new field of adult education.

Little is known of Eduard's year in Detroit except that he was lonely in his rented room. He burst into print with his first book, *College Characters I Have Met*, which he seems to have induced the *Gleaner's* printer to publish.[11] In this thoroughly interesting—if simple—volume, Lindeman drew intriguing portraits not only of professors but of a librarian, secretary, gardener, and judge.

Eduard was already thinking in terms that would speed his intellectual entry to the world of adult education. In the preface to *College Characters*, he indicates that the nonprofessional characters whom he portrays may not be "teachers of books and facts," but they are nonetheless "teachers of life." He did not mean to imply that their influence upon him and other students had been greater than that "which emanates from those who conscientiously regard their obligation as a teacher, but it wishes to emphasize that which is too often slighted."[12] This was a theme that would be important in Eduard's future—and in the future of adult education in the United States.

College Characters contains the faintest of clues to what might be the most painful memory in Lindeman's repressed past. It comes in Eduard's sketch about the college gardener and concerns a letter:

> One night, very late, I went to post a letter. It had been a hard letter to write, and I had waited until the dormitory was quiet before I made the attempt to begin. I was certain that I was right in saying what I had said, but still I was not satisfied. I knew that that letter would hurt the feelings of my dearest relative. . . I do not know how long I sat [in the garden] that night, but suddenly I started at the sound of footsteps near me. I quickly rose to my feet and started for my room. As the man behind me came nearer, I turned and was recognized by The Gardener. He put his hand on my shoulder and said, "Well old man, what are you doing out this time o'night?" He seemed to understand that there was something wrong.[13]

His dearest relative? A sister? Brother? And what might that pain have been?

No clear dissatisfactions sift out from the *Gleaner* experience, but like most intelligent young men, Eduard must have been restless. He was also struggling to define and articulate his religious faith. This spur, and the presence of Hazel, also, must have moved him to seek and secure a position with the Plymouth Congregational Church in Lansing.[14] And besides, he had started later than his peers. There was time that had to be made up. Eduard Lindeman was a young man in a hurry.

Levi Taft disliked Eduard, considering him too liberal.[15] But his daughter's mind was made up. Hazel Charlotte Taft and Eduard Christian Lindeman were joined in marriage on August 29, 1912. After the ceremony, the newlyweds left for Charlevoix in Northern Michigan where the Tafts had relatives and a summer home on Pine

Lake (now Lake Charlevoix).[16] This was a spot that Hazel and Eduard would love all their lives. It is where their ashes are buried.

As they honeymooned and later returned to their small home at 627 Sparrow Avenue in East Lansing, the young Lindemans must have assessed each other with some degree of awe on both sides. Eduard undoubtedly thought himself lucky to have won so attractive and capable a woman for his wife. He had clearly married above himself economically and socially. Was his new wife not well connected, being related even to the President of the United States? Not that she was a snob. Ever practical, with a no-nonsense approach to the business of life, Hazel Taft Lindeman was truly an uncomplicated person. She asked little of life except that she be allowed to live in the manner expected for a woman of her time.

Clear-eyed, direct in manner, with a fresh and warm face, Hazel walked with the brisk stride of an athlete. Here was a strong woman, Eduard may have reasoned, someone who could be the rock that had been denied him in his earlier life.

For her part, as she contemplated the man who was now hers, Hazel must have wondered from the beginning just what she had gotten herself into. His mind worked so differently from hers—asked questions she would never think to ask and often didn't even understand. Yet, certainly he was brilliant and surely would be an adequate provider. To be sure, he was a bit rough on the edges, but he seemed amenable to selective polishing.

The young Lindemans, in truth, each had good qualities and had much to offer each other. Yet theirs was not destined to be the easiest of partnerships. Like many other married couples, the Lindemans would find marriage to be a series of tests for which there were not always facile answers. Growth, when it occurs, is not always in parallel, or even compatible, directions. But these would be events in the days ahead of them. In the fresh new weeks of September 1912, there is no evidence that Hazel and Eduard took anything other than delight in each other's company.

Plymouth Congregational Church, located on Townsend Street in Lansing just opposite Michigan's domed Capitol, occupied an exuberantly Victorian Gothic structure. Its congregation, many of them executives in the embryo automobile industry or faculty at M.A.C., included some of the first citizens of the city.[17] The pulpit at Plymouth Church was occupied by a Scot, Dr. James S. Williamson, whose slightly burred speech had a particular fascination for the congregation.[18]

Eduard became "assistant in charge of church work" in September

1912, at a salary of $1,800 a year. His charge was that of organizing clubs and similar work among the young people. Both young Lindemans joined the church upon confession of faith on January 15, 1913.[19]

Though records from this era are scant (many were consumed in a fire that destroyed the original building in 1971), Lindeman seems to have done a good job. But the church was having financial troubles, and in February 1914 the Board of Trustees found it necessary to accept Lindeman's resignation, though not until they had conducted negotiations in an effort to get him to stay on with a reduced salary. Eduard's successor was paid only $1,000 per year.[20]

It was undoubtedly a boost from his father-in-law that enabled Eduard to join Michigan Agricultural College's Division of Extension as State Leader of Boys' and Girls' Clubs on October 1, 1914.[21]

Since passage of the Smith-Lever Act in 1914, the land grant colleges had been busy organizing their statewide Cooperative Agricultural Extension Services. In Michigan this task, directed by Eben Mumford, a sociologist, was proceeding apace, with the generous grants of federal money being supplemented by an equal amount put up by the Legislature. Each county was to receive an Extension agent as soon as funds were available.[22]

Some fifteen county agents had already been appointed, each with half his salary paid by combined state and federal funds, with the balance coming from funds appointed by the county board of supervisors. Eduard Lindeman was one of a number of special agents appointed to assist the various county agents and to work in counties where no agent had yet been appointed. The Cooperative Extension Service would grow to become one of the largest adult education systems in the world. Interestingly enough, Eduard Lindeman's job was with the youth arm of this evolving adult education giant— though his involvement with parents and adult leaders may have been the initial locus of his lifelong interest in parent education. Lindeman's job, under what would eventually evolve into the 4-H Club program, was that of organizing clubs in which farm boys learned to grow healthy crops and livestock and girls learned to sew and can fruits and vegetables.[23]

It was wholesome, useful work, and Eduard was good at it. His reports of Junior Extension work roughly parallel the period of World War I. Food was essential to the war effort, and Eduard's boys and girls were prodded to do their share—as they apparently did.

Great quantities of corn were raised by the young people in these clubs, to say nothing of potatoes, poultry, livestock, beans, apples, birds, flowers, and alfalfa. Girls plunged into projects in canning and gardening, housekeeping, and garment making. There were some 374 organized clubs with 5,952 enrollments in all of these activities reported for 1916.[24] The Service must have placed great confidence in Eduard to charge him with the full statewide responsibility for this work.

By 1917, Eduard was hitting his stride and churning out the kind of figures that made his program look good—as it undoubtedly was. Eduard and his apple-cheeked charges from Michigan farms that year hurled some 456,873,430 bushels of corn in the general direction of the German Kaiser. The sugar-beet clubs sent 28,864 tons, and the pig clubs weighed in at 1,797,196 pounds (10,583 animals).[25] It was a good year.

By 1918, Lindeman had almost an empire. Because of the war-imposed demand for food production, the staff of Junior Extension work was increased so that at the close of the fiscal year there were thirteen leaders employed on the state staff and sixty-four with the various counties. A total for all projects was an impressive 22,396 boys and girls.[26]

Lindeman began to show promise as a writer on serious subjects while he was with the Extension Service. His first article in a major national publication appeared in *Survey* in 1915. Its title: "Legislature That Did No Harm." The young writer was a little naive (he felt that Michigan's legislators were "free from undue lobbying pressure"). The people's elected representatives were benign in that they "did very little that can possibly be harmful to the welfare of the state."[27] Lindeman would sharpen his critical skills in the years ahead. He was at least off to a good start. Lindeman's first major book, *The Community*, was also a product of the Michigan years though he would not write it until 1921.

Eduard Lindeman resigned from the Extension Service effective September 30, 1918, after exactly four years.[28] What was his reason for leaving what would become America's proudest adult education institution? The apparent answer lies in a 1924 article appearing in *Survey*. Lindeman's remarks were brutally sardonic—a rare form of expression for him.

He proposed that "an expedition be sent to study agricultural methods in Siberia and that the personnel be composed of 90 per cent of the deans of agriculture in the agricultural colleges, 85 per cent of the directors of extension, 80 per cent of the agricultural agents or farm demonstrators, 50 per cent of the home demonstration agents and boys' and girls' club leaders, and a like number of 'bosses' and office-holders in farm organizations. While the expedition is away it might also be beneficial if the United States Department of Agriculture could be reorganized into a school of rehabilitation or re-education for mis-educated specialists." He added that the most obvious objection to the expedition might come from the Siberians. "In this connection one can only hope for the best."[29]

His quarrel with the Extension Service? "Its impact upon rural people is overwhelmingly materialistic, prosaic, dull and uninspiring." The Extension instructors "are uniformly persons who have been trained to view life through the lens of some technical specialty . . . They look at the farmer in relation to hogs or alfalfa, but they almost never see hogs and alfalfa in relation to the total personality of the farmer."[30]

Still, Extension's adult education thrust must have left its impression on Lindeman, for the idea of adult education, or lifelong learning, was already within him and begging release.

As he contemplated his future, Eduard could not be casual for there were many more mouths for him to feed. Doris was born to Eduard and Hazel Lindeman in 1913. This happy event was closely followed by three others as Ruth, Betty, and Barbara presented themselves to the world in 1915, 1916, and 1918 respectively.[31]

As his responsibilities increased, so, too, did Eduard's self-confidence. Moreover, he was acquiring a circle of admirers. Eduard Lindeman had the gift of charisma—and he was showing that he could attract the great as well as the small.

It was undoubtedly during his stay in Detroit that Eduard met and was befriended by one of that city's most influential citizens. Harriet Robinson McGraw was fifty-three in 1912. She was the first of a series of wealthy, intellectual, and civic-minded woman patrons who would be drawn into the orbit of a magnetic Eduard Lindeman.

Eduard must have been awed not only by the wealth but by the accomplishments of this aristocratic supporter of the unpopular causes that were also his own. The intelligent and strong-minded Mrs. McGraw was a pioneer in a number of social service movements. She was an opponent of capital punishment and worked for its abolition at both state and national levels. She was a delegate representing Michigan at the first birth control conference in New York and sponsored Margaret Sanger's appearance in Detroit to speak on that then almost unmentionable subject. She was a board member of the National Women's Party, an ardent pacifist, a defender of civil liberties, a campaigner for the freedom of political prisoners.[32]

From her suite in Detroit's Pontchartrain Hotel—and later in the new Statler Hotel—she quietly directed or supported the kinds of causes that would not receive favorable consideration or even hearings in the drawing rooms or clubs where her wealthy social peers gathered. Through financial aid or other support, Mrs. McGraw encouraged the efforts of idealistic young people, Eduard Lindeman among them.[33] Mrs. McGraw's daughter, Kathleen (Mrs. Donald) Hendrie, would also become a close friend of Eduard's.

What sort of man was it that drew Harriet McGraw and so many men and women of all ages to Eduard Lindeman? Someone meeting him for the first time in this period would immediately notice that he possessed a commanding physical presence. He was arrestingly handsome—though it was not of the movie star variety.[34]

The face, often roughly sunburned (a by-product of hours on the tennis court and in his garden), was animated, strong, and open. A jutting jaw was counterpointed with high cheekbones that helped give the visage of a patrician appearance. The generous shock of hair was a sandy brown, not quite blond. Ironically, in light of future events, Eduard Lindeman possessed to an inch all of those characteristics that would be ascribed to the perfect Aryan type by Adolf Hitler. Behind his penetrating blue eyes seemed to march generations of North European ancestors.

He was six feet tall; his body was raw-boned, lean, and gave the appearance of male vitality. He moved rapidly. There was just a trace of awkwardness in his posture and movements, but its effect was such as to lend a certain distinction rather than raw eccentricity.

He dressed carelessly. Unless Hazel's latest ministrations to his shirts and suits were just minutes in the past, he looked rumpled. Ties were apt to be worn with the knot askew or loose.

He could also be physically clumsy at times. "I can't get through a meal without breaking at least a glass or a saucer," he once told a friend. A few nights before he'd attended a country club party. Someone knocked an ash tray off a table, "and you should have heard the chorus shout: 'Eduard Lindeman, I know.' And, it wasn't."[35]

But it was Eduard's mind and demeanor that would be central in riveting the attention of Harriet McGraw and so many others. He could immediately command attention with a strong and vibrant bass voice, but the mood it summoned was that of welcome, never intimidation. He gave the same warm attention to the world's little people as he did to the rich and powerful. The person he was addressing would be made to feel important. There was an immediate sense of personal empathy.

In spite of his plebeian background, Eduard Lindeman had by this time acquired a high degree of polish. Was it Hazel who had taught him good manners? He spoke well and with restraint. It was years before he could bring himself to use even the word "damn" in letters to close friends. Before that, he would say only "darn" or would write "d——n." He never raised his voice, nor was he often sarcastic or insensitive to the feelings of others.

He had a great capacity for friendship though he kept many relationships at low levels of emotional engagement. There was an air of enticement surrounding Lindeman, which invited personal approach. He had the genius of interchange. It was very easy to talk to Eduard Lindeman.

Lindeman was also a man who loved the good life. He liked food and drink, socializing informally, jokes and laughter, baseball and tennis. An avid gardener, he also had a passion for bird-watching and pursued this hobby in spare moments during his travels in the United States and around the world. He liked to dance and to sing and was good at these sociable arts.

Lindeman was persuasive in a way that went beyond pure logic. A longtime friend recalls that it "didn't make much difference whether he said anything or not, he sounded wonderful."[36] And he always appeared to be in such dead earnest—so much so that Bonaro Overstreet remembers him whimsically beginning one lecture with this statement: "Nothing is ever as true as I say it is when I'm talking earnestly."[37] Still, one instinctively knew that Eduard Lindeman meant what he said.

He was an inventive man. John Hader, a close colleague, remembers him as picking up "little bits of ideas and the first thing you know he *had* something."[38] His relentless pursuit of emerging issues was legendary. He would be on the scene in a hurry, and the outlines of the problem, along with developing answers, would quickly find their way into his speeches, articles, and conversation.

The line between work and recreation for Eduard Lindeman was indistinct. He loved teaching, speaking, reading, and even writing when the words flowed easily (as they frequently did). At the same time, he played hard. He would discharge great bursts of energy in relentless games of tennis. Such a man would not have difficulty in finding a new employer.

After a short temporary assignment in New York City with the War Camp Community Service in the closing months of World War I, Lindeman accepted a position with the YMCA College of Chicago.[39] The transition to Y work would certainly have been smooth for this collegiate YMCA president. Also, he had worked extensively with YMCA workers in Michigan's counties.

The YMCA College in Chicago was then rapidly expanding what it called its School of County Work. As "specialist in country life and rural leadership training," Lindeman joined the staff on January 1, 1919, and the family took up residence in an old house on South Drexel Avenue in Chicago. He was charged with training leadership for county Y work in the future.[40] In practice, this involved teaching courses in rural life. Half of his time was to be spent at the College, with the balance in the field in developing leadership training. Lindeman's "contribution to the student" at YMCA College was to be that of aiding him "to understand the forces constructive and sinister in American life and to become a forward-looking thinker."[41] As it turned out, Eduard's articulation of this mission was to be quite different from that expected by the College.

For Eduard, it must have been heady to be addressed now as "Professor Lindeman." It was a title he would continue to hold with only a single interruption for the rest of his life—though he never earned a degree higher than his Michigan Agricultural College baccalaureate.

Lindeman's tenure with the YMCA College was unexpectedly brief. His resignation "on account of ill health" was announced after only one year of service. The College newsletter, in announcing Lindeman's resignation, went far beyond what would routinely be expected in praising the young faculty member. Professor Lindeman's work had been "of extraordinary brilliancy. We recognize in him one of the most gifted minds that has ever been attached to our teaching staff." It seemed fitting that his going-away present was a lamp presented by students "to one whose torch-like intellect had lighted their way with its flame."[42]

This ebullient outburst may have been more typical of student reaction to the departure of Professor Lindeman than it was of his administrative superiors at the College. The trouble began even before Lindeman assumed full-time duties at Chicago with an incident at the Y's Summer School and Conference at Williams Bay on Wisconsin's Lake Geneva.

The setting was peaceful, even if the atmosphere was not. The Lindeman family, including the newest baby, Barbara, was ensconced in a small cabin on the camp grounds above Lake Geneva, one of the handsomest lakes in America's Midwest. Eduard would typically move his portable Corona with its tripod outside under a tree when he wrote letters detailing his worsening situation to Mrs. McGraw.[43]

His problems had begun with a speech so controversial in content that some of his friends had worried that he might have to leave the auditorium by a back door afterward rather than from the front. He had begun earnestly: "On an occasion like this one is tempted to say those things which are pleasing and soothing rather than those which ring true to the inner conscience. With God's help I shall not yield to that temptation this morning." He was proud of that beginning which "the men about camp" were still repeating the next day.[44]

The text of Lindeman's speech does not survive, but it seems to have turned on theological concepts that were antithetical to those espoused by the Conference administrators. In any event, "it stirred up the lions"[45] to the point where they would not permit it to be published, an action necessitating the issuance of refunds to students who had already paid to receive copies.

The administration, supported by the older cadre of faculty members, would have been pleased had Eduard resigned on the spot, but he had support from the younger group, who put up a fight on his behalf. A number of students, too, had threatened to boycott the College had Lindeman not been allowed to remain on the staff. Lindeman was allowed to stay on until the Conference sessions ended on July 24.[46]

Eduard admitted that he rather enjoyed the ensuing altercation though he was disconcerted at its impending effect on his career. He recognized that he would now probably have to leave the YMCA movement; yet he wanted to "see the thing through since I have been the cause of the precipitation."[47] Though he did not say so, Eduard must also have had more than a few nervous tremors as he looked into the faces of his four young children. It would not be the last time their father would place the family's economic well-being at risk for his adherence to principle.

In this ambiguous environment, Lindeman moved on for a second YMCA Summer School and Conference, this time at the Y's summer colony at Silver Bay on New York's Lake George. Eduard was initially put off by the reserve of the easterners who peopled this establishment. They had a disinclination to speak with anyone to whom they had not been introduced or whom they "hadn't known for at least ten years." They were, it seemed to him, an altogether "queer lot."[48]

He loved the Adirondack Mountains, however, with their sharp, craggy rocks. The wide variety of trees intrigued him—mostly spruces and white pines but also maples, beech, and occasional patches of clear white birches. The scene compared favorably with that at the Y

Camp at Estes Park in the Colorado Rockies where he had attended a conference the summer before.[49]

In time, he even warmed to the people of the East. Their group song services under an outstanding leader seem to have done it. He picked up some pointers that he had promised Mrs. McGraw he'd carry back to her Twentieth Century Club crowd, which also enjoyed singing. One night he rented a boat and drifted on the lake as songs from the camp poured out over the water, which seemed to "purify and harmonize" the music remarkably. Never before had he realized the "simple grandeur" of "Just a Song at Twilight."[50]

He grew to appreciate his students, most of them "high calibre teachers," but he was annoyed by an atmosphere that seemed pervasively conservative. "What," he asked his class, "shall be the position of an industrial Y.M.C.A. Secretary in the case of a strike?" He was amused at their "trimming, shilly-shallying, straddle-the-fence" answers. "You may be sure," he reported, "that I did not permit them to be comfortable in this attitude."[51]

Lindeman's "liberalism" did not create quite the stir at Silver Bay that it had at Lake Geneva because here he had clear support from a Professor Hayes, a Yale faculty member, who was teaching a class in economics. Both were doing the same kinds of reading. The only difference was that Eduard had practical experience whereas Hayes had none.[52] It is a mark of Eduard's growing confidence that he felt himself favored over Hayes on grounds of his greater store of experiential knowledge. A less confident man would have been intimidated by Hayes's undoubted superiority in credentials.

If Eduard had *provoked* controversy at Lake Geneva, he enlisted Hayes and others to *start* an insurrection at Silver Bay. Some of the faculty "or rather a small group on the faculty, was attempting to dictate the method of teaching that is to be employed by all teachers." In the service of "democratic ideals," Lindeman was elected to make the rebel speech at a faculty meeting. In the attending melee "all of the blame for the fight" centered on him. Eduard, clearly in an upstart mood, pronounced it all "very amusing."[53]

Not so amused were his superiors at YMCA College, who had on their hands an unwanted boat-rocker. The situation was delicate. They wished to ease themselves out of any commitment to young Lindeman, who was scheduled to begin teaching duties at the institution's Chicago campus in the fall. But they did not want the impression to get out that he was leaving because of a difference of opinion, which they correctly perceived would be injurious to the College. Eduard was rather contemptuous of what he perceived as hypocrisy on the part of the official who conducted negotiations with him, admitting that he'd "like to hit him in the nose. . . ."[54]

College officials needn't have worried. Lindeman had no desire to make difficulties or remain where he was uncomfortable and unwanted. He had already ascertained that he did not want to go back to Chicago to teach.[55] The resignation on account of illness announcement was undoubtedly a situational mask that served the needs of all concerned.

Considered in the context of the whole of his life, this series of incidents was atypical behavior on Lindeman's part. While he never shrank from a battle that he felt needed to be fought, he grew to hate "contentiousness" in human affairs. He would never again provoke a fight in just the way that he had provoked these.

There is a further anomaly in these encounters with YMCA officials. The anger that is evident in Eduard as he turned on his older colleagues and administrative superiors is almost meanspirited, and it is of an intensity that goes beyond the circle of its announced cause. Could this have been displaced anger—aimed at targets in the YMCA but stemming at its roots from individuals and events closer to Eduard's person and Eduard's past?

If the YMCA College at Chicago did not want to retain Lindeman, there was another institution waiting in the wings to take him on. The North Carolina College for Women in Greensboro offered Eduard a position in the Department of Sociology and Economics at a salary of $4,000. It was more money than Eduard had ever seen, and he hastened to accept—though he had great reservations about teaching in the academic backwater then associated with a college for women.[56]

Eduard plunged with his usual zeal into his work as Director of the College's Sociology Department and quite soon tangled with older faculty members. As at Silver Bay, the problem, as Lindeman viewed it, was that these persons wanted to impose particular teaching methods upon others.[57]

Eduard Lindeman never quite fit in at North Carolina College for Women. But Greensboro was not all bad from the Lindemans' perspective. In Charles Shaw and his perky wife, Dorothy, Eduard and Hazel Lindeman would acquire lifelong friends. Shaw, the college librarian, was a match for Eduard in both intellect and wit. Their personal correspondence between the year 1924, when Lindeman left Greensboro, and his death in 1953 records a jewel of a friendship.

As he had left the YMCA College in Chicago in a cloud of controversy, Lindeman's departure from North Carolina College for

Women, too, would be traumatic. The details are meager, but the basic fact was that the College president seems to have felt forced to release Lindeman because of an ugly racial incident in which the Lindemans incurred the enmity of the Ku Klux Klan and its prominent allies in that officially segregated Southern community. The offense: allowing their black cook to entertain a fair number of her friends at a birthday party in the Lindeman kitchen.[58] Finding themselves in physical danger, as well as in emotional turmoil, Eduard and Hazel decided to get out of the Klan's way without delay.

But adversity may have hastened the approach of good fortune. Two persons entered Eduard Lindeman's life in this period—both of them to become close personal friends. Both too, had the sort of connections that would make it possible for Lindeman to extend himself far beyond the world of Greensboro—or any other small American city. Those new friends were Dorothy Whitney Straight and Herbert Croly, editor of one of America's most prestigious magazines, *The New Republic*.

CHAPTER 4

Another World

Herbert David Croly was older than Eduard Lindeman by sixteen years. His background, solidly genteel, had given him a strong base from which to launch himself professionally. Croly's mother, Jane Cunningham Croly, a prolific writer on topics of interest to women, had been one of America's best-known syndicated columnists under the pen name "Jennie June."[1] David Goodman Croly, Herbert's father, had been editor of the *New York World*.[2] Herbert Croly followed in the journalistic footsteps of his parents, becoming the founder and first editor of *The New Republic*.

The New Republic's chief executive was an extremely shy man and one who was difficult to know.[3] To those who did not know him well, he could also seem humorless and even a bit strange.[4] "A tight mouth" was how civil libertarian Roger Baldwin described him, adding that "he'd never talk, he wrote."[5] Croly tended to depend upon his more outgoing wife, Louise, to carry on necessary personal diplomacy. To his friends, Croly revealed real personal warmth and a true sense of concern for others—a concern which was translated into calls for action on social issues on pages of *The New Republic*.[6] Brilliantly intellectual, he also had a mystical and religious side.[7]

Croly probably became acquainted with the young professor at North Carolina College for Women when Lindeman was preparing to submit his first article to *The New Republic*, a piece on tobacco cooperatives,[8] though his attention might also have been drawn to

Eduard's book *The Community: An Introduction to the Study of Community Leadership and Organization,* which was published in 1921.

It is odd in a way that Lindeman and Croly would strike up a friendship as close as it was according to all accounts, including their own. For the childless Croly, the attraction must have been generative in part, that of a need for a retiring man in late middle age to play the role of mentor to someone as brilliant and charismatic as the young Eduard Lindeman. For the younger Eduard, Croly became a father figure. Theirs was an affinity of minds—with Croly finding himself more closely allied intellectually with Lindeman than he had ever been with any previous friend.[9] But there was laughter as well in their relationship—something infrequent in Croly's interactions with others.[10]

With Eduard at hand to run interference, Herbert could sometimes relax enough to enjoy some of life's informal pleasures. On one occasion, he was able to unbend enough to play a game of bridge with some of the Lindemans' homespun neighbors. Another time, he even allowed himself to talk politics with someone who had driven up to the Lindeman home to present Eduard and Hazel with a basket of fruit.[11]

Largely on the basis of his book *The Promise of American Life,* published in 1909, Herbert Croly qualifies as one of the most influential political theorists of the twentieth century. His assertion that the national government should consciously and systematically advance social welfare was one of the cornerstones of Franklin Roosevelt's New Deal.[12] The ideas in Croly's book also influenced Lindeman as he wrote *The Meaning of Adult Education.*

Lindeman's departure from Greensboro was made possible by another new friend, one whose role in his life would be pivotal. The place and manner of the meeting of Eduard Christian Lindeman with Dorothy Whitney Straight is unknown, but it was quite likely through introduction by Herbert Croly. The meeting probably took place in 1921 or 1922, and by 1923 Eduard and Dorothy were writing each other long and affectionate (though determinedly platonic) letters. It was a lucky star for them both that brought the son of Frederick and Frederecka Von Piper Lindemann into the orbit of the daughter of William Collins and Flora Payne Whitney.

Dorothy Payne Whitney was born in Washington, D.C., where her father was serving as Secretary of the Navy in the Cabinet of President Grover Cleveland. The child's godmother was Frances Folsum Cleveland, the President's newly acquired young wife. The year was 1887.[13]

Navy Secretary William Whitney was hardly the prototypical Washington bureaucrat. He was one of the nation's wealthiest and most powerful men. According to Henry Adams, who knew him well, Whitney "had . . . gratified every ambition, and swung the country almost at his will; he had thrown away the usual objects of political ambition like the ashes of smoked cigarettes; had turned to other amusements, satiated every taste, gorged every appetite, won every object that New York afforded, and, not yet satisfied, had carried his field of activity abroad, until New York no longer knew what most to envy, his horses or his houses."[14]

Flora Whitney, through her Payne family heritage, was fabulously wealthy in her own right. According to *The New York Times*, Mrs. Whitney "reigned supreme" as a Washington hostess. "Always a leader, she sounded the keynote and society followed. . . The coming to Washington of Mr. and Mrs. Whitney was coincident with a style of entertaining which . . . had been unknown in this city."[15] Flora Whitney had plenty of rooms to fill with guests. At one time, the Whitneys possessed no less than eight homes.[16]

As the world measures good fortune, little Dorothy Whitney appeared to have everything. But tragedy struck early. Flora Whitney died when Dorothy was only six. William Whitney died in 1904 when his daughter was only seventeen.[17]

One of the nation's richest women and already on her own as a mere teenager, Dorothy was expected to take her place in the society world of New York, which was her principal home. Social concern, if any, within this group tended to focus on the charity ball. Between these and other social events, women of this station led basically indolent lives. For a time, it appeared that Dorothy's transition to womanhood as defined by this world would occur without undue delay.

Her debut was made with much fanfare in January of 1906, with the most notable guest being President Theodore Roosevelt's tempestuous, imperious, and spoiled daughter, Alice.[18] Dorothy was, as a matter of course, named to the Four Hundred in C. W. deLyon Nicholls's *The Ultra-Fashionable Peerage of America*—this at only age eighteen.[19] There were opulent balls, gay house parties, elegant dinners, horse races, and extended grand tours. It was a superficial, tasteless, mindless, selfish kind of existence—the same that produced so many superficial, tasteless, mindless, selfish women and men among America's economic elite at the turn of the century.

But great wealth produced a curious inversion inside the mind of this young woman. If life had meaning, wouldn't it involve more than the narrow frivolities of the blatantly vulgar world she had inherited from her parents? This woman of wealth acquired a social conscience and a sense of mission that would be lifelong.[20]

Michael Straight asserts that his mother's belief that her great wealth must be stewarded as a public trust was strengthened after she had read a series of newspaper articles containing the charge that William Whitney had acquired his great fortune at the expense of small investors.[21] She may also have been influenced by the egalitarian plan for the democratic life that was presented in Herbert Croly's book *The Promise of American Life*.[22] Dorothy became, in any event, a close friend of Croly, whom she came to revere and whose advice in all matters—including those involving donations from her great wealth—she took very seriously.[23]

However it was acquired, Dorothy's social conscience was alive and growing as she moved into life's mainstream as a woman of means. She did not sell all her goods to feed the poor. Neither did she desert Fifth Avenue Manhattan to live in the Borough of Queens. Though she did not allow herself to be dominated by the more acquisitive values of her parents, Dorothy accepted her position of wealth and status and occupied it with confidence and comfort.[24] For a time, Dorothy's concern was expressed in quite conventional ways. She helped found the Association of Junior Leagues of America and was its first president.[25] As Dorothy Payne Whitney, and later as Mrs. Willard Straight, her photograph was frequently in the New York papers as she participated in this or that charity event.

Later, Dorothy took it upon herself to dig deeper into the roots of poverty and misery than was the usual wont of the Junior League. In the company of Emma Goldman and Rose Schneiderman, she visited the notorious sweat shops of New York. With Lillian Wald, she worked at the Henry Street Settlement.[26]

It became clear to Dorothy that poverty and its ugly companions would not in any permanent sense yield to patch-and-fix-it solutions. She set about the task of educating herself about what the nature of sounder and longer-range solutions might be. It was to be an adventure that would cost her dearly in its dampening effect upon her relationships with her wealthy family. But she would gain many times what she lost in richer and more satisfying relationships with persons who were then pushing forward the frontiers of human social development. Dorothy Whitney's place in history was to be assured in a way that her parents' never would be.

Dorothy Whitney was pursued by many moneyed suitors in her own set, but she rejected them all in favor of an urbane and charming, but not wealthy, financial diplomat named Willard Straight. The pair were wed in Geneva on September 7, 1911.[27] Willard Straight was a man of feeling and warmth. He shared with Dorothy an interest in working for a better world.

One of the most influential and lasting of Dorothy Straight's gifts to the people of the United States is *The New Republic*, which eventually became a vehicle for some of Eduard Lindeman's best work. It was born in an almost offhanded manner.

Shortly after he had met and become friends with the Straights (probably in 1913), Herbert Croly visited the pair at their home on Long Island. Croly was discouraged about what seemed the "ineffectuality" of *Harpers Weekly* in presenting the positions of America's liberal left. "Why don't you get out a weekly yourself, Herbert?" Dorothy asked.[28]

Herbert's response: "Where would I find the money?" "I will find it," Dorothy said. Croly warned that it might take five years before the publication could be self-supporting. Undaunted, Dorothy said: "Yes, I understand. It may take longer, much longer. But let's go ahead."[29] And they did.

Dorothy Straight was also one of the founders of the New School for Social Research, a unique adult education institution, in New York. She was a director and substantial financial contributor.[30]

With its stable of distinguished editors and writers, *The New Republic* became in the 1920s a cutting edge of expression for those who, unlike President Coolidge, believed that the business of America might be something more than business. Croly recruited such lights as Felix Frankfurter, John Dewey, and Lewis Mumford in America— and in England Virginia Wolff, Bertrand Russell, John Maynard Keynes, H. G. Wells, and Rebecca West.[31] In 1922, Eduard Lindeman made his first appearance in *The New Republic;* he would follow this with many more articles in the decade ahead.

If Dorothy Straight was generous in bankrolling *The New Republic*, she never sought to control its editorial policies. The journal possessed complete editorial independence from its wealthy benefactress. After World War II, Dorothy's son, Michael Straight, became editor. The publication was sold in 1953, but not before Dorothy had poured in some $3,700,000 or an average of about $95,000 per year during its more than thirty-eight years of publication.[32]

Dorothy's marriage to Willard Straight was quite happy, and she was devastated by his death in Belgium in the great flu epidemic of 1918.[33] Thus, it was with the serious-minded young widow that Eduard Lindeman developed a friendship. Though it was her great wealth that instantly set her apart, it was the luminous character and personality of this remarkable woman that made her a continuing center of interest for the young philosopher and many others.

Dorothy was not beautiful by conventional standards. Yet she had most pleasing facial features, good skin, and often displayed a warm smile, all set off by fine dark hair. She was slender, had a soft and graceful manner, and carried herself well.[34] As she grew older, Dorothy's features became more angular—she appeared less soft—though she retained an aura of gentleness and charm.

Dorothy Straight radiated energy derived from dimensions of real inner strength. She was eminently sensible while retaining—indeed cultivating—an adventurous physical and intellectual life. She was direct, honest—though tactful, always—incapable of jealousy.[35] Importantly, because of the intellectual circles in which she placed herself, she was a good listener. Self-effacing at times, she often tried to compensate for her elevated economic status by assuming less-favored positions in group situations. As her friend Ruth Morgan said, "She always takes the hard chair. . . ."[36] Though cooperative and sensitive, Dorothy was no willow in the wind. She had firm and decided opinions, though it was characteristic of her that she expressed them gently.[37]

A certain air of sycophancy inevitably surrounds wealthy persons—especially if they are individuals known to be open and generous. Dorothy did not encourage this kind of attention—though she often got it. Felix Frankfurter was one such flatterer.[38] She did, however, attract genuine friends of both sexes in great numbers during her entire lifetime. She had a great capacity for friendships and wrote warmly, affectionately, and frequently to many of them.

Swanberg, one of her biographers, and an objective one, was hard pressed to find in Dorothy any major flaws. If she "had a fault, it was the ease with which she bestowed praise."[39] Her second son adds that she was sometimes given to "wishful thinking"—reading into other people qualities she was looking for but that possibly were not there.[40] A member of her personal staff who greatly admired her employer, when pressed, recalls that she sometimes was overcasual in issuing invitations. When the invitees later appeared she might have forgotten not only the invitation but the identity of the visitors. "Who on earth are they?" she would ask as the guests were being shown to their rooms.[41]

But these are small imperfections. One is forced to wonder whether a woman as worthy as this one really existed. The evidence, as gathered from review of Dorothy's correspondence, interviews with friends and colleagues, and hard looks at her record of accom-

plishments is overwhelmingly in favor of the most generous judgments of her character. Dorothy Straight was not perfect, but she was
very, very good.

Because it was quietly exerted, the full extent of Dorothy Straight's
positive influence on the United States of America may never be fully
known. She did not draw attention to herself. Her goals often were
realized in an indirect way through her support of more visible
others. But any full accounting of social reforms in America during
the 1920s and 1930s would be incomplete if it did not devote major
attention to the role of this noble and venturesome woman.

While Dorothy was a very intelligent woman, she did not have the
brilliance that marked the minds of Lindeman, Croly, Walter Lippmann, Felix Frankfurter, and others of her activist friends. But she
had something just as useful—a determination to use every cell of the
mind she did have to its fullest capacity. In this effort she succeeded;
her rate of intellectual and moral growth never slowed.

Dorothy would never willingly settle for an unsatisfactory status
quo if she thought there was the slightest chance that new options
should be tried. She read avidly. Her letters to Lindeman and others
are filled with accounts of the books she had been reading and
recommendations for books they might want to read. She also
accepted many of their recommendations for books.

Her formal education had been limited, but she shared with
Eduard a passion for continuing and continuous adult learning. By
the time she met Eduard, she was already on familiar terms with such
writers as Ralph Waldo Emerson, G. K. Chesterton, and William
James.[42] As her circle of friends who had a life of the mind increased,
she participated with them in discussions. She heard their lectures,
read their books, and developed with them the habit of critical
thinking.[43]

Dorothy Straight would have been among the first "adult students"
at Columbia, where she enrolled in courses during the days of her
widowhood. "Oh Leonard—the psychology courses are *such* fun!" she
wrote her soon-to-be-fiancé, Leonard Elmhirst, in 1921. In the same
letter she enclosed an announcement describing one of John Dewey's
courses at the New School for Social Research in which she apparently
was also enrolled.[44]

Later, instructed by Eduard, she would seek to use even illness as
a growth experience.[45] Her opportunities to do this were limited,
however. For, unlike Eduard, Dorothy enjoyed quite good health for
most of her long life.

Though she avoided the gross excesses that were characteristic of her parents, Dorothy Straight lived in an Edwardian manner. At the time Eduard met her, she had four homes. The elegant townhouse at 1130 Fifth Avenue in New York (now the International Center of Photography) she had built in 1912 after her marriage to Willard Straight. Applegreen was her ninety-acre estate at Old Westbury, New York. A staff of ten gardeners maintained the grounds there, which included a racetrack and polo field. Inside, it took between ten and fifteen servants to make the house functional for Dorothy and her three children, Whitney, Beatrice, and Michael.[46]

In the Adirondacks, Dorothy shared with a nephew and niece ownership of Camp Deerlands, a converted hunting lodge on Raquette Lake. A month or two of each summer were spent here, though she might also extend her children's vacation time by renting a large shingled summer residence at Quisset Harbor at Woods Hole, Massachusetts.[47] The Lindeman children recall a number of joyfully spent summer days as guests of Dorothy at both of these establishments.[48]

About seven blocks from her Fifth Avenue townhouse in New York, Dorothy maintained a large apartment at 1172 Park Avenue. Guests would often stay here at Dorothy's invitation—even when Dorothy was not in residence. Dorothy had offices on the twenty-sixth floor at 120 Broadway, where her manager, Oswald Gorton, directed her financial affairs, assisted by a staff of three or four. Edward Grove, who looked something like America's bald eagle emblem, was Dorothy's butler and presided over her household staff with an iron hand. Harry Hutchinson and Matthew Hamel, the chauffeurs, had charge of Dorothy's cars. In the 1920s she favored Stevens Duryeas with their handsome caned sides. Later there were Packards[49] and at least one Cadillac.[50]

Dorothy's personal affairs were delegated to Anna Bogue, a tough, domineering executive secretary who ran a tight ship—so tight that it sometimes cramped the style of her employer. A tall and massive woman with a pair of badly fitting false teeth that she needed periodically to push up,[51] Anna Bogue could be a great help—or an immovable obstacle—to anyone wanting access to Dorothy. Miss Bogue might sometimes be annoyed by Eduard Lindeman's casual attention to the details of his business dealings with her employer, but she was also susceptible to his charms.

No record of the initial arrangement exists, but it can be said with certainty that it was Dorothy Straight (prompted by Herbert Croly) who financed Eduard's liberation from his difficulties at North Carolina College for Women.[52] By mid-1924, Eduard was receiving from Dorothy a half-time stipend of $250 a month plus $1,200 a year for secretarial support and $900 for expenses.[53] Between 1922 and 1924, when he was otherwise unemployed, Eduard was able to do his own research and work as a free-lance writer as a result of Dorothy's largess. This interruption in regular employment, a generous sabbatical, enabled him to find himself intellectually and to begin what would be the most productive years of his life.[54]

❧

The early summer days of 1922 found the Lindemans frantically busy as they prepared to leave Greensboro. For Eduard there were examinations to grade and the windup of his work at the College. There was packing to do, moving arrangements to make, and, of course, farewells.[55]

Eduard by this time had developed the habit of keeping a scrapbook or journal. The first was contained in a looseleaf binder. For all others, he used bound volumes. Like the diarist Anaïs Nin, Lindeman carried his current volume with him on his travels, filling the empty pages with words while on trains or in hotel rooms. He never used a cursive writing style; most scrapbook entries are printed in capital letters. When he was at home or had access to a typewriter, he typed materials for the scrapbook. Many printed items were pasted to scrapbook pages.

The scrapbooks are basically intellectual journals—filled with random thoughts; articles and speeches in draft form; newspaper and magazine articles, usually accompanied by Lindeman's marginal notes; quotes from individuals as diverse as Confucius, Abraham Lincoln, Henry Ward Beecher, and Thomas Mann; travel itineraries; poetry (much of it bad); jokes; diagrams; notes or excerpts from books; conference programs; photographs; even doodles and maps. The Bill of Rights occupies the first page of Lindeman's scrapbook for 1941–1942.

Unfortunately for the biographer, Lindeman almost never included personal notes in his scrapbooks. Daughters might get married. Grandchildren would appear. There would be long periods of illness with hospital stays. Professional traumas, the midlife crisis, marital tension, and love affairs might come and go. But in the scrapbooks, these landmarks of life would be nonevents.

The scrapbooks do, however, constitute elegant records of the twisting and turning of Eduard Lindeman's intellectual journey. In general, the scrapbook entries are reliable records of his lectures. In speaking, he would have the scrapbook open in front of him, referring directly to his handwritten notes.[56] All of Lindeman's published works were mere outcroppings of a vastly larger and less polished base in the scrapbooks.

Lindeman was eager to claim his new future as he prepared to leave Greensboro. But already he was becoming aware that his body would not necessarily serve the desires of his mind. Though he looked perfectly healthy—rugged, really—Eduard Lindeman was a very sick man.

Nephritis, a kidney disease, is cruel and insidious as it works its path of destruction through each organ's approximately one million nephrons with glomeruli capillaries that act as filters for the blood. Chronic renal disease is regarded as a situation in which many of the kidneys' nephrons are destroyed and replaced by scar tissue. The advance of disease in the serious forms of nephritis is progressive and irreversible.[57]

When he took a physical examination to assess his fitness for military service in World War I in 1917, Eduard Lindeman learned that he had nephritis, or Bright's Disease as it was generally called then.[58] He presumably learned as well that the disease was incurable, that his blood would slowly be poisoned by waste products that increasingly impaired kidneys could not remove. Advanced medical science has brought drugs, dialysis, and even kidney transplants that can save or prolong the lives of nephritis patients. But during Eduard Lindeman's lifetime, persons afflicted by the disease lived under an immutable sentence of death.

During the middle and later years of his life, Eduard Lindeman suffered greatly from this illness and other maladies. Though his many periods of hospitalization or homebound illness often bore other labels (thyroid, sinus trouble, influenza, gall bladder, heart attack, lymphatic infections, and the like), it is likely that many of these were related in some way to problems brought on by his failing kidneys.

Most friends and associates knew that Eduard's health was precarious, but few, if any, knew how serious the difficulties were. Though most of Eduard's letters to friends contained references to various illnesses, none of the many that survive mentions kidney disease specifically. Perhaps Eduard kept the full knowledge of his house of pain a secret even from himself. Nephritis can exact from its frightened victims an involuntary vow of silence.

CHAPTER 5

The Social Action Dimension of Adult Education

Is self-improvement for the individual the purpose of adult education? Eduard Lindeman's answer to this question was yes, but with an important qualification which was derived from the adult education philosophy then prevailing in Denmark and Germany.[1] Adult learning involved more than putting additional knowledge into one's own behavior. The learning adult would find mere self-improvement to be a delusion unless it was pursued with understanding of, and in harmony with, the surrounding social context.

Modern human beings functioned within groups. Individuals engaged in joint enterprises with others because they believed that in so doing their own interests would be advanced.[2] Enlightened self-interest, then, called for attention to the related improvement of societal groups. Adult education should take into account and beckon "more intelligent responses" from individuals in their roles as members of organized groups.[3]

If individuals needed to be conscious of the importance of groups, groups needed to acquire a comparable consciousness of individuals. One of Eduard Lindeman's basic beliefs was that adult education was the most reliable instrument for social activists. Only by educating the adherents of a movement could such persons "utilize the compelling power of a group and still remain within the scope of democratic behavior."[4]

Every social action group, he thought, should at the same time be an adult education group. Conversely he went "even so far as to believe that all successful adult education groups sooner or later become social action groups."[5] This progression was inescapable. Consequently, adult education would become "an agency of progress" if its short-term goal of self-improvement for the individual could be made compatible with "a long-term, experimental but resolute policy of changing the social order."[6]

Three vehicles were extensively used by Eduard Lindeman in his effort to explore the age-old question of the individual and the group and to articulate the social action dimension of adult education. He was aided in generating his ideas and thinking them through as he participated in, and helped lead, a group called The Inquiry. In addition, Lindeman used the pages of *The New Republic* and another publication, *Survey,* to share his ideas with a larger public.

The Inquiry was another in the arsenal of social action efforts backed financially by Dorothy Straight. It was essentially a loose confederation of free spirits chaired (to the extent this was possible with so freewheeling a group) by Edward C. (Ned) Carter. In 1926, the organization had offices at 109 East Fifty-second Street in New York with desks for some twenty staff members and consultants.[7]

Inquiry members met in conference or workshop settings to discuss issues of the day. Projects were developed. Monographs and articles were written. But what counted at The Inquiry was a state of mind hospitable to experimentation leading toward social reform.

In practice, the group took on just about any problem or issue any significant cluster of its members might choose—community development, international relations, racial conflict, "business ideals," class conflict. They even talked about talking. Systematic and considered attention was given to analysis of such arts of democracy as discussion and conference methods.[8]

At times, the goals of the Inquirers were at least diffuse if not totally unclear. Lindeman himself admitted as much when he described the dangers of "perpetual tentativeness" as he surveyed the workings of the group for which he was a consultant.[9] He wryly turned to Emerson for support. Had not that great philosopher believed "an erroneous vitality to be superior to a deadly accuracy?"[10]

For persons wanting definitive goals and task assignments, contact with The Inquiry could be vexing. "Unless you were at the inside of [the] organization," remembers one Inquiry employee, "it was difficult to get any appreciation of what in the devil was going on. . . "[11]

It probably didn't help much when Lindeman advised that The

Inquiry was engaged in "a persistent effort to disentangle from the complex web of culture those situations which realistically revealed unadjustment."[12]

The Inquiry had been started as "The Conference on the Christian Way of Life," with motivations that were unmistakably religious. The idea was to stimulate American church members toward "recognition of their responsibility toward certain social problems." Meetings were opened with prayer.[13] But troubles arose within the first year when a great gulf opened between those who believed that an existing Christian ethic, for realization, simply needed arousal of "slothful Christians to apply it" and those who felt that "the discovery of new sanctions for behavior . . . might somehow fuse the best of social idealism with religious aspirations." Gradually, though only after much stormy debate, the group drifted toward the more secular approach and became simply The Inquiry.[14]

The list of consultants and staff members for The Inquiry serves almost as a directory of prominent thinkers and doers among American liberals and pragmatists in the 1920s. Walter Lippmann and Colonel Edward House (President Woodrow Wilson's chief advisor), along with Herbert Croly, were among the organizers.[15] Felix Frankfurter was also involved, as were Lindeman's friends Alfred Dwight Sheffield and Mary Parker Follett.

Bruno Lasker, an intellectual and social worker long active in settlement house work in New York, was also active in The Inquiry. A farsighted thinker in the realm of racial problems, he served as secretary of the Commission on Race Relations that functioned under Inquiry sponsorship.[16] Lasker, through The Inquiry and other channels, endeavored to raise the consciousness of social workers and their social reformer allies on the explosive problem of racial discrimination.[17]

In 1929, Lindeman wrote a statement of "Inquiry Principles" in which he took on the difficult task of concisely summarizing the collective thinking of his diverse group of colleagues. Lindeman found first of all that the inquiring group believed themselves to be expressing "a way of looking at people and at situations which is to be found neither in the accepted textbooks of education nor in the practices of most adult education institutions." Yet there was great hesitancy in concluding that they had yet come up with "anything so explicit as a 'school of thought.' "[18]

The Inquiry's philosophy, amorphous as it was, needed to be made more straightforward before it could "find full expression in programs and activities." And, like the true pragmatists that most of the

Inquirers were, they required validation before anything more could be claimed for Inquiry methods "than a passing effectiveness within the limited scope of situation and surrounding conditions in which they have been experimentally applied."[19]

With respect to the questions of conflict—an Inquiry target topic—the "distinctive Inquiry view" was that no factors in a situation, "whether of personality or of circumstances, are so 'jelled' as to be no longer pliable within a process of growth." All elements of "wish, policy and organized structure" are "plastic" and all of them are "manageable by methods that reset the stage for new educative experiences." Where differences between protagonists seem well rooted, "the educational solution lies along a course of fresh stimulations and redistributed emphases that bring out unsuspected needs on the basis of which employees and laborers, or any other parties to a dispute, can learn cooperation."[20]

A second view of conflict that Lindeman labeled as characteristic of the group reveals The Inquiry effort to have anticipated "life stage" or "crisis" theories of adult education motivation. Or, as Lindeman said it, this view was "one in harmony with a scientific conception of strain and upset as phases in a creative life-process." Any living organism "is continually undergoing upset by forces developing either from without or from within. Each 'upset' brings into play the energies that set up a new equilibrium among the tensions and pressures involved." Creature satisfaction becomes "a sense of restored equipoise—of *reset* after upset, usually at a new status or level." Violent or "too protracted upset" might produce "reactions which overtax and wear out the organism, but normal upsets produce enriching compensation and adjustments to on-going experience."[21]

Growth is a process by which the individual "is stirred to enriching and expanding activities, and finds 'the good life' in continued progressive new equilibriums after successive disturbed situations."[22]

In their approach to education, as to other aspects of life, the Inquiry group strove for a logic that was "plastic," i.e., "befitting the actual shifting, commingled complexities of things." Nothing in life was "purely this and not that." "In the 'autocratic' employer *some* motivations spring from democratic influences; in the 'democratic' labor union *some* procedures savor of autocracy. Things are *both* this *and* that." When human character was viewed in this light, "education becomes a matter of fostering shifts among the elements of [the person's] dominant attitudes." The individual "grows to be *less* of this and *more* of that in learning new appreciations and sensitivities. The process is one not of conversion but of steady inner reorganization."[23]

The Inquirers also believed themselves set apart from most other educators in their attitudes toward convictions—"toward points of fact and principle on which as 'settled issues' the mind comes to rest." To the mind of the Inquiry group, it was necessary to challenge the prevailing view that "the advance of social understanding and appreciation" was a "process of accretion." Under this process, a given item or act or principle, after being questioned and, over time, validated, "is to be treated as part of an irreducible minimum of fixed assumptions from which new learning starts but which is itself not to be reopened for dispute." All assumptions were not reopened by this group of thinkers because to do so would "simply ignore the intellectual work of the past, and start with a world of skidding relativities." "Conviction" and "open-mindedness" become "terms of contrast" with open-mindedness becoming "a proper attitude only where a due phase of testing is not yet complete."[24]

To members of The Inquiry, on the other hand, a movement forward in social understanding was "not a process of accretion upon an inherited deposit, but a process of *revision.*" Inherited principles would have the benefit of a "strong *presumption,*" until challenged within the current situation. Principles and convictions would not be challenged "apropos of nothing, in a spirit of wayward skepticism." They could, however, be "challenged by the *situation,* which then reopens questions as to their meaning." All "facts" were "permeated with interpretation." A fact or principle could therefore be invoked "*both* open-mindedly *and* with conviction." However strong the presumption in favor of facts or principles, The Inquiry would recognize "(1) degrees of *more or less* in his convictions, and (2) new elements in the present experience." The "*state of the circumstances*" dictated the degree of conviction and open-mindedness.[25]

Lindeman was coming into his own with an ability to synthesize the thinking of others, presenting it in a way that could be understood by a more broadly based group. Recognizing this skill as a "great gain" for *The New Republic,* Herbert Croly began tapping Lindeman for major editorial contributions.[26] In July of 1924, Herbert shared in a letter to Dorothy his view of the contribution that Eduard was making.

Croly's goal was that of rewarding the attention of *New Republic* readers "by adding something to their insight" into a subject. But, he said, articles of that kind were not easy to get "when it is necessary to demand also some measure of readability and some appeal to an audience which seeks chiefly to be distracted and entertained." Bruce Bliven, then managing editor, was "one of the best men in the world

. . . but like most journalists he has the mind of a medium rather than the mind of a self-starter." Eduard Lindeman had the kind of "indefatigability and strenuousness of spirit" that was required except that in the past it had been "canalized into perfunctory expressions." Eduard was "growing now very rapidly" because of the opportunity Dorothy had given him to "make a fresh start." Eduard, Croly said, would "get better as he gets older. I would trust him more completely in more relationships than any man I know."[27]

"I still have a great deal to talk over with you," Croly wrote Lindeman in 1926.[28] Sentences similar to this one were now frequent in Croly's communications with his younger friend.

The New Republic editorial group was a kind of collective body in Croly's eyes.[29] He tried to foster a sense of lateral, rather than vertical, responsibility.[30]

Lindeman often attended Croly's intimate luncheons or occasional dinners at *The New Republic* offices on West Twenty-first Street.[31] On these occasions, any editor could invite anyone. Philosophers, social reformers, politicians, businessmen, artists—anyone rich in mind or spirit—were the usual guests. The discussions, often supplemented by a speech at the dinner sessions, were fruitful in generating ideas for later appearance in *The New Republic*.[32]

Lindeman was thoroughly at home in the editorial realm of *The New Republic* by the time he served as editor for a special section on adult education in the February 22, 1928, issue. Heralding adult education as a new means of social change for liberals, Lindeman himself wrote the first of nine articles. As his point of departure, Lindeman took his cues from John Dewey, citing "intelligence" and "ideas" as the "supreme force in the settlement of social issues."[33]

The question for liberals was this: What kinds of intelligence and what sorts of ideas were needed to overcome social inertia in promoting social change? Democracy, for example, was "a goal to be reached and an end to be consummated."[34] It was the public school, presumably, that would nurture the "reconditioning procedure which was to transmute raw democracy, with its rough egalitarian fundamentals, into a creative fellowship." Yet the American system of public education did not "merely fail to fulfill the liberal faith." In reality, it "came to be one of the barriers which stood in the way of such fulfillment."[35]

Educational activity might have multiplied, but intellectual reflection "lacked depth." Liberal ideas "ceased to be social forces" even while schools, colleges, universities, and compulsory-education laws piled one upon the other. Eventually, the places of honor were held, "not for those who possessed ideas capable of social regeneration, but rather for those who had won pecuniary success." Meanwhile, the liberal idea "withered" or fell into the "complete decay . . . now heralded by fascists and communists everywhere."[36]

But there was hope. The foregoing criticism of American life was no longer wholly true. A "sure though subtle revaluation of values" was proceeding apace. One aspect of this was the development of "experimental," i.e., progressive, schools for children. Here, the whole conception of education was being "revamped." No longer was education being conceived as "a process of inducting children into the accumulated wisdom of adults." Rather, education was being conceived as "egress, not ingress, experiencing, not imitating experience."[37]

The concern for subjects and curriculum was giving way to increased attention to experience and method. Rather than the external ends, e.g., the service of state, citizenship, or industry, it was the interests of the individual pupil that were receiving prime attention.[38]

But there were limitations to the role that the schools could serve from the liberal perspective. Education might be finely conceived and executed for children, but it was adults who would always manage affairs of importance. And at last, for the first time in America, "grown-up people" were beginning to "inquire seriously about the state of their intelligence."[39]

The new movement which had, Lindeman thought, been awkwardly and misleadingly labeled "adult education" was being viewed through two sets of theories. The "culturalists" were perceiving adult education as simply a "handy article to have about." There was no telling when it might "become useful, or at least conversationally appropriate." The "problem-solvers," in contrast, viewed education as a valid process only when "the learning person knows why he wants to learn." Such learning had its own "tests and criteria" and was immediately usable.[40]

The crux of Lindeman's argument was that liberalism would be effective only when it was derived from "a valid learning process which is continuous, co-terminous, with life itself." Even with the best of will and the warmest of feeling, the liberal could not solve social problems "if he is incapable of calmly appraising his own behavior." Self-knowledge was "the beginning of all wisdom," but it did not come from a "textbook" or "oracle." Neither was it to be "plucked from mystical trees."[41]

Self-knowledge *would* come from experimentation, exercises in "self-awareness in which acting and thinking are kept integral to each other." Thinking without acting was "wasted energy." And the thinker-actor would "recognize the necessity of watchful vigilance over his own behavior." This would be a person capable of self-criticism. Each act, each reflection would be "pregnant with learning possibilities." The individual would "always be creating a world of progress within himself and within the circle of his vital interests."[42]

True intelligence was "both critical and functional." Continuing education was "the new means for attaining liberal ends." So conceived, education was not "a door which opens and closes at stated periods." Rather, it was the "very air essential for intelligent living . . . " As such, it should quicken the spirits of those who were standing "disillusioned and bewildered in a world where the supreme force which settles many social issues is still so largely infused with fear rather than intelligence."[43]

With this thoroughly Deweyan introduction, Lindeman opened *The New Republic's* February 28, 1928, special section with its range of articles across a wide sector of adult education concerns. Albert Mansbridge followed Lindeman with an update on world aspects of adult education. Free folk-education and library functions in Germany were described by Guenter Keiser and Hans Hofmann respectively. H. M. Kallen's "Between the Dark and the Ivory Tower" was a proclamation of adult education as incorporating "a change so radical that it requires a new stuff, and proclaims a new god" and a new way of living that "must overthrow and shatter the godhead of the Successful Business Man and sit in his place." Joseph Hart in "Education and the Folk-ways" cited extra-school learning and wondered whether the new breed of educators might "even, in time, teach the schools what education is." "Learning to Learn," a subject that would lie almost moribund for more than forty years, occupied Helen J. Mayers. Tom Tippett wondered: "Will Workers Study?" and Britisher Harold J. Laski closed *The New Republic's* special section with a piece, "On the Prospects of Adult Education."

In 1933, *The New Republic* published in book form Lindeman's interpretation of the principles and methods developed by The Inquiry between 1923 and 1933, under the title *Social Education*.[44] Much of this piece was a further elaboration of the 1929 article "Inquiry Principles," but there were some additions of particular interest to adult educators.

In his preface, Lindeman defined "social education" for The Inquiry's purposes as "a process *and* a goal, but not necessarily a technique *for* a preconceived goal. It represents a continuing sort of learning, or reconditioning, which moves toward social adjustment with instruments derived from social experience."[45]

For teachers "baffled and perplexed" in striving to "accommodate themselves to a social ideal and purpose," Lindeman had advice. They should begin "with the self as learner and participator." Effective inquiry was to be "directed both inward and outward." The scientist, scholar, technologist, or teacher "who has not yet begun to realize that it is he himself who needs to be re-conditioned and re-educated has not taken the first step in confronting the modern world." It was through participation, "by taking the risks of exposing himself, his knowledge and his feelings in the arena of social conflict," that such re-education would occur.[46]

One of The Inquiry's basic assumptions (among sixteen) was that "true learning is always insight or understanding derived from the interpretation of facts with feelings."[47] One of four "central ideas of the social education which [The Inquiry] was committed to test" was "that we need a new kind of education to meet this tide of ever-coming problems, an education that sees itself not as preparatory, but as continuing throughout life."[48]

If The Inquiry was long on principles and on advice about social reform and even organization theory, it was short on management savvy in its own household. Eduard Lindeman was one of The Inquiry's consultants. As such, under the generous (perhaps overgenerous) terms of Dorothy's grant, whatever interested Lindeman or others of its leaders at the moment became, for a time, the main agenda. Laissez-faire creativity was the unspoken administrative motto. All else came second.[49] A glance at the mechanics of The Inquiry's administration is enough to capture Eduard Lindeman's perennial ineptness as an administrator.

One of the first outsiders to enter The Inquiry's chaotic environment was John Hader, who met Eduard Lindeman when he took his class in adult education at the New School for Social Research. A sturdy young man with an open face, quick smile, and hands hardened by manual labor, Hader was drawn like a magnet to the then forty-one-year-old Eduard Lindeman. He was immensely flattered that an older man of Lindeman's accomplishments could be interested in him. Eduard Lindeman probably saw in the twenty-nine-year-old John Hader a kind of diamond in the rough—perhaps of the same genre as a very young Eduard Lindeman of St. Clair of several decades back. In any event, they took to each other.[50]

Lindeman hired Hader in 1926 under Inquiry funds to assist him with project research. His job, Hader relates, "was to shuffle papers and dig up fundamentals and do something that you could get published." Lindeman put Hader to work as a kind of ferret to find out what was happening around New York City in the various workers' education organizations. He also sent him on an information search at the Rand School, which was considered as a radical, probably Marxist, organization.[51]

But too often, from his point of view, Hader had time on his hands. Young and inexperienced, he knew little of the overall purposes of The Inquiry. "The thing was so informal you wondered what held it together at all." But the worst aspect of the situation for Hader was the fact that his boss, Eduard Lindeman, didn't show up at The Inquiry's offices very often. "I wouldn't see him for days, sometimes for weeks. I had trouble keeping the ship going—for direction." All Hader knew was that Lindeman was often traveling outside New York. When he returned, not much was said about where he had been. "We didn't ask too many questions," remembers Hader. It didn't seem as if such questions would be encouraged.[52]

"I have never had a clear picture of what Lindeman wanted or what we were doing. I had the feeling the ship is going on the rocks, I'd better find the captain," Hader recalled more than fifty years later. There was not much camaraderie among ever-shifting occupants of the desk chairs at The Inquiry offices at 19 East Fifty-second Street. Bruno Lasker was often there, but he was an ascetic-appearing older man and seemed to find it hard to talk informally with the young Hader or others. There was no one on the scene to whom Hader could convey his problems.[53]

In his frustration and desperation, Hader acted rashly. "I did a very uncreditable thing." He couldn't talk to Lasker. Heading the office was Chairman Edward C. Carter, but he, too, seemed to know little about what was going on in the shop. Besides, he was "a former YMCA man"—a breed that discomforted Hader. Whom could he see? Herbert Croly.[54]

Hader knew that Lindeman "saw more of Croly than of Carter," so he decided to visit Croly at his offices at *The New Republic* and pour out his difficulties. The conference took place and though Hader could not have known it, the content came as no surprise to Croly, who was well aware of his friend's frailties. What later transpired between Lindeman and Croly is unknown, but Hader's comments were passed on to the peripatetic Eduard.[55]

Lindeman did not display overt anger or even irritation at his young assistant. His manner, however, was atypically correct when he confronted him with "what amounted to a betrayal," in Hader's words. Hader defended himself: "Eduard, I didn't know what to do. I hadn't seen you for six weeks! Where are we? What's the score?" After a discussion that was very uncomfortable for them both, the matter was dropped.[56]

Hader's action was not the "awful mistake" that he would afterward call it. It was Eduard who was in the wrong, as Eduard must have known. Neither Lindeman nor Hader ever mentioned the incident to the other again. They remained friends and went on to cooperate in authoring *Dynamic Social Research.*[57]

After Herbert Croly's death in May of 1930, Lindeman's ties with *The New Republic* diminished to nearly nothing. He had little personal or intellectual affinity with the new editor, Bruce Bliven.[58] But by this time, Lindeman was hardly dependent upon a single publication for placement of his prolific output. In 1928, he had written a textbook for college use, *Urban Sociology,* with Nels Anderson, and speeches and journal articles continued at a steady flow.

As the 1930s wore on, however, Lindeman strengthened his ties with *Survey* and its more broadly focused companion, *Survey Graphic.* Like *The New Republic,* *Survey* took on social issues such as impairment of civil liberties, freedom of speech, racial discrimination, industrial exploitation, commercialization of culture, employment insecurity, problems of aging, and urban problems including slum housing.[59] These topics, plus Editor Paul Kellogg's announced purpose of reporting and interpreting social movements, made the publications natural outlets for Eduard Lindeman's work on the social dimensions of adult education. It was, after all, the "processors of mutual education," i.e., "educators, lawyers and jurists, doctors and nurses, engineers, ministers, public administrators, social scientists, business managers, technologists, social workers" who read *Survey* who would move the nation "down the path of welfare and progress."[60] Kellogg would often recruit Lindeman's help in planning special issues.[61] He also accepted frequent contributions from Lindeman as a book reviewer.

％

None of Eduard Lindeman's views on adult education as an instrumentality for social action could be classified as radical—even in the crisis environment of the 1930s. The high-water mark of his youthful radicalism had come much earlier—in 1924, when he had contributed to a civil disturbance in the usually peaceful city of Toronto, of all places.

Lindeman had delivered a provocative speech in Toronto at the National Conference of Social Work—where it was received with considerably less enthusiasm than a talk he had given to the same group a year earlier in Washington. Part of the problem was that the previous speaker, cooperative marketing advocate Aaron Sapiro of New York, had spoken for more than an hour—over twice his allotted time. By the time Lindeman began his talk, darkness was descending; he could hardly see his general session audience of fifteen hundred, seated out of doors on the University of Toronto campus. Speaking for only fifteen minutes, he had eliminated all of his illustrations.[62]

If the initial reception to the talk was tepid, there was nonetheless "discussion and disturbance" when the effect of what Lindeman called this "radical" paper was felt. The reporter who covered the conference for the *Toronto Globe* did "an excellent piece of work" in covering the talk, Eduard wrote Dorothy. It was much better than he had expected in "Tory Toronto."[63]

Eduard had reason to be pleased, for the *Globe* reporter gave him top billing and the lion's share of space in a lengthy article bearing the headline, "Predicts Farmers and Tradespeople Soon Are To Rule." Lindeman had given a "scholar's description of the maladjustments of the existing social and economic order, a logician's analysis of the nature and cause of those maladjustments, and a courageous prophet's portrayal of what he believed would be the outcome of a class struggle."[64]

Although he predicted capitalism's decay, Lindeman offered his listeners no Marxist antidote. Marxism would not win in North America because the necessary impetus—an ever-increasing disparity between the wealth of the few and the poverty of the many—was lacking. Rather, millions of industrial and agricultural workers would become the "new capitalists."[65]

Canada was at that moment in the throes of one of its now-famous and endemic postal workers strikes. The strike leaders learned of Lindeman's remarks through the newspaper article, and he was drawn into strike-related mass meetings and some joint meetings with governmental representatives. He made a speech at the Sunday mass meeting just before the government agreed to take all of the strikers back. Within minutes, Lindeman found himself being "carried in a parade down through the streets of Toronto." Alas, on the following morning, the government "repudiated its promises." It struck Lindeman as ironic in the extreme that while his government "was playing this sad part Premier MacKenzie King was at Yale receiving an honorary degree for his contribution to the solution of industrial disputes."[66]

But if Lindeman found time to take to the streets of Toronto with the striking postal workers, he did not neglect a comparable controversial role at the conference itself. Lindeman and Roger Baldwin had prepared a report on "Sources of Power for Industrial Freedom." The chairman of the Industrial Session, Miss Mary Van Kleeck of the Russell Sage Foundation staff, was a "brick," Lindeman wrote Dorothy, in that she managed to get the Lindeman-Baldwin report read and discussed in the face of great opposition." Unfortunately, most of those who might have objected most strongly had stayed away from the meeting. As it was, there was only "mild dissent" from Jane Addams, Mary McDowell, and "other radicals of the last generation."[67]

"Miss Addams insists that there is no class struggle in America." Before leaving Toronto, the increasingly confident young man had luncheon with her and found the great lady of social work "quite confused about a great many things." She nonetheless urged him to come to Hull House in Chicago for a week in the autumn, "and I fear that she has designs looking toward my conversion."[68]

If the conference's industrial section had been disturbed about Lindeman's thinking or activities, such concern was not reflected in the democratic processes of the group for it elected the thirty-nine-year-old Lindeman as its chairman for the next year. Lindeman was pleased.[69] What the citizens of Toronto may have felt about an American being involved in a strike against their national government was not recorded.

His professional role might at times be unsettling for Eduard, but his life had stabilized in other ways. The Lindemans' search for a home after they left Greensboro had ended happily. In the fall of 1922, Hazel and Eduard had rented a massive stone house in the town of High Bridge, New Jersey—the former residence of the president of the Taylor Wharton Iron and Steel Company. Spacious inside, it had eleven rooms—twelve if one counted the rooftop observatory. Two large porches at each end of the first floor plus a sleeping porch on the second level gave the family an abundance of elbow room. Luvina and Ben Lewis, the cook and handyman (and only black residents of High Bridge), had a small suite consisting of a bedroom, living room, and bath on the third floor.[70]

On the thirty-four acres outside was plenty of running room for Eduard's healthy girls. There was a large garage, a barn, and garden space. Eduard enjoyed raising flowers and vegetables, but he took particular pride in creating his own rock garden, in which he lovingly placed a number of rare plants. Eventually, the Lindemans would add a tennis court.[71]

Eduard installed himself in two third-floor rooms. In one, lined with shelves, he kept his books and periodicals. In the other was the desk where he did most of his serious writing. As he worked, he could look out the window and see the foothills of the Alleghenies.[72]

Everyone thought the place was just about perfect—and it was. Some of Dorothy's great homes had names—Applegreen, Camp Deerlands. Eduard and Hazel called their home Greystone after the New Jersey fieldstones from which it was constructed.[73]

Greystone served another function for the two older Lindemans. It gave them breathing room in a marriage that had become increasingly difficult to manage. For Eduard, Greystone would become a weekend retreat. When not traveling, he lived in Manhattan, a fifty-mile train and ferry ride from High Bridge.[74] "The sad mariners of New Jersey," Eduard called his fellow travelers on the Manhattan ferries.[75]

In 1928, he took a very small three-room apartment at 21 Minetta Lane in Greenwich Village, which he shared with the American Civil Liberties Union's admittedly radical and controversial founder and director, Roger Baldwin, who was then unofficially between wives.[76] Later, when a speakeasy located downstairs became too noisy, the two friends moved to a large apartment on West 12th Street, which they shared with various others.[77] One of these, the young Robert Gessner, married Eduard's oldest daughter, Doris.

It was in this period that Eduard began the dual existence that would continue until the early 1940s. On weekends, he was husband to Hazel and beloved father to Doris, Ruth, Betty, and Barbara. For the balance of the week, Eduard, Roger, and a teeming and frequently changing throng of friends lived what was then called a Bohemian existence in the Village. Tom Cotton, writer and early consumer advocate Stuart Chase, and artist Robert Hallowell were close friends of Eduard's on the Village side of his living arrangements.[78]

There was very little connection between the two lives. Though there was no elaborate effort at deception, many participants in one knew little or nothing about the other.

What sort of woman was it that Eduard Lindeman had married? Photographs show that Hazel Lindeman in middle age was an attractive woman who retained the firm, athletic body that was hers by inheritance. Her features were softer, though certainly as finely turned as those of her husband. She was attractively and immaculately dressed—though never in the latest fashions. She retained an easygoing, comfortable, unpretentious middle western appearance and demeanor.[79]

A candid snapshot of life at Greystone with Hazel in charge is provided by Louise Croly who, with Herbert, spent a week there with the Lindemans in September of 1927. Louise's portrait of the assembled Lindemans in a letter to Dorothy is just the slightest bit condescending in describing the Lindemans as "such a perfect type of middle class American" family. Even so, the portrait that emerges is one that is complimentary to Greystone's mistress.[80]

The Lindemans had a Hudson automobile, a Frigidaire, a washing machine, and a mangle. There was no radio, Louise was glad to note.[81]

The four little girls were "charmingly dressed in light summer dresses." They had "most extraordinary freedom and lack of repression and promise which is characteristic of American children."[82]

For Hazel, with her college training in "household economics," Louise had great respect. She kept the Greystone menage functioning and "really holds everything together." Hazel did all the laundry herself. There was a maid-cook, "a Negress," who would hang it out. Hazel used the mangle for doing all the flat pieces of laundry and imported a laundress for a half day a week to iron shirts and the children's dresses. Aided by Luvina (and by the girls as they grew older), Hazel also did the house cleaning. She was a competent seamstress and made many of the children's clothes. With Eduard's help, she canned fruits and vegetables for the winter.[83]

Like so many others, Louise found Hazel very strong and "not a bit nervous." She exuded no sense of pressure. She managed the children "so well and so quietly." The food was "excellent, and you feel no anxiety about ways and means."[84]

In summary, Hazel Lindeman was a good mother. The girls were well taken care of. She presided over her household with quiet confidence and impressed others as outwardly content with the role of homemaker. Unassertive, she deferred to Eduard in most things and was in some ways quite dependent upon him after the manner of respectable married women in those times.[85]

From a contemporary feminist perspective, however, it was Hazel more than Herbert, Dorothy, or other suppliers of mere cognitive and material sustenance who made possible Eduard's professional success. Where else could he have obtained so competent and willing a helpmate to provide for his domestic needs and bring up his children?

Guests in the Lindeman home were welcomed by Hazel though she must have been intimidated by some of the more esoteric of Eduard's friends. One of these, Roger Baldwin, found Hazel to be something of a puzzle. "I never knew what was there because so little came out."[86] Roger was not the first to make this observation. Hazel's classmates at Michigan Agricultural College seem to have had a comparable impression; the inscription under her graduation photo in the yearbook was "The Riddle of the Universe."[87]

John Hader's intelligent Norwegian-born wife, Mathilda, a frequent visitor at Greystone, also remembers Hazel as very quiet but found her "well-adjusted" and "easy-going." It was obvious that she loved her home and generally prefered staying in it.[88] She might appear reserved at times, but basically Hazel Lindeman had a warm and affectionate nature.[89]

While she was hardly the type to sit down for long, or even short, discussions of great issues or abstractions of any kind, Hazel Lindeman was no cipher in comparison to her more outgoing husband. She was intelligent and had interests beyond the affairs of home and hearth. She was elected to the High Bridge School Board and was a conscientious member of the Parole Board at Clinton Farms State Reformatory for Women.[90]

Eduard was fond of Hazel and respected her. Certainly he had no desire to break up his home. Still, his needs were such that Hazel could not supply them all—nor could he apparently supply hers. Eduard's shuttle on the High Bridge–Manhattan axis was the way that the Lindemans chose to make their life together possible and tolerable.[91]

%

Snow, which gave the countryside its "double aspect of strength and purity," covered the hills around Greystone by December 1923 as Eduard wrote Dorothy about his search for the permanent employment that would be necessary once Eduard's "mutual undertaking" with Dorothy came to an end.[92]

He told Dorothy that he had eliminated a proposal from *Collier's* magazine. After seeing people at their office several times, he concluded he "could not possibly fit in without sacrificing too much."[93]

Columbia University had apparently expressed some interest in the promising (though uncredentialed) scholar, "but again I find myself unable to make the necessary adaptations." Discussions, however, continued. The New York School of Social Work, later to be merged with Columbia, was more promising. They had made a tentative offer for a part-time teaching position. Cornell University, however, seemed the best opportunity. They would allow half-time for research, a major advantage. While visiting farmers in New York state the week before, Lindeman had learned that farmers and their wives had sent a request to Cornell's Dean Mann "asking him to secure me." Because of its "genuineness," this movement had especially pleased him.[94]

Eduard was scheduled to talk with Herbert Croly soon about his plans for the future. What he really wanted was to continue on the projects he'd started with Dorothy's financial sponsorship "so that your investment and your faith will be justified." He would "select my future work with this aim in mind." A part-time teaching, part-time research position would be the ideal arrangement.[95]

In the meantime, Eduard was delighted, he told Dorothy, that "New York seems to have at last taken me in." "Invitations of all sorts" kept arriving, "most of which I am obliged to decline." There was "something terribly unreal about city life with all its conferences, meetings, and talking. I enjoy watching it all, but I am sure that I shall never be an integral part of it. My relation is destined to be 'to' and not 'of' city life and ways."[96]

It was the New York School of Social Work position that finally met Eduard's specifications, and in 1924 he accepted the position as faculty in social philosophy, with a schedule of teaching five hours each week and a period of three months free for study and writing. He told Dorothy he had already talked over his plans with Herbert and Miss Bogue. He was mailing Miss Bogue a written statement to be submitted to Dorothy. "It will be quite ideal," he thought, "to do a bit of teaching and also be able to do what I want most to do, namely watch and study and write."[97] Eduard Lindeman had found his professional home base.

The correspondence between Dorothy Straight and Eduard Lindeman, which began in 1922 and continued intensively for most of two decades, is a record not only of their friendship but of the issues and concerns that occupied others in America's social action coterie during this period.

Eduard's letters to Dorothy were invariably typed on his faithful Corona. The flow from his end was frequent, sometimes running to several in a month. Most years, there was an annual summary letter written at New Year's time.

The often-roaming Dorothy wrote Eduard from wherever she happened to be at the time. If it was from one of her homes, she would have stationery personalized to that address. When in New York it was a handsomely simple: "1130 Fifth Avenue" letterhead that would grace Eduard's mailbox. An uncharacteristic commercial note crept onto her writing paper at Camp Deerlands, where this name was followed by the words "Whitney Realty Company" and then "Raquette Lake, New York." Many of Dorothy's letters also came on stationery of the transoceanic liners or elegant hotels.

Dorothy's letters were handwritten in flowing script that was assertive but apparently produced rapidly enough that it was not always firm and clear. Periods tended to become dashes. T's might be crossed sweepingly or they might not be crossed at all. She had an irksome (to a biographer) habit of dating a letter with the month and day but no year.

Eduard was living in Greensboro when their acquaintanceship and correspondence began. His first letters, in which the salutation was "My Dear Mrs. Straight," were halting, very much the product of a man unsure of himself in the presence of a person of Dorothy's exalted position.

Gradually, they grew less formal. Dorothy asked Eduard not to call her "Mrs. Straight" anymore. It was from then on to be "Dorothy." She wondered if she might call him "Ned." "I know I shall find the perfect name for you someday!"[98] Eduard's response to this request does not survive. It would be interesting to see what it was, for thereafter Dorothy would never refer to her friend as anything except "Edward," the original spelling of his name, though he signed each of his letters to her using the spelling "Eduard" that he had adopted on his own.

Dorothy's longing for a substitute for the dead Willard is revealed in many of her early letters to Eduard. She thought the two men would have been friends: "Oh—how often I wish that Willard had known you—I cling always to the hope that those opportunities come again."[99]

If Eduard was disquieted at first by Dorothy's wealth, she stood in awe of his powerful mind. In the early stages of their acquaintance, she hung on his every word and might read his letters over many times, pondering their messages.[100]

For a noble-spirited woman born to wealth, Eduard's rapid climb from the bottom of America's economic and social ladder was also a drawing card. It was an endorsement of the promise of American democracy. She was inspired by him and was grateful for all that he gave of his "most glorious self."[101]

The two friends were equally devastated by Herbert's death in 1930. In a letter to Dorothy, Eduard's grief showed as he became uncharacteristically maudlin in describing his feelings. The "entire direction of his life had been altered by the contact with Herbert [and] in this respect you and Herbert stand apart." His "saintly purity refined and cleansed so many motives, and his glowing disinterestedness was to me as a great light."[102]

Herbert was gone, but Dorothy was alive. "How I long to see you, Dorothy," Eduard wrote. "There is no one I can readily talk to about Herbert save you. . . I've never been so lonely since childhood, since those early years when I started forth to do battle against the world without my mother. Mine are the 'Tears from the depth of some divine despair' and you alone understand."[103] There was more in this same vein, much more.

Dorothy's letters to Eduard must be read in the context of her whole life and of the times. Terms of endearment came naturally to her. Her letters to other friends, male and female, are filled with affectionate references. Then, too, it was an age in which a certain hyperbole of expression in letters between friends was common. Hazel Lindeman could have read most, if not all, of the surviving letters without experiencing undue concern. Dorothy usually was careful to include a kind word to be passed on to Hazel in her letters to Eduard. Still, some of these exchanges suggest a pair for whom the attraction was more than intellectual.

Referring to a recent illness of Eduard's, Dorothy said, "It made me realize how much I cared for you and how important you had become in my life as well as in the larger life of mankind."[104] Writing from Woods Hole, probably in 1924, Dorothy gushed a bit about how she had kept about eleven of Eduard's letters to her. "Did anyone ever have such a friend? I have longed many a time . . . to be able to give you some idea, an inkling even, of what these letters have done for me. . . I can't bear to cast even one away—they are all going to be kept and treasured."[105]

Theirs was a meeting of minds. From Dorothy's perspective, it was Eduard's "original thought" and his ability to fire "peoples' hearts as well as their minds" that was compelling.[106] She admired also "that clear, clear quality in you—the absolute sincerity and purity of your actions—the uncompromising honesty that is yours." She tried "oh so feebly" to follow. "And you are always an example."[107]

Eduard most certainly was strongly attracted to Dorothy, but it is unlikely that Dorothy allowed herself to respond with anything more than warm letters and conversation. Her moral code was exacting, and her respect for the marriage bond was great. Moreover, her full sensual nature apparently had not been awakened during her marriage to Willard.[108]

Meanwhile, high above Cayuga's waters, the man who was to become Dorothy's second husband was hard at work on a degree in agricultural economics. Like Willard Straight, he had no money of his own. Like Eduard, he had a dream. Unfortunately for Eduard, this man's dream was an expensive one. Even worse, its realization lay across the sea in faraway England. It was a dream that was to change the course of Dorothy's life—and Eduard's.

CHAPTER 6

1925: The Turning Point

Dorothy Whitney Straight met Leonard Elmhirst in the same way that she met so many other people. He asked her for money. He had just been elected president of the Cosmopolitan Club, a student residential organization at Cornell, only to learn on his first day in office that the Club, despite its grandiose name, was deep in debt and likely soon to be declared bankrupt and sold at auction.[1]

Dorothy's interest in the Cosmopolitan Club, to which her late husband had belonged, was minimal though she did promise to give the organization some help in getting back on its feet. Her real concern at the time was that of providing the university from which Willard Straight had graduated with a memorial to him that would make Cornell "a more human place."[2] This objective would eventually be achieved on campus with the presence of a handsome and well-appointed student union building—Willard Straight Hall.

While planning and implementing her first husband's memorial, Dorothy found herself spending more and more time with the young Englishman who had diverted her attention to the staggering Cosmopolitan Club. Younger than she by six years, Leonard Knight Elmhirst was the son of a Yorkshire Methodist farmer-parson.[3]

Educated at Repton and Cambridge, Leonard had gone to India

during World War I, where he had met Sam Higginbottom, the American missionary leader who founded the Allahabad Agricultural Institute. Interested in the work of this institution, which was designed to assist poor Indian farmers in improving their practice of agriculture, Elmhirst, driven by a desire to provide real assistance to the rural poor, worked his way to the United States. He enrolled at Cornell and began work on a degree in agriculture, which he earned in 1921.[4]

After leaving Cornell, Leonard returned to India, and his romance with Dorothy, which was driven by intellectual and aspirational affinities more than passion, stalled. But Leonard was gently persistent, and there was something about this idealistic man which greatly appealed to Dorothy. Lindeman and other American friends would have been apprehensive had they known that by October of 1924, Dorothy had begun asking Leonard to advise her about where to donate her money.[5]

In 1923, Dorothy had given Leonard Eduard's address and suggested he write to her friend. And, from Rio de Janeiro, write he did—a very full twenty-seven pages of what Leonard described as "a spring cleaning of the mind."[6]

"Will you excuse me," he asked Eduard, "if I shake the dust out of a somewhat cobwebby brain pan into your lap—for dissection & examination, if you will, or for, what it deserves, ultimate dumping into an incinerator?"[7]

What followed was the letter of a very earnest man and a very young man. Its discursive narrative ranged from the concerns of the British Empire to the law of supply and demand, to the cyclic appearance of ideals, to God, to defects in school-based education, and to societal reform. Leonard laid bare his soul almost, and all to a man whom he'd never met except through description from Dorothy. "Except for our own little family group in India," Leonard wrote, "I know only one or two in the West to whom I would dare risk a letter such as this."[8]

When they later met, Eduard passed muster with Leonard as some of Dorothy's other friends did not. "I'm glad I met Lindeman," he wrote Dorothy in August of 1924. "He's the first man among the few of your men acquaintances I have met over here [in the United States] whom I really wanted to ask to keep his eyes open on your behalf." Some of the others "had so many eyes open that one seemed to be unable to miss a glimpse of their insides at work, and it wasn't always so pleasant. So I thank heaven and America for Lindeman."[9]

Dorothy, writing from Woods Hole in September, gave Leonard

Eduard's comparable impression of him. Eduard had written her "such a nice letter the other day and this is what he says about you— 'Mr. Elmhirst and I had a long meeting and we discussed his book on India. He has made a deep impression on me.' "[10] Dorothy would have been less sanguine about the future relationship of these two men had she been able to plumb those depths.

During the entire period of his rather desultory and long distance romance with Dorothy, Leonard laid himself open for friendship with Eduard—seeming not to recognize (or perhaps choosing to ignore) Eduard's feelings of jealousy. He continued, in any event, to carry on a correspondence with Eduard, encouraged by Dorothy, who had been told by Eduard that he wanted to know "what's going on in [Leonard's] mind—impressions, ideas and experiences."[11]

While Leonard Elmhirst did not possess the intellect or the inventive mind Eduard had, he had a passion for growth that rivaled Dorothy's, and he found Eduard's ideas stimulating. Moreover, unlike Eduard, he was secure enough to welcome criticism. He urged Eduard "to say things direct to me, about my own failings, with myself, (the person I have got to get-right with), & with Dorothy's friends."[12] His letters to Eduard were invariably warm, friendly, and open.

Dorothy confided in Herbert and Louise Croly as she made her decision about whether to marry Leonard. She was concerned, however, about the possible disruptive effects of implementing Leonard's vision of developing an experimental community that would incorporate rural rehabilitation, education, and the arts. Should she and her three children leave America for England, where Leonard, with Dorothy's money, wished to bring his dreams to life?[13]

Croly was skeptical, counseling Dorothy that without a firm American base, "your life may develop into a series of excursions tied together by a purpose which will have but little relationship into any national affiliation or background either for yourself or the children." It was possible also, Croly warned, "that if you live in England the major part of your wealth will be demanded by the British government for the support of the British Empire."[14]

According to Michael Straight, his mother's other American friends were pursuing much the same tack as was Herbert. Beset by indecision, Dorothy became quite ill for a time, but eventually she made up her mind. She would marry Leonard, and they would go to England, where she would put her financial resources to work for his dream, which would become hers as well.[15]

※

The promise of Lindeman's professional life in 1925 had never looked better. He had been befriended and helped by Herbert Croly, one of America's most distinguished intellectuals. Warm friendship supplemented with much-needed financial support was coming his way from one of the world's wealthiest and most influential women. The son of poor immigrants was in the company of those who were leading the nation in thought, if not always in action.

The six Lindemans were handsomely ensconced within the spacious walls and grounds of Greystone. To an outsider looking in, Eduard Lindeman's life must have looked very good indeed. But there was that dark though often hidden stain—his health.

Eduard became quite ill in the early days of 1925—a "thyroid deficiency," his doctor called it. His temperature would go up nightly, though it would not be high.[16] The prescribed cure was plenty of "rest and iodine."[17]

Dorothy talked of sending Eduard to a sanitarium, but everyone knew he would have none of that.[18] Then came a better idea. She would send Eduard with Hazel and the four girls for a rest cure in Italy.[19]

Martha Anderson, a bright young woman whom Eduard met when he gave a speech at Bryn Mawr College, had been engaged by Lindeman (with funds from Dorothy Straight) to assist him in translating extracts from French and German. When Lindeman was stricken, she became a part of Dorothy's grand design for speeding Eduard's recovery. Not only would Dorothy continue paying Martha's salary, but she would send her to Italy with the Lindemans so that Martha could be on hand to assist when he felt like working. She would principally be occupied with translating extracts from French and German.[20]

Martha welcomed this opportunity for adventure with the man who had become a "vital, humane, interesting, loyal friend." She was excited about being for so extended a time in the company of the handsome man with the "very warm personality which made him the idol of the women's clubs . . . the preferred speaker." Miss Anderson and Lindeman worked well together; she would stay on as his personal assistant for five years.[21]

There was great excitement at Greystone as all of the six Lindemans got ready for the trip. It must have been a lark to tell friends that their mailing address while in Europe would be c/o Dorothy's bank in London, the Guaranty Trust Company, 30 Pall Mall.[22] Eduard had already been to Europe in 1920 and again in 1922, but for the others it would be the first trip. It was a thrill for them all when the *Conto Rosso* sailed from New York with them aboard on March 24, 1925. The destination was Naples.[23]

The land portion of the trip, which began in the south of Italy, got off to a bad start. For one thing, Eduard's health was not improving. If anything, he felt less well than he had two months previously in the United States. The weather was bad—a lot of rain with frequent changes in temperature—hardly the climate to benefit a semi-invalid. Travel in Italy was expensive. Because of the Roman Catholic Holy Year, everything cost much more than usual.[24]

About the Italian people, Eduard had a similar bleak impression. It seemed to him that the Italians too often focused on the form or exterior aspects of individuals, ignoring the spirit. To him, form was important only when it revealed something important inside.[25] Lindeman would gain a more favorable impression of the Italian people by the end of his visit.

There was a pause in Naples at the Hotel du Vésuve where Mount Vesuvius was visible from the hotel windows. "As a really red-blooded volcano, I don't think much of it," he wrote Charles Shaw. On the other side, the Bay of Naples, with its iridescent waters, was "entrancing."[26] But Naples was destined to dose Eduard with a bitter pill, along with visual delights.

Eduard was hurt and enraged when he learned from a newspaper story that Dorothy Straight had married Leonard Elmhirst in the garden of her home at Old Westbury in April. He fired off to Dorothy and Leonard a letter in which he spilled out some, though not all, of his real feelings with regard to their new status. After a few forced words to communicate "my blessings to you both," his letter, written from Naples, took on another cant.[27]

"It would be useless to attempt a concealment of the great shock which the news brought. I read the London Mail and then walked up the hill of Via Santa Lucia with tears blinding my eyes. The event for which I had often wished . . . quite upset me when I learned of its consummation. But, the tears of joy outnumbered the selfish ones which were merely tokens of certain things come to end. When calm returned I was assured that far better things were at beginning."[28]

His "two hurried contacts" with Leonard had been sufficient to "imbue" him with his "high purposes." Perhaps they would come to know each other better. "In any case, I want you to know that my feeling for you is one of sincerity. You will, I am sure, understand my present attitude of intimacy."[29]

Eduard would have been less than human had he not been upset about the Straight-Elmhirst nuptials. His feelings for Dorothy were intense—perhaps crossing the boundaries of love. Now she had been co-opted by another man—and a foreigner at that. Surely he had now lost Dorothy, and her interest in his projects would wane.

Life, however, had to go on, and after numerous tribulations— many of them associated with traveling about with small children— the Lindemans eventually settled in at the Hotel Bristol in the resort town of Rapallo on the Ligurian Sea. Here, things began to look better. The sheer beauty and peace of the place helped heal Eduard's damaged emotions.[30]

Friends were writing about old problems that Eduard, from his Italian context, was unable to see as realities: Spencer Miller and workers' education, Owen Lovejoy and child labor, Roger Baldwin and free speech, Porter Lee and social work, Tom Cotton and immigration, Ernest Johnson and the church, Alfred Dwight Sheffield and discussion. All of them with their inventories of problems seemed unreal.[31]

The letter writers all wanted their friend to return to health so that he would be able to plunge with them into the fights again. But Eduard was not in a fighting mood. He knew he would eventually have to return to a fighting world, but for the moment he was going to sit tight and catch his breath.[32]

Eduard wrote Charles that he had settled into a relaxed routine. He tried to get in about three hours of reading daily. He worked also on a new essay, "Liberalism and the Scientific Spirit." Martha Anderson would be joining them in two weeks. Eduard wasn't certain he would be ready to work by the time she arrived, but he took note of "mountains of letters" which would occupy her for some time.[33]

In Rapallo it was easier to relax than to work. Eduard ate, swam, and tanned in the warm Italian sun. The somnolent pace continued even after Martha Anderson arrived. She noted that the usually frenetic Lindeman had little inclination to work. She knew also that he was ill, though she was never told what his illness was. What little work they did together was accomplished in the shade of the trees on the spacious grounds of the Hotel Bristol.[34]

Martha lived intimately with the Lindeman family during this period, serving as babysitter as well as assistant to Eduard. She found them all thoroughly likable. Eduard was warm and affectionate with his daughters, and they responded in kind. The "red-headed" Hazel was an "excellent mother and a lot of fun to be with." Eduard and Hazel teased each other in a lighthearted way, and it seemed to

Martha that the two had a "companionable relationship" in spite of differences in personal makeup and interests.[35]

The Lindemans played bridge nightly with other guests. Martha, who disliked bridge, took refuge in concerts and the theater. She also learned how to play chess and took Italian lessons given by the owner of the hotel.[36]

An unexpected trial beset the Lindemans when Barbara came down with the measles. Since she had exposed all of the other children, Hazel and Eduard decided to remain in Rapallo for another three or four weeks. Eduard didn't mind. The climate was moderate, and he was feeling better.[37] As Ruth, Doris, and eventually Betty also acquired the measles—in serial sequence, not concurrently—Eduard had plenty of time to think.[38] He had some recuperating of his own to do—not all of it just of the physical variety. Eduard was engaged in sorting out the pieces of his relationship with Dorothy Straight Elmhirst—an effort which may explain his surprising reluctance to pursue intellectual disciplines with his usual vigor.

There was an air of pained nobility as well as petulance as Eduard reminded the new Mrs. Elmhirst, in a letter that seemed designed to test the strength of her ties to him, that the time was coming when they must discuss "a discontinuance of your financial help. I must . . . be true to my convictions in this region. Your interests will henceforth lie in other directions [Leonard's ambitious school-community dream], and you may recall that I made mutual interest one of the conditions of our original arrangement." But the "original plan" had come to an end. "You not only carried out your promises but far exceeded them. I am saying these things with an air of coldness which is not consonant with my feelings. I could weep at every word. But, you will understand. Always I count on your understanding heart. I want you to be free for your own experiments, and I am one of those troublesome persons who demands a great deal from friends. In short, I cannot go on with my projects and accept help from you unless I can also have your interest, and under present circumstances it would be unfair to ask for your interest."[39]

Dorothy's reaction to this letter was the very sensible one that Eduard was behaving childishly. How could Eduard say that her interest in his work would diminish? "I could spank you for such a thought." Did he think that because she happened now to be living in England that she cared "one whit the less" about America and her American life and friends? "I think I care just about twice as much."[40]

Eduard was properly chastened after absorbing Dorothy's verbal spanking. "Yes, I did deserve it, but not for my meaning—only for my awkward manner of expression." What he'd really wanted to say was that with her present concentration on starting the school, it would be unfair of him to expect a continued interest in his projects. "Of course, I didn't expect you to cut yourself off entirely from affairs in America."[41]

Dorothy's response was sincere, but she could not foresee that her interest in what her son calls "the Ruth Morgan issues" would diminish over time. Still, she set aside money for these causes though she would no longer have a significant emotional engagement with them.[42] She would instead make a comparable commitment to her adopted land, Great Britain.

Though he often felt unwell, Lindeman was studying with care the new Fascist government of Benito Mussolini, which was settling in for what would be a long stay. Italy was the first major European nation to install the kind of government that would give its name to a generic political system. The world was watching the experiment with interest.

Roger Baldwin had asked Eduard to get information regarding political prisoners and to get details of a new press censorship bill. By July, as Lindeman wrote Dorothy, he had been in touch with the International Committee for Political Prisoners but had thus far been unable to secure reliable information. He had invited Benedetto Croce, Italy's distinguished philosopher-statesman-critic-historian, and an editor of the Milan liberal daily paper to come to Rapallo for a few days and brief him about "Fascist coercive measures."[43] Croce was just beginning to revise his earlier opinion that fascism was a transitory stage through which Italy must pass while en route to higher levels of political consciousness.[44]

Lindeman was preparing himself to edit the *Survey's* special issue on fascism which would appear in March of 1927. *Survey* editor Paul Kellogg cabled Lindeman and asked him to let Martha Anderson go to Rome, where an interview with *Il Duce* himself could be arranged. Unaccountably ["I preferred not to"], Miss Anderson declined.[45] Was she too shy? Had she heard perhaps of the dictator's reputation as a seducer of women? Kellogg seems to have assumed—perhaps correctly—that the state of Eduard's health would not have permitted his making the trip himself. Certainly it was not in Lindeman's nature to let such an opportunity pass. In any event, the *Survey's* otherwise excellent issue on fascism was not enriched by information gleaned from a first-hand interview.

❀

In spite of its political climate, which was rife with the stench of incipient fascism, the Italy of 1925 had captured all six of the Lindemans, and they were sad to leave.[46] Of course, there had been bad moments—the news of Dorothy's marriage, the ordeal with measles—but happy memories of Italy would long remain with Eduard, Hazel, and their brood.

If Dorothy's prescribed (and financed) rest cure for Eduard in Italy had been unsuccessful in meeting its announced objective of improving Eduard's physical health, there were other unplanned benefits. Eduard felt his mental health was better than it had been upon his arrival four months previously. He thought he had learned much about himself. To his benefactress he wrote that it had been "very wise of you" to send him to Italy.[47] With this sentiment, Hazel and the girls would have concurred with heartfelt amens.

The Lindemans were traveling home via Paris, then England, where they had been invited by the newly married Elmhirsts to view their budding Dartington Hall educational, social, and economic establishment. Paris in August of 1925 was a different Paris than the one Eduard remembered from his visit five years previously. Then, he'd thought the city ugly, with its "mongrel architecture, mock politeness, and post-war cynicism." But things seemed so much better now, and Eduard felt a real affection for what he was seeing and feeling. Was Paris really different, or had he changed more than the city?[48]

Eduard answered his own question in a letter to Charles. In other places, life was "sufficiently external" to allow one to talk about it. But in Paris, life changed "when people have learned to know who one is." Before, he had been "only a tourist—and an American one at that— than which none worse can be said about anyone in Europe." He was pleased with his new and more prominent place in the world, but ironically could not avoid "a slight feeling of cynicism concerning attentions."[49]

While Eduard pondered over his emerging identity, Hazel and friends from Michigan days were enjoying themselves thoroughly with visits to museums and the usual tourist sights. They also did the shops. For the Lindemans, six months away from home had been enough to deplete the family's wardrobe.[50]

Hazel and Eduard both enjoyed the Paris art galleries. Eduard's friend, Bob Hallowell, had work on exhibit, and Eduard thought it much beter than what Hallowell had had on display the year before. The new Hallowell had "more variety, more strength, more subtlety." Hallowell's Venetian things he dismissed as "too pretty," but the work with Swiss and Tunisian settings seemed to him "superb in coloring, drawing and imagination."[51] He talked with Leo Stein, the art critic and brother of Gertrude, about Hallowell's work and was happy to find that Stein thought highly of it. Apparently a number of Parisians shared this view for many of the paintings were marked "sold" at the time of Lindeman's visit. Hallowell himself had been in Paris but left town before his friend learned of his presence.[52]

Eduard decided after viewing what Paris had to offer in the way of art that his inclinations were decidedly in the direction of post-impressionism. His favorite room in the Louvre was the one featuring Monet. Manet's work came second. "With them," he wrote Dorothy, "I begin to see where the distinction resides." His "tenacious inhibitions" were indeed being dissipated and his tastes elevated—undoubtedly under the influence of his new friend, Leo Stein, with whom he had been visiting the galleries.[53]

Lindeman's favorite pastime while in Paris—and the one that occupied most of his time—was that of "debate" as he described it to Dorothy. With Floyd Dell, Dick Mount, Carl Chapman, Thorstein Sillin, and a few others on occasion, he met almost daily at the Cafe de la Paix at noon. "We argue ourselves to a restaurant on the left bank and from there [we are] back to Luigi's for beer and sandwiches at five." The starting point for discussion was usually an assumption of "some absolute position in regard to realism, Gothic architecture, socialism, etc." The friends would then "proceed to discuss ourselves back to reasonableness." Sometimes the group took excursions together—the cathedral town of Chartres being the goal of one such day trip. Eduard especially enjoyed the company of Floyd Dell, an editor, novelist, and playwright—and fellow contributor to *The New Republic*. "He retains the odor of mid-western soil, the flavor of rural psychology, and consequently I understand him."[54]

There were other sights in Paris that Lindeman found impressive, the Folies Bergère for one. Eduard was also a bit goggle-eyed about the "half-dozen dukes and countesses" one tended to "bump over" while en route to a restaurant seat.[55] By any standard, he had come a long way from the village of St. Clair and even from Michigan Agricultural College.

The French were fighting a colonial war in Morocco, but Lindeman had to buy British papers to learn anything about it. He speculated that the reason for silence in the French press was that the war had thus far been a "continuous defeat" for the French. "There is apparently no enthusiasm for the war here," he reported to Dorothy, "although many efforts are being made to manufacture some."[56]

In mid-August, Martha Anderson left Italy and rejoined the Lindemans in Paris. After talking with her, Lindeman arrived at the mistaken conclusion that fascism in Italy was "on its last legs." He based this belief on two events that he interpreted as evidence of weakening support for Mussolini's Fascist government, the retirement from political life of former Prime Minister Vittorio Orlando, who had decided to live in France, and the brutal beating of Giovanni Amendola, who had opposed Fascist policies.[57] Orlando had made an unsuccessful attempt to reconcile fascism with the democratic process.[58] Amendola, a professor of theoretical philosophy turned politician, died of his injuries in 1926.[59]

Crossing the channel to England, the Lindemans first spent a week with the Elmhirsts, who were temporarily living in the Seymour Hotel in Totnes, Devonshire. Dartington Hall, the 1,600 acre estate they had just purchased, was only a mile away.[60] The buildings at Dartington were little better than ruins—but they were grand ruins going back to the late fourteenth century.[61] There was a magnificent tiltyard that would eventually be restored as an outdoor amphitheater for the Dartington School. Handsome trees on the estate—among them some spectacular twisted old Spanish chestnuts—awaited discovery by the visitors from America.[62]

When the Lindemans visited, Dorothy and Leonard were hard at work creating their dream community. While there, Eduard roamed the Dartmoor countryside and gained a deep feeling for its beauty. Inside, however, he fought feelings of hostility toward Leonard. How irked he was at the sight of this Yorkshire clergyman's son who carried a walking stick as he surveyed the grounds of his own estate and behaved as if he were lord of the manor—as in fact he was.[63] And Dorothy these days seemed to talk and write of nothing except her future with Leonard and what was now their joint project.

Still, he tried to quash these feelings and, accepting a defeat of sorts at Leonard's hands, allowed himself to be drawn into the great planning effort that would culminate within a year in a school at Dartington. In the years ahead, Eduard would figure prominently— if painfully at times—in the experiment at Dartington. The Lindemans would make a further contribution to the experiment that was building on the hills of Devon. In 1928, an excited and venturesome Betty Lindeman would become a student at Dartington School. Her transportation and tuition for the first two years were a gift to the Lindemans from Dorothy Elmhirst.[64]

Recovered from the worst of his earlier pique caused by the news of Dorothy's marriage, Eduard planned to discuss renewal of the arrangements under which Dorothy had been supporting his work. Eduard had earlier talked with Herbert Croly about his plan and had asked his friend's advice about how to proceed. He cannot, however, have been pleased with Herbert's response, which was that it would be advisable for him to cease the financial arrangement with Dorothy and depend upon his own earnings for carrying on his work. Herbert frankly told Eduard that he would be giving Dorothy the same advice.[65]

This word from his best friend was unsettling enough, but Eduard would have been even more disturbed had he known the entire content of Herbert's August 13 letter to Dorothy. Herbert indicated to Dorothy that he had talked with Eduard but that he had not told him all of his reasons for giving Dorothy advice "different from what it was a year ago." "It seems to me clear," Croly wrote, "in the course of the last winter, that he is getting into a dependent frame of mind. That he is passing on to you responsibilities which are essentially his own, and that he needs for awhile at least not to feel as if he had someone to depend on." In part, this attitude might have been the result of illness, "but it may still survive now that his illness is over, and I think it would be rather unfortunate for him if it did survive."[66]

Between his work at the New York School and the part-time job that Ned Carter had offered him [at The Inquiry] he could perfectly well earn as much money as Dorothy had paid him while he was writing *Social Discovery*. Herbert continued: "I think he could carry that same amount of work without straining himself and without placing any obstacles in the way of a certain amount of outside writing which he ought to continue."[67]

Perhaps, after Eduard had taught a few years, he might "then have something in his head which he would like to have the leisure to express." If so, and if Dorothy were still interested in him, she might offer him the opportunity of writing a book "free from financial worries." In any event, it would be better, Croly went on, if Dorothy's assistance were to be "occasional and limited to a particular time and to a particular piece of work than that it should be permanent and irrespective of a definite job."[68]

Croly had been "really deeply troubled last winter, particularly during the last two months before he went abroad, at the indications of an increasing sense of personal irresponsibility on his part." Had the episode reported by John Hader been part of this? Croly, however, concluded that Eduard had experienced a "temporary weakness" now past.[69]

So that there could be no misunderstanding, Croly concluded his letter to Dorothy with the assurance that "what I have said does not diminish in any way my regard for him nor my confidence in him, but he suffers a little bit from a sense of inferiority and I think that his illness combined with the help that you have given him has developed this sense of inferiority in a somewhat undesirable direction. The chances are . . . that he will recover his balance, but he needs to be watched."[70]

Considering the riptide of currents that surged within his mind and coursed through his heart, Eduard was probably glad to leave Devon to attend the Trade Union Congress in London. He found the city to be in vivid contrast to Paris, where life was lived on a "sprightlier plane." In London, pessimism seemed pervasive everywhere. The industrial situation, marked by shockingly high unemployment, grew worse daily. Worst of all, in Lindeman's view, was the lack of leadership in the country. The Labour Party, he thought, was growing more conservative while the "minority radicals" were moving steadily further to the left. Still, the British seemed to "enjoy living in an atmosphere of impending doom." Lindeman told Charles Shaw that he liked to "spoof" them about it.[71]

He found the Trade Union Congress disappointing. It seemed to him that there was "no leadership" in the older group, while the younger men "are the victims of phrases." He was especially irked at the seemingly endless debates over resolutions that were "nothing more than futile words." And always there had to be a "general principle: if they wanted a program for organizing shop committees they were obliged to include in the resolution a sentence affirming that by this means the capitalist system could best be overthrown."[72]

Eduard conveyed to Dorothy his impressions of some of the union leaders. He very much disliked Arthur Cook of the Miners' Federation, who appeared to be "neurotic and muddle-headed." James Thomas, John Clynes, Robert Smillie, and the older group of men "served merely as wet blankets." All of them, including former (and future) Prime Minister Ramsey MacDonald were "so frightened by the Bolshevik bogey" that they couldn't think in "constructive terms." Emanuel Shinwell, leader of the seamen, "made the deepest impression" upon Lindeman, who also noted that he had great power "but is mistrusted by everybody." Ernest Bevin, who had spearheaded merger of thirty-two unions into a national organization (Transport and General Workers' Union), also possessed power "but his thinking does not go deeply enough."[73]

He became "very fond" of Arthur Greenwood, then a Labour Party

M.P., but thought he had nothing more to give. As for the American fraternal delegates to the Congress, they could only be described as "awful, and the least said about them the better."[74]

America's inquisitive philosopher was not idle professionally while in the British capital. He made appointments with numerous government officials and Labour Party people. To him, it was an "entirely new crowd." Persons who had been powerful during his previous visit in London had dropped out of the scene.[75]

Lindeman took particular care to become acquainted with Waldo McGillycuddy Eager, who was the "land policy man" advising former Prime Minister David Lloyd George. Addressing Britain's newest great landholder, Eduard pointed out that the Liberals had worked out a far-reaching program that was designed to "eliminate the landlord altogether." This land plan was to be the main plank in the Liberal Party's platform in the next general elections, which were expected to take place in 1927. "What a canny old schemer L.G. is!" was Eduard's reaction.[76]

Eduard's room in London looked out upon the courtyard of the British Museum, into which poured daily a steady stream of "serious looking students, antiquarians with frayed frock coats, and at hourly intervals caravans of American tourists who rush in and out." Eduard himself went in only occasionally and then only to look at some particular exhibit. His chief interest was the anthropological section.[77]

Just around the corner was Mudie's book shop, which Eduard knew would interest his academic librarian friend. He wrote Charles that it was a place that "not only consumes much of my time but relieves me of most of my funds." There were specialty book shops which tempted him even more.[78]

If Hazel and the girls had outfitted themselves in Paris, it was Eduard who splurged in London. Yielding to the pleas of friends who deplored his dated attire and habitual dishevelment, he had four suits and an overcoat made. Included were a grey tweed with plus fours, dark blue and dark grey business suits, and a new dinner suit. His suits might need pressing—as they invariably did when Hazel wasn't on hand to see to it— but at least he had a decent wardrobe for the first time in his life.[79]

Awaiting Lindeman in London were letters from Alfred Dwight Sheffield, who was "full of plans for the winter," and from Frederick Keppel, president of the Carnegie Corporation. The days of relative leisure in Paris and London had been nice, but Eduard was getting restless. The letters from across the Atlantic stimulated him; once again he felt "very much like plunging into something."[80] He had the itch to go home.

Eduard and Hazel Lindeman—with Doris, Ruth, Betty, and Barbara in tow—were aboard the liner U.S.S. *Leviathan* (once Kaiser Wilhelm's *Vaterland*)[81] as it steamed out of Southhampton on September 21.[82] Except for the steady Hazel, perhaps, none of them would ever be quite the same as they were upon their arrival in Europe four short months before.

As the ship's great propellers boiled the grey Atlantic, Eduard in particular had much to think about. He had experienced a quality of happiness in Italy that summer that seemed in retrospect to have been possible only because youth had definitely been abandoned.[83] He was forty. He was a man increasingly confident of his abilities. He was winning recognition from people who counted. And in the shining city at the mouth of the Hudson, excitement awaited. His letter from Carnegie's Keppel was full of news about Keppel's adult education plan, which was slated to become a landmark of the American adult education movement.[84]

The America to which the *Leviathan* returned the Lindemans in 1925 was, on the surface, hardly Eduard Lindeman's kind of place. The flapper society actually masked a nation that was deeply conservative—even reactionary.[85] The United States had refused to join the League of Nations. The Scopes trial, which rocked the nation, had ended in July. Most Americans were soundly approving of presidential success in reducing the national debt. The absence of a comparable national commitment in other areas of need was not noticed by most citizens.

Economically, the nation had erected a Potemkin village that looked like prosperity. But the banking system, as well as the stock market, was totally out of control—though who cared so long as it was possible for nearly everyone, it seemed, to make money? The day of reckoning for the nation's economic system was still four years away, but Warren Harding's "return to normalcy" had suddenly exploded as Teapot Dome, the Watergate of its era. The President's seedy and greedy friends had enriched themselves and misused their positions of public trust. Harding conveniently died as the scandal was about to break and was replaced by his honest but lackluster Vice President, Calvin Coolidge.

In spite of Teapot Dome, Coolidge had been able to win the White House on his own in the 1924 election, soundly defeating both the Democratic candidate, John Davis, and the Progressive Party nominee, Wisconsin Senator Robert M. LaFollette. "The business of America is business," the new President had solemnly declared as his second term began. Hardly anyone laughed, and a substantial majority of the people in the world's largest democracy appeared content that no higher goals were being set by their nation's chief executive.

But appearances, in an America that could produce Thomas Jefferson, Franklin Pierce, Abraham Lincoln, and Calvin Coolidge, were, as always, deceiving. Beneath a somnolent political surface in that year of 1925 bubbled a veritable cauldron of intellectual, scientific, and creative energy. It was the year in which Willa Cather produced *The Professor's House;* for John Dos Passos, it was *Manhattan Transfer;* Edna Ferber and Sinclair Lewis garnered Pulitzer Prizes for *So Big* and *Arrowsmith* respectively. From his base at New York's Union Theological Seminary, Harry Emerson Fosdick preached a gospel that was shaking the foundations of American Protestantism. On the musical scene, the young Aaron Copland, who received the first Guggenheim Fellowship, weighed in with his Symphony for Organ and Orchestra. An American physicist, R. A. Millikan, discovered the presence of cosmic rays in the upper atmosphere. Even social reformers were making more progress than they knew.[86]

For thinkers and dreamers of all kinds, these were good times. If a man had his wits about him he could flourish. Eduard Lindeman's mind was fixed in this mid-decade year on a soon-to-be-fashionable notion—the idea that adult human beings were inveterate learners. It seemed to him that this simple fact was of crucial importance for anyone with faith in social engineering—and that it ought to be recognized and understood in all its dimensions. The coming realm of adult education was territory that he had staked out for himself, and he was not about to leave the task of exploration to others.

CHAPTER **7**

The Meaning of Adult Education in Its Time

When he finished writing *The Meaning of Adult Education* in mid-1926, Eduard was jubilant. For one thing, he was feeling well both mentally and physically, though some dimensions of his mood were puzzling. The slightest events sometimes seemed important, even thrilling, but adversity could be shrugged off. His friends noticed a change. As someone at *The New Republic* said, "You've always had a don't give a damn attitude toward life but now you've come back from Italy with a go-to-hell one."[1]

His new book had been completed in record time. His career was picking up steam. He was in demand as a lecturer and writer. Next year, he would once again be in Europe for reasons that were important and exciting. It would be back to Denmark for more studies of adult education, then to the new League of Nations in Geneva for some observations and writing. Then he was scheduled to cross the Channel to England, where he would assist Leonard and Dorothy in a weeklong training session for their newly recruited staff at Dartington School.[2]

Money was no problem. "Shall you need further funds before starting over here [Europe]?" Miss Bogue had written. "You can cable me c/o Guaranty in London if you do."[3] It was going to be a hopping, skipping, and jumping year, America's young philosopher thought.

In his 1924 book *Social Discovery,* Lindeman attempted to develop a technology which could bridge the gap between academic research and the realities of organized social life. The book, which was based largely on Lindeman's work with The Inquiry, was a critical success. "It cannot be said too emphatically that this is a book to be reckoned with by every sociologist [and] by every social scientist intelligent enough to recognize his responsibilities to methodology" was how one critic began his review.[4]

Could he now repeat and even improve upon this achievement with his planned new volume, *The Meaning of Adult Education,* which would be much less carefully crafted? The book that almost wrote itself on Eduard's typewriter in 1926 was a product of his intuition. He had soft-pedaled for these moments his usual canons of logic.

The critical reception to *The Meaning of Adult Education* needs to be understood in the context of the times in which it took place. The adult education movement received its first major stimulus just after what many historians were calling the Great European War, as a weary world searched for ways to put backbone into the idea that "the war to end all wars" was not mislabeled. So vibrant and widespread was the search for knowledge to make a better world that Everett Dean Martin, one who was experiencing it, sensed that he was part of a mass movement of educational hunger that had not been exceeded in strength since the thirteenth century.[5]

This urge for the better life through lifelong education was felt with particular strength—even passion—in Great Britain, where the Ministry of Reconstruction's Adult Education Committee released in 1919 its report on the role and significance of adult education in a free society.[6] Christened *The 1919 Report,* this document made a strong case for adult education, not as a luxury but as a national and international necessity.[7]

In America, the movement found focus in the mind of Frederick Keppel, president of the great foundation that Andrew Carnegie had established for advancing his philanthropic concerns. With awesome financial resources at his disposal, Keppel could do more than think about adult education. He could act, and he did.

The Carnegie Corporation, in June 1924, convened in New York the first American conference on adult education. To this gathering were invited twenty-eight persons considered "most competent to advise" the Corporation with respect to the nascent adult education movement in America.[8] The chief outcome of the conference was a decision to institute under Carnegie sponsorship a series of studies of adult education which would focus at the outset on *nonvocational* endeavors,[9] a decision consistent with one of Lindeman's four basic assumptions about adult education.

Eduard Lindeman was invited to attend this conference in his capacity as secretary of the American Country Life Association.[10] Ironically, in light of his contempt for the breed, his advice was sought as a "technical expert" who had "experience in the development of techniques that would help disseminate information or knowledge."[11]

Though he did not attend the conference[12] Lindeman was one of seven men selected as members of the Corporation's Advisory Board on Adult Education. The others were the historian Charles Beard, as representative of the National Institute for Public Administration; Alfred Cohn, Rockefeller Institute; John C. Dana, Newark Public Library; C. R. Dooley, Standard Oil of New Jersey; Everett Dean Martin, People's Institute of New York; and James E. Russell, Teachers College, Columbia University, who served as chairman.[13]

The committee kept no minutes of its meetings, but memos written by its members have been preserved in the Carnegie Corporation Archives.[14] As cited and analyzed by Amy Rose, they provide intriguing insights into the crosscurrents of thought extant in the earliest days of America's adult education movement.

The Carnegie Corporation, in October 1925, convened a second national conference on adult education in Cleveland. To this conference, subsequent regional conferences, and another national conference in Chicago in 1926, Keppel invited a variety of thinkers and doers, among them Eduard Lindeman, to address this question: "How shall we use our wealth and leisure properly save as we have knowledge of the proper uses of wealth and leisure?"[15]

The adult, midstream in the responsibilities of life, "must be helped to an educational analysis of his own problems," was one "opinion" presented at the Carnegie conferences. Among other such opinions presented by adult education leaders: college courses should be spread over longer periods in the form of extension courses; individuals should cooperate in self-analysis; finding thirst was more important than satisfying it. One such opinion that could not have come from Eduard Lindeman at this stage in his life: "Youth from 18 to 20 should be helped to develop a sense of sin."[16]

There was a further outcome of the Carnegie initiatives. At the Cleveland conference, a constitution for a proposed adult education association was drafted. Reactive regional meetings followed in New York, San Francisco, Nashville, and Chicago.[17] In April 1926 at a Carnegie-sponsored conference in Chicago, the American Association for Adult Education was born. AAAE, or "Acubee" as its members would generally call it, was given a healthy $137,500 start-up grant from the Carnegie Corporation.[18] As a member of the advisory committee that antedated the Association, as a direct participant in many of the discussions that led to its birth, and as a member of the original AAAE Executive Board,[19] Eduard Lindeman qualifies as a founding father of AAAE and its most recent incarnation, the American Association for Adult and Continuing Education (AAACE), now headquartered in Washington.

The initial aspiration of AAAE, which had offices at 41 East Forty-second Street in New York, was modest—merely that of serving as a clearinghouse for adult education matters. Its first executive director was Morse Cartwright, a candidate Lindeman had initially opposed. Lindeman's candidate had been Ned Carter, but Carter felt he could consider the job only on a part-time basis, with The Inquiry as his other interest.[20] Doubting the wisdom of this option, Lindeman seems to have written Cartwright, assistant to the president at Carnegie Corporation, telling of his initial opposition but now offering his support.

In acknowledging Lindeman's letter, Cartwright said he had not known of Lindeman's opposition at the meeting of AAAE's Executive Board and accepted his offer of support as "generous and fine." He was delaying a decision, however, "until I am convinced that I represent as near a unanimous choice as the Executive Board is able to make."[21]

Lindeman may not have been completely candid with Cartwright about the reasons for his belated support. In a letter to Leonard Elmhirst, he said he feared the Executive Committee had "drifted toward Everett Dean Martin [who] wants it and he has been on the ground from the beginning." With Carter out of the running, it would be awkward, Eduard said, for him to suggest any other candidate at this point. He wasn't sure just what direction the new organization would take. "With Carter at the helm, I think we might have made it something really creative for American life."[22]

The able, though aloof and hard-to-know, Cartwright got the job, but his relationship with the more gregarious Lindeman was never comfortable. It was common knowledge within the AAAE leadership that Lindeman was almost never invited by Cartwright to play any prominent role in any of the organization's forums or annual meetings. The differences in style were matched by those in philosophy. Lindeman viewed Cartwright as too elitist in his approach. Cartwright was equally skeptical of Lindeman's more egalitarian direction—and feared an activist role for AAAE. Herbert Hunsaker, who knew both

men well, believes the differences in philosophy were not as significant as either of them imagined.[23]

Some of the stepchild legacy of vocational education as a member
of the adult education community can be traced to the victory within
the AAAE of the liberal education wing as represented by Cartwright
over forces that would have encouraged a more far-ranging base of
educational concern. AAAE wrote into its bylaws a clause that its
membership was not available to persons representing for-profit
institutions. In practice, most of these were proprietary schools
offering vocational instruction.[24]

While he rejected the exclusivist tendencies of the liberal education
faction, Lindeman shared their concern that vocational education was
a special case. It was too easily corruptible so that the job rather than
the person became the central concern. Adult education for self-
fulfillment tended to get lost in the process. Public education might
include vocational education but should not "be primarily vocational
in purpose."[25]

Lindeman's contributions were not generally encouraged by the
AAAE's first executive director. But many years later, Lindeman's
advice would be sought by the administrative coordinator of a newly
formed AAAE successor organization, the Adult Education Association of the U.S.A. (AEA/USA). In 1952, Malcolm Knowles sought
Lindeman's advice in the earliest days of his incumbency. With
Dorothy Canfield Fisher, he visited Lindeman, then in the terminal
stages of his illness, at his home. How should the new association be
different, Knowles asked, from both AAAE—allegedly too theoretical—and the rival National Education Association Department of
Education (later to become the National Association for Public
Continuing and Adult Education), which emphasized the nuts and
bolts of practice?[26]

As usual, Knowles found himself in complete agreement with his
old friend and mentor. AEA/USA should avoid either wing of a false
dichotomy and instead seek to bridge the gap between intellectual
leaders and practitioners.[27] Lindeman would certainly smile from the
grave if he learned of the merger in 1982 of the Adult Education
Association of the U.S.A. (AEA/USA) with the National Association
for Public Continuing and Adult Education (NAPCAE).

Eduard Lindeman has emerged in the decades since the 1920s as
one of the leading conceptual architects of the modern practice of
adult education. In 1925, however, Lindeman was just one of a
number of American intellectuals to be taken with the notion that
adults not only could learn but must learn if they are to survive as

anything other than empty human beings in a complicated world. Consequently, *The Meaning of Adult Education* was to have a number of competitors within the educational commonwealth for the attention of the public. A number of these projects—though not Eduard Lindeman's—were supported wholly or in part through Carnegie Corporation grants.[28]

Lindeman's chief rival—as measured by attention from the critics—was Everett Dean Martin, whom Lindeman knew well. Both served as members of the Carnegie Corporation Advisory Committee on Adult Education. Martin was then drawing audiences of one thousand for his Friday night lectures at the People's Institute of New York.[29] In his book *The Meaning of a Liberal Education,* he laid out a case for adult education from the tradition of the liberal arts.

In Martin's view, the aim of liberal education was to produce the "cultivated amateur."[30] It was pursuit of this goal that would save adult education from "degenerating, like Protestantism, into a conflict of narrow orthodoxies." Any "passing fancy or popular prejudice, however ungrounded in philosophy," might become serviceable as a "dominant ideal" in the absence of appropriate guidance by qualified educators.[31]

Seeming to qualify as passing fancies in Martin's eyes were short-term institutes for farmers and "instruction to industrial workers which will improve their efficiency and deepen their loyalty to the company." Much of the "Americanization propaganda which gave employment to uplifters during the years following the war" was also being called adult education, much to Martin's disgust.[32]

In marked contrast to Lindeman's egalitarian views about education for adults, Martin articulated the often-elitist liberal education view that adult education was selective. "Its aim is not to provide a slight increase of information and a few noble sentiments for the rank and file, but to select out of the undifferentiated mass those who are naturally capable of becoming something more than automatons." Opportunities in adult education should be for "people worth educating."[33]

Yet even these select few would often be "very opinionated—especially when they first come to class." Indeed, they have "violent prejudices and are extremely 'advanced.' " The adult educator, "if he is to *keep his hold upon* these persons, must gain their favor and sustain their interest." (Emphasis added) How would this be done? Simply "make a concession to popular prejudice," Martin advised his readers. In common with the reading public, adults in classes "like to be told what they would like to regard as true." Ultimately, Martin seems to say (though he never quite does), the group could be brought around.[34] Considering this context, Martin's parallel assertion that the teacher of adults "must make himself a student with the others" has a rather hollow ring.[35]

Beyond this concern about curriculum, Everett Dean Martin was suspicious of the adult education movement itself. Was the "alleged general interest . . . evidence of a spontaneous and growing desire for knowledge?" Or could it just possibly be "something promoted, worked up by interests which would 'educate the masses' in order to attain certain economic ends, individual or social." After all, "popularization of knowledge is not the same as humanization of knowledge," he continued huffily.[36] Martin's position, which was essentially that of philosophers who emphasize liberal arts as the centerpiece of education, would be taken up and pursued with superior skill in later years of the twentieth century by Robert Hutchins.

Martin's book was durable and did well for its publisher, W. W. Norton. More than 18,000 copies were sold before it went out of print in 1945. A reprint edition by Garden City Press generated additional sales of more than 33,000 copies.[37]

Joseph K. Hart, who served for a time as education editor for the *Survey*,[38] was the most prolific of writers in the field of adult education during the 1920s, turning out no less than three books. In addition to *Adult Education*, which appeared in 1927, Hart wrote *Inside Experience*, a thoroughly serviceable account of adult education through the lens of pragmatism. Earlier, in 1924, Hart had provided Americans with an overview of Nikolai Grundtvig in a book engagingly titled *Light From the North*.

Setting aside a tendency to erupt in bursts of semicolons and an occasional gush of wordiness, Hart demonstrated in his book *Adult Education* that he was in most ways a better writer than Lindeman was at this stage of his career. Hart does not contribute significantly more than Lindeman, but he is often more precise and speaks with great clarity—if less poetically.

Hart's ideas merged with Lindeman's to a remarkable degree. Like Lindeman, he had a passionate devotion to democracy and believed that it was adult education that would help Americans "realize the meanings, still latent, unexplored, even unsuspected within that democratic future. . . "[39] The scent of democracy would never rest in the neighborhood of a mechanistic "pedagogy" which Hart termed responsible for the production of "this greatest liability of the modern world—the chief obstacle to democracy—the 'ad-ult'; the pluperfect, completely finished, unintelligent member of the community."[40]

Experience as a factor in adult learning was another axiom shared by Hart and Lindeman. The new industrial order required intelligent participation by the citizenry. And each individual, before teaching anyone else how to live in the new order, "must learn how to live the new order. . . ."[41] Eventually, there must be adult education "to prepare adults who will have the capacity to grow their own ideas out of the sorts of their own experiences—at their own need, and risk, too. . . ."[42] He was, in short, as much the pragmatist as Eduard Lindeman.

With Lindeman, Hart took a slap at education designed as "*credit* toward some future life. . . Rather, adult education takes the 'cash' of actual meaning and use, and lets the credit of 'eventual standing' take care of itself."[43] Moreover, the real task for Americans was "not that of endlessly re-educating adults who were badly educated in childhood." Rather, it was that of "making sure that we shall eventually get generations of adults who will have escaped the deficiencies, the inhibitions, the blockings, the frustrations of our present adult generation. . . ."[44]

Lindeman's *The Meaning of Adult Education* appeared first. It was shorter and had for that reason perhaps a broader based appeal than Hart's *Adult Education.* And, as subsequent events would show, Eduard Lindeman had a missionary zeal about him, coupled with a developing ability as a speaker, that propelled him ahead of his rivals for the role as chief conceptualizer of the new and growing force.

Joseph K. Hart was a professor of political science who had a troubled career at the University of Wisconsin and later at Vanderbilt and Columbia Universities. He presents rather a puzzle for the historian of adult education.[45] His efforts are respectable pieces of work. Yet he disappeared from the adult education community—and from the memories of adult educators—leaving hardly a trace.

With Lindeman, Martin, and Hart carving out the philosophical high ground, it remained for William S. Learned to sketch more of the outlines for adult education practice. Learned's book, *The American Public Library and the Diffusion of Knowledge,* was financed by a Carnegie grant.[46] It was not, however, an independent study but was done by Learned in his capacity as executive assistant in the Corporation. As such, it constitutes a view of the adult education world that was shared by officials of the Carnegie Corporation.[47] Learned presented a no-nonsense—yet startlingly prescient—view of the coming adult education world. Like Martin, Learned was skeptical of much of what passed for adult education in the fad atmosphere of the early 1920s. Although "commendable in spirit," much of this activity, he thought, "lacks purpose, and the greater portion of it, certainly, lacks the cumulative sequence necessary to give it significant and lasting value."[48]

Learned's vision was of nothing less than an information society—this in the world of 1924. "There are everywhere indications that our American society is on the eve of a much more thoroughgoing organization of its intelligence service than has hitherto been attempted. . . " No longer could the "acquisition of orderly and trustworthy knowledge . . . be considered as an esoteric mystery locked up in an institution and available only for the young." On the contrary, "self-education with intimate relation to daily interests and activities must be recognized as a natural process of mental growth. . . " Properly gratified, such "constant and legitimate craving of the intelligent adult" would continue throughout life. "The existing borrowed and imperfect methods" for satisfying this hunger were insufficient. The problem: "to develop a technique suited to the satisfaction of its peculiar demands."[49]

Pressures toward adult education, Learned believed, were appearing in "the rapid accumulation of vast masses of information which makes imperative some means of selection, digest, or abridgment whereby any one who needs them may gain possession of essential facts. . . " Every form of human activity was being stimulated "by the phenomenal improvement in speed and accuracy of communication, and by the consequent increase in area over which experience may now be readily assembled and compared."[50] It was the library, Learned said, that should be staffed with "intelligence personnel" who could facilitate the acquisition of knowledge by its users.[51]

Society was changing so rapidly that adult education was becoming a necessity rather than a luxury. But there were problems. Was it not true that the American adult was "not generally well trained . . . in the technique indispensable to self-education, namely the getting of ideas independently from books?" It was the library—conventional, yet in need of reorganization to better serve adults—that Learned saw as the primary agent for problem resolution and effective realization of adult education opportunities.[52]

Dorothy Canfield Fisher's *Why Stop Learning?*, published in 1927, captured a large readership among the general public. It is notable chiefly for its vivid description of existing adult education activities in the United States as gathered under Carnegie Corporation auspices and for its explicit and sensitive treatment of informal learning efforts by adults. Like Lindeman, she asked questions from a humanistic perspective: "Is there any educational activity for wage-earners in this country where the purpose of both teacher and grown-up student is neither to make more money, nor to fight a more winning battle for recognition and power, but to develop each individual personality as harmoniously as possible?"[53]

Lindeman reviewed the Fisher book in *Survey*. He found it refreshing that she "breathes new life" into the newly assembled facts. But he sounded a bit peevish as he continued by saying that "those of us who have already assimilated them wish that she might have devoted herself wholly to interpretation. The great danger now confronting those who are determined not to stop learning is that they, too, will become parts of a quantitative movement." Not everything calling itself education was "leading us into the light."[54]

That a novelist of the stature of Mrs. Fisher would interest herself in adult education is indicative of the attraction of the idea in the late 1920s. By the early 1930s, the *Journal of Adult Education* was publishing articles by other well-known Americans, among them Charles A. Beard, Nicholas Murray Butler, John Erskine, Harry Elmer Barnes, Harry A. Overstreet, E. L. Thorndike, Glenn Frank, and Jane Addams.[55] Unhappily, as the Depression wore on, this widespread enthusiasm waned. Only a persistent group of believers, Eduard Lindeman among them, retained a full commitment, as measured by a continuing flow of articles, speeches, and leadership in adult education organizations.

The Meaning of Adult Education came off the presses in late 1926. It eventually garnered six full-fledged reviews in major publications and at least five short reviews or mention in minor or specialized publications. With few exceptions, the general reaction of mainline critics was poor, or lukewarm at best. There wasn't the slightest indication that any reviewer sensed himself or herself to be in the presence of an adult education classic.

Evans Clark in *The New York Times* reviewed it in the same column with Everett Dean Martin's *The Meaning of a Liberal Education* and drew comparisons between the two which could not have warmed the heart of Eduard Lindeman. Clark cited the "general stampede" in the direction of adult education and noted that both Martin and Lindeman "are deeply impressed by the spectacle. They see its moving drama and sense its implications. But they both are alarmed by some of the crude and bizarre effects; and both of them . . . are dominated by a passion to set the feet of the multitude in the paths of decency and reason."[56]

Martin, according to Clark, "writes brilliantly. Mr. Lindeman, on the other hand, writes with a heavy hand—although his faults are undoubtedly thrown into abnormal perspective by Mr. Martin's exceptional gifts. Where Mr. Martin is specific and concrete, impelled by images, Mr. Lindeman is schematic and abstract, moved by logical consistency rather than by the play of the drama."[57]

After devoting twenty paragraphs mostly to praise of Martin, Clark turns to Lindeman and his "conviction that education is not set apart from life: a goal or an ornament that is acquired in youth along with manners and the ability to play tennis and bridge." Getting to adult education, the reviewer noted that Lindeman, like Martin, laid down no program for its implementation. "On the contrary, Mr. Lindeman's book is nothing more than a sketchy outline of his conception of how modern life might be lived with more intelligence and grace."[58]

Several paragraphs of summary are then capped with the judgment that Lindeman's book "has the fascination of an ideal and the neatness of a logical pattern, but much less of the bite and challenge of reality than has Mr. Martin's own. Mr. Lindeman is a philosopher at heart: which is a serious handicap in this age of the concrete."[59]

Clifton Fadiman of the *New York Evening Post* at least refrained from gratuitous insults aimed at Lindeman's profession. Yet the scope of his coverage of *The Meaning of Adult Education* was in itself demeaning. In a nine-paragraph review, eight paragraphs mostly praised Martin's effort. "To read 'The Meaning of a Liberal Education' is almost equivalent to receiving one." So good was it that it was "one of the few volumes on modern educational tendency which are free from the bias of any particular school or philosophy"—which must have come as news to Martin himself.[60]

Fadiman dispatched Lindeman in a single paragraph. The author had written a book that "contrives to be at once brief and wordy. It aims to provide a sort of formula which shall sum up the meaning of adult education. Adult education aims to organize intelligence toward the securing of power. Power in turn enables us to express ourselves and thus acquire freedom which may be translated into terms either of creation or appreciation. The book is not distinguished for any particularly concrete application of any of these very dignified and worthy phrases."[61]

As if this weren't enough, the hapless Lindeman suffered in comparison with Everett Dean Martin at the hands of Lewis Mumford as well in *Progressive Education*. Two other volumes were also subjects of Mumford's review: *The Path of Learning*, essays on education selected and arranged by Henry W. Holmes and Burton Fowler, and William Heard Kilpatrick's *Education for a Changing Civilization*. Lindeman got a backhanded compliment in the way of comparison with Kilpatrick: "Mr. Eduard Lindeman begins with something like the same attitude as Professor Kilpatrick but by dint of a rather arduous and sometimes obscure criticism of every step in the educational process he reaches what seems to me a more adequate point of view."[62]

Amy Hewes, a professor of economics and sociology at Mount Holyoke College, reviewed *The Meaning of Adult Education* for *Survey*, along with other books on the new trend of "Education for Everybody." Included were *Educational Opportunities for Young Workers* by Owen D. Evans; *New Schools for Older Students* by Nathaniel Peffer; *The University Afield* by Alfred L. Hall-Quest; *Correspondence Schools, Lyceums, Chautauquas* by John S. Noffsinger; *Libraries and Adult Education*, a report on a study made by the American Library Association; *Light from the North* by Joseph K. Hart; and, once again, the ubiquitous Everett Dean Martin with *The Meaning of a Liberal Education.*[63]

Professor Hewes presented few value judgments on any of these volumes except for offering a paean of praise "to the pleasure of reading [what else?] Mr. Martin's book." A quick summary of *The Meaning of Adult Education* was preceded by acknowledgement that "a man whose formal education began at the age of 21 . . . [and who undertakes] to explain the meaning of adult education is in possession of a point of view others can not bring."[64]

The only really positive review was that of John E. Kirkpatrick in the *New York World*. Kirkpatrick congratulated Lindeman for producing a "significant discussion of education conceived in the large." At last someone had done something to "help intelligent people see that adult education is not merely vocational education for the worker but 'an agitating instrumentality for changing life,' and that it is wholly indispensable if our democracies are to be saved from the threatening Mussolinis and other 'power-grabbers'."[65]

There were three basic themes running through the unfavorable reviews of *The Meaning of Adult Education* published in the 1920s. First, the topic, new as it was, remained fuzzy in the minds of critical readers. What was adult education anyway? In the absence of a clear-cut definition of adult education, it was hard to grasp just what was meant by the concept. Second, Lindeman's writing style got in the way of critical understanding, rather than aiding it. Third, some critics were profoundly suspicious of the adult education movement itself, and Lindeman's effort apparently did nothing to allay these qualms.

As has been seen, Lindeman's omission of a straight-out definition of adult education in a volume purporting to explain the meaning of adult education was deliberate. This may have been a decision shot through with intellectual integrity, but it was fatal for anyone hoping to communicate with the critics.

As for writing style, on technical grounds the critics were right, of course. Still, it is strange that none of them sensed the poetic lilt that several generations of adult educators have experienced upon first reading *The Meaning of Adult Education*. It is possible—even probable—that the reader will simply *feel* good after savoring the book. It is this intangible affective dimension permeating the book's eccentric syntax that distinguishes Lindeman's creation from those of his competitors.

Eduard's friends generally liked *The Meaning of Adult Education* though a number of them agreed with the critics that Eduard should improve his writing skills. Writing from an ocean liner in mid-Atlantic, Roger Baldwin teasingly told his friend the book should be called " 'The Resurrection of the Boobs.' " Thanks to Eduard, it would be necessary "to get out of our graves and start running somewhere with our souls on fire, our roots trailing behind us, our homes abandoned, bound for glory." Though his language was "restrained," Eduard was "really quite drunk. . . You have taken education from its lofty perch and made it a vulgar accompaniment of the day's chores." He then took Eduard to task for writing that was "involved, cloudy and sometimes obscure." His talk, in marked contrast, was "vivid, pointed, clear." Why couldn't Eduard write as he talked?[66]

Leonard Elmhirst also criticized Eduard's writing style, so it must have been deliciously satisfying for Eduard when he wrote Leonard that some eight hundred copies of *The Meaning of Adult Education* had been sold just three weeks after its release.[67] He must have done something right.

Beyond the generally unfavorable comments about his writing style, Lindeman must have noticed the strand of disdain that was often present within the reviewers' discussions of adult education. Condescension was the norm in most of these critical essays. Adult education, whatever it was, might be all right for the masses (assuming rebellion was not being incited), but the place to get a real education was still while one was young and in school.

H. E. Buchholz (or more likely his editor) revealed much of this attitude in the title given in his review of six books on adult education in *The Nation*. The choice: "Teaching Adults To Read."

Buchholz's review is chiefly interesting in that it illustrates explicitly, rather than implicitly, the attitudes about adult education that were pervasive among many of the nation's intellectuals. In a six-paragraph piece, Buchholz managed to attack not only the announced scope of adult education ("comprising everything in life from puberty to senility, with liberal extensions across the borders at either extreme"), but its clients ("those who went into professional work with inadequate preparation"), its institutions ("mail-order houses [that] distribute doctorates in philosophy and chiropractic"), even the Carnegie grant, which he termed an "investigation indecently elaborate."[68]

"There is a feeling in this country," Buchholz noted, "especially among those who live in the suburbs of intellectual America, that all citizens should be required to partake of the intellectual life. Mr. [Nathaniel] Peffer [in *New Schools for Older Students*] points out the danger of making this endeavor a form of uplift, and then himself tumbles into the very pit against which he has warned others. He grows hot for rescuing 'the great sodden middle class—college graduates, owners of $3,000 cars, members of country clubs,' all of whom, he doubtless wishes to imply, have no brains at all." But neither Peffer, nor Lindeman, nor any of the other chastened authors of the books under review had "the courage or vision essential" to answer "a few pertinent questions" before "any concerted effort is made to rescue these people. . . ."[69]

By this time, the *Nation's* reviewer seems to have worked himself into a paroxysmal frenzy. He continued: "Allow that a large part of the people show no inclination to lead intellectual lives, and it may be found that the fault, in its entirety can be traced to inadequate schooling. If so, the problem becomes one of elementary, not adult, education. Again . . . what evidence has so far been adduced to prove that a large part of the people cannot be happier as individuals and more useful as citizens if permitted to own $3,000 cars, belong to country clubs, and talk golf than if they should be transformed into collectors of first editions and members of Browning societies who will take to talking adult education."[70]

Having settled the matter, Mr. Buchholz was able to close his review with no further comment.

This suspicion—even fear—of the spontaneous and growing adult education movement was probably the reason behind the extremely favorable view of Everett Dean Martin's work that was taken by most critics in the 1920s. Martin was safely academic. To him, adult education would be traditional—a kind of extension of the best forms of a liberal education. Educators would not have to waste time trying to work with people who were uneducable, or nearly so. Lindeman, on the other hand, had the idea that adult education was for everybody; at least that's what came through to most critics from the jumble of words that an author had labeled *The Meaning of Adult Education.*

Lindeman must have been distressed by his near-total defeat by Everett Dean Martin in the book review columns. So far as can be determined, he never challenged Martin's views directly in any public forum. However, in a 1944 article in *The New Republic,* he described the "division in education" between two traditions (liberal arts, presented by Robert Hutchins, and his own, embodied in pragmatism) as "at war with each other." We must, he said, "decide which is integral with the basic American spirit."[71]

The settled elites might be suspicious of adult education and the reviewers critical of his work, but Eduard Lindeman was right. A fresh hope was astir. From many quarters *was* coming a new kind of education, with its initial assumption affirming that *education is life*—not a mere preparation for an unknown kind of future living. There was a new hunger for the nourishment that could make a person grow—self-improvement, as they called it then.[72]

Progressives generally, and even a generous share of the thoughtful public, liked *The Meaning of Adult Education,* if evidence suggested in Lindeman's correspondence is reliable. The original publisher was New Republic. Harvest House of Montreal issued a second edition of what it called "A Classic North American Statement on Adult Education" in 1961.

What Adult Education Means: Discovering and Rediscovering the Concept of Andragogy

In *The Meaning of Adult Education,* Eduard Lindeman wrote with something less than crystal clarity in stating the assumptions about adult education that undergirded his work. Moreover, he never restated these assumptions so that they took into account the evolution of his thinking in the years between their initial presentation in 1926 and his death in 1953. Further explanation and amendments are clearly necessary if Lindeman's work is to be understood in its full dimensions.

The four original assumptions were: (1) that education is life—not a mere preparation for an unknown kind of future living, (2) that adult education revolves around nonvocational ideals, (3) that the approach to adult education will be via the route of situations, not subjects, and (4) that the resource of highest value in adult education is the learner's experience.[1]

Education is life. On its face, this statement seems nonsensical, and one sympathizes with those reviewers who found *The Meaning of Adult Education* to be abstruse. Lindeman's subsequent assertion that "education is life and . . . life is education" does nothing to help.[2] What do these statements really mean? For the full answer, it is necessary to draw upon additional Lindeman writings.

Lindeman's point of departure in developing his philosophy of education was to reject the premise that education is "preparation for life," or something that one acquires in youth and merely draws on as an adult. Education conceived as preparation for life "locks the learning process within a vicious circle."[3] It was this assumption that led to "stop-go" educational systems in which one was expected to complete an elementary education, a secondary education, and perhaps a college education, with abrupt transitions at the end of each phase.[4] Under this concept, learning is supposedly turned on and turned off at successive stages and appropriately terminates as the person becomes an adult. Such learning, in addition, was associated with organized classroom-based study under specified institutional arrangements.

In contrast, Lindeman proposed sundering the "vicious separation between life and learning."[5] Adult education could take place anywhere—in or out of institutional settings. Education is not preparation *for* life; properly conceived, it *is* life, or more precisely, "a process coterminous with life."[6] It is not just "a few breathless years of fact-hunting" preceding a time when the individual settles down to collecting "dollars, automobiles, satisfactions."[7]

Each individual, just by being alive, has a desire and a need to learn—to use experience for learning. The aim of adult education must be that of encouraging, facilitating, and nurturing the desire for learning that is innate within the individual—"to put meaning into the whole of life."[8]

Adult education occurs when an individual confronts life's situations; it is not an external tool given to an individual by a teacher or someone else.[9] Rather, adult education becomes the way in which an individual learns to work within or out of life's situations; it is the practical use of experience. At its highest, it can be the *intelligent* use of experience.

Adult education, so defined, is a part of the repertoire of every human being. One learns as one survives. Learning is derived *from* life. Furthermore, there exists a total learning system that transcends adamantine boundaries established by schools, universities, and other overt educational arrangements. Human beings need not go to school in order to learn something of significance.

Adult education had, of course, always existed in some form. It was conscious recognition of its methods and goals that had been missing. Lindeman sought to bring about a reconceptualization of education that took into account the full scope of adult learning.[10]

Adult education and its orientation to the total human learning system is made explicit in Lindeman's work. Given this recognition, it becomes logical to examine the process of adult education within individual lives. The individual who understands this can appreciate, cultivate, and build upon the essentially continuous learning process and more intelligently approach life's survival and developmental tasks. Such an individual will also find it easier to learn constructively those things that will make life more whole, more creative. The educator who understands it can do a better job of designing learning systems that take into account the real learning styles and needs of adult clients.

Education as a process "coterminous with life" revolves around nonvocational ideals. Adult education "begins where vocational education leaves off" as Lindeman rather inelegantly puts it.[11] Because of this statement, which he hardly bothered to explain, Lindeman must assume some of the blame for the continuing stepchild relationship of vocational education within the adult education family. If adult education is life, why should education bearing on one's vocation, a central concern of life for most adults, be excluded? Where, too, does vocational education "leave off?"

The narrative of *The Meaning of Adult Education* is less than satisfying in setting forth Lindeman's thinking about vocational education. To fathom his thought in this area, it is important to arrive at a concurrent understanding of the context within which *The Meaning of Adult Education* was written. In 1926, as now, there was great pressure for education to be "efficient" and "practical" in the sense of equipping a person to fit a particular job slot.

To Eduard Lindeman these pressures were distasteful, for as a child and young adult he had lived in communities where "the fear of economic insecurity is so great that the entire educational enterprise is thought of almost wholly in the light of its relation to vocations." In this environment, young people especially "are compelled to concentrate on earning a livelihood at the very time in life when their natural inclinations might lead them to explore nature and the various arts."[12] In like manner, adults in their vocations were faced with a demand that they perform "specialized, partial functions."[13]

It was all "a gigantic conflict between interest, rights and values." On one side stood "the machine, industrial technique, with its utilitarian, dynamic materialistic set of values." On the other side stood "human nature with its unquenchable desires for freedom and release, representing values which are social, cultural and ethical." Men and women endeavored to free themselves from this dilemma, but these efforts were, in turn, "heroic and pathetic."[14]

The motivations toward vocational education became related to the "crass 'success' motto."[15] This did not need to be the case. A vocation is so central to existence that each person "will of necessity learn to do his work," and it can be a "high order" of education that will be at the center of this effort. But the province of adult education must be what lies beyond vocational training. The purpose of adult education "is to put meaning into the whole of life."[16]

The peril, i.e., the unbalanced application of vocational education to produce generations of empty people, was real. If Lindeman could help it, the new movement was not to be co-opted by those who would place the vocational needs of the Industrial Age ahead of needs as determined by each human being. In retrospect, the cure seems to have been prescribed in gross overdose.

Though he did not explicitly say so in *The Meaning of Adult Education,* Lindeman also believed that adult education "begins where academic education leaves off." If academic education did not "motivate its participants for adult education," then it was incomplete. One purpose of adult education was to "prevent intellectual statistics." The "arrested development of individuals who have been partially educated cannot be prevented otherwise."[17]

Lindeman's third assumption was that the approach to adult education was via the route of situations, not subjects. The adult person "finds himself in specific situations with respect to his work, his recreation, his family-life, his community-life," etc. These situations call for adjustments; adult education begins here as the individual's way of learning how to confront situations.[18]

Pervasively humanistic, Eduard Lindeman's adult education would begin with people rather than subject matter. What does this mean in practical terms? It means that in teaching economics, for example, the adult educator might start not with "a subject called economics [which] exists and needs to be studied," but rather with the economic situation in which the prospective learner finds himself or herself. What are the economic factors in this total situation? Given this setting, how may the individual come to know how to deal with these factors in advancing through "progressive sequences of living"? For example, might there be some skills or knowledge that must be acquired before a family's standard of living can be enhanced?[19]

In an article appearing in a 1929 issue of *Progressive Education,* Lindeman cited two additional examples of life-centered adult education drawn from his own experience in work with adults. One involved a group of workers in the building industries of a midwestern city who evolved a course of study "derived from their separate and integrated experiences as builders." The other was a discussion and study group of young married women who discovered they had "common interests and also some common fears," who wanted learning experiences that would prepare them for "child-rearing obligations." In each case, adults were learning "in order to adjust themselves to pertinent features of their lives." The subject-matter focus came from their own experience. They acquired their own materials and developed their own study plans.[20] Lindeman served such groups more as facilitator of learning than as teacher in the traditional sense.

This conception of curriculum development was, of course, greatly at odds with prevailing practice in education in 1926. In Lindeman's view, America's academic enterprise was not putting first things first. The starting points were "subjects and teachers," with students being secondary. Students of whatever age or life situation were required to adjust to an established curriculum. Adult education, on the other hand, with life as curriculum, derives its content from individual and group needs. Content will be influenced by the sponsoring agency, the setting, teacher availability, and learner capacities. With their wide varieties of need and motivation, adult learners will present a wide range of demand for curriculum content that may or may not be satisfied by a mere adaptation of existing academic curricula.[21]

After all, life does not present itself "in the form of experiences some of which may be labeled economic, some psychic, some social, some linguistic. . . " While some phenomena might be "predominantly economic . . . there can never be a purely economic experience."[22]

Books and subject-matter experts remain important, but "they will come into learning not formally but naturally and when needed."[23] The setting is therefore one of reality. The starting point is not history or an abstraction but the contemporary situation. The educated person becomes one who knows how to use knowledge in vital situations.[24]

There was a further benefit to be derived from an adult education "free from the yoke of subject-tradition." Such freedom would make it possible to "experiment boldly even in the sacrosanct sphere of pedagogical method." The adult educator's major concern might therefore address "method and not content."[25] Concerns attending the learning process, which he deemed of crucial importance in and of itself, were always central in Lindeman's work. He was interested not at all in what would come to be called behavioral objectives. It was the means, more than the ends, of adult education that concerned him. In addition to Malcolm Knowles, among contemporary adult educators who have followed in Lindeman's tradition in this respect are Allen Tough, with self-directed learning,[26] and Robert Smith, with his exposition of the art of learning how to learn.[27]

Lindeman's fourth basic assumption was that the learner's experience is the resource of highest value in adult education. If this is true, then experience is "the adult learner's living textbook." Adult experience is "already there waiting to be appropriated."[28]

Eduard Lindeman had firsthand knowledge of the frustrations inherent in having one's experience ignored in a supposedly educational process. Entering college as a young adult, but as one who had little formal education, he spent "frantic hours" over books which mystified and confused him. Somehow none of what he was being asked to learn bore "even the remotest relation to my experience" which was, in fact, rich in potential build-on learning experiences.[29]

In the years of youth, Lindeman conceded, it might be necessary to "anticipate objective experience." But too much of conventional learning for adults "consists of vicarious substitution of some one else's experience and knowledge" for that of the learner himself or herself. "Authoritative teaching, examinations which preclude original thinking, [and] rigid pedagogical formulae" should be shunned by the adult educator. The setting for adult education, rather, is established when adults "begin to learn by confronting pertinent situations," and explore the "reservoirs of their own experience before resorting to tests and secondary facts." All of this may be guided by teachers "who are also searchers after wisdom and not oracles."[30]

If one is to start with experience, it is much better to start with the situation close at hand. "The affairs of home, neighborhood and local community are vastly more important educationally than those more distant events which seem so enchanting."[31]

Real learning proceeds outward from experience. Learning does not build in; rather it leads out.[32] In parallel, growth comes from within the individual. It does not come by "inculcation from without."[33]

Strangely, in light of later events, Lindeman did not use the term "andragogy" in reference to the method for teaching adults anywhere in *The Meaning of Adult Education*. He had, however, introduced the term to Americans for the first time in an odd one-paragraph article published in the journal *Workers' Education* in 1926. This article, which was omitted from the publication's table of contents, is reproduced in its entirety below:

Professor Eugen Rosenstock of the Frankfurt Academy of Labor has coined a new word: Andragogik. He distinguishes between Pedagogy, which is the method of learning for children and youth; Demagogy, which is the method for miseducating adults; and *Andragogy* [emphasis added], which is the true method by which adults keep themselves intelligent about the modern world. Andragogik represents the learning process as one in which theory and practice become one—a process according to which theoretical knowledge and practical affairs become resolved in creative experience. The word, Andragogik, is perhaps a bit awkward, a bit artificial but the meaning behind it is significant for those who would be either learners or teachers. Workers' education will make a qualitative difference in the life of our time only if it discovers a learning method which is more dynamic than that of conventional education.[34]

This language suggests that Lindeman might have considered "andragogy" as too pretentious a term to use in a book designed for general readership. He did, however, use the term again in an article coauthored with Martha Anderson in 1927 when the two researchers published *Education Through Experience* in the Workers' Education Research Series. In this piece, the term was used almost casually:

Schools are for children. Life itself is the adult's school. Pedagogy is the method by which children are taught. Demagogy is the path by which adults are intellectually betrayed. *Andragogy* is the true method of adult learning. In andragogy theory becomes fact; that is, words become responsible acts, accountable deeds, and the practical fact which arises out of necessity is illumined by theory.[35]

The new term seems to have impressed itself upon no one, not even its originators. So far as is known, Lindeman never used it again. Martha Anderson, who worked in close collaboration with Lindeman for five years, could not recall using the word in 1927. "I don't even know what it means," she said, when interviewed just before her death at the age of eighty-seven in 1984.[36]

Forgotten by its original American midwives, andragogy lay buried in America (though not in continental Europe) until resurrected by Malcolm Knowles in 1968. Using some of the same European sources earlier tapped by his old mentor, but with no knowledge of Lindeman's earlier use of the term, Knowles independently arrived at an application of the word that was similar to that earlier proposed by Lindeman. For Knowles, andragogy meant "the art and science of helping adults learn."[37] This time the linguistic transplant was successful, and andragogy became a word used frequently by American adult educators to describe the process of adult learning.

Eduard Lindeman's links to the past, the present, and indeed to the future of American adult education are often subtle, yet they are real.

The Lindeman assumptions are manifest in the work of nearly every American adult educator—including those who are pioneering the newest instrumentalities for facilitating adult learning.

Education is life—or a process coterminous with life. The time is long past when anyone can make a serious case for learning as a function relevant or practical only during the years of youth or while someone is in school. Not only is learning a process integral with life, it is a process that is *essential* for the maintenance or creation of a civilized lifestyle in a world of future shock, megatrends, and "third waves" (Toffler 1980).

True, learning skills are not identical across all age groups. Learning in middle and mature adult years has a different quality and different dimensions than learning in youth. But there are ways and means of understanding and facilitating the adult learning process. So-called "nontraditional" education for adults, with its instrumentalities designed to enable persons with adult responsibilities to learn at times and places of their convenience and in modes of their choosing, is built upon Lindeman's assumptive base. Eduard Lindeman would be as comfortable with contract learning and intensive weekend programs as he was with night courses and independent study.

The approach to adult education should be via the route of situations, not subjects. Eduard Lindeman said that arbitrarily divided subjects of learning should not be taken as the point of departure for adults engaged in learning activities. This assumption is a direct or indirect bulwark for individualized majors, individualized learning modules, and programs involving internships, work-study, and apprenticeship training for adults.

The extensive use now being made by adult educators of life-stage or crisis theories is a further extension of Lindeman's situational learning assumption. He recognized that change events such as marriage, parenthood, job change, divorce, and the like enhance readiness to learn and present opportunities for growth. In 1937, Lindeman even worked out a rudimentary "life-stage" scheme pointing toward crisis theories of learning.[38]

As early as 1951, Lindeman called on professional schools to adjust their curricula to take into account learning already acquired by practitioners.[39] With this statement, he clearly anticipated the now-common practice of granting credit for prior experiential learning. Professional schools may still be lagging in their adoption pattern, but at the baccalaureate and associate degree levels, credit for prior learning under noncollegiate sponsorship is facilitated by reputable colleges and universities under appropriate academic protocols.

If a prospective student already knows something as a result of a learning experience; if this is of direct relevance in the educational program for which application is made; if such learning can be appropriately documented—should it not then be recognized, with the student receiving credit for it? This is a sequence of argument that flows from Lindeman's assumption that the resource of highest value in adult education is the learner's experience.

The assumption about learner experience, with its implicit challenge to the traditional role of the teacher, is also Lindeman's boldest statement about adult learning. The relationship between teacher and learner is to be informal. No special threat here. But there is more. The teacher is concurrently a learner. Not only that, the best teacher is one who "knows more than his subject" and who "dares to reveal his special subject in the context of the whole of life and learning."[40] Teachers are to reveal themselves as human beings. Each partner has something to give as well as to receive. And the teaching-learning transaction is democratic territory. This Lindeman assumption lies squarely in the center of the contemporary trend toward the instructor as role model—someone who shares student perspectives and who strives to teach in a way that helps students learn from each other.

If Lindeman's assumption about the value of adult experience in a teaching-learning transaction threatens a traditional teacher, it poses problems for the traditional institution as well. If experience counts for so much, perhaps the best locus for learning in many instances may be outside an educational institution in places closer to the sources of experience—at work, in the home, at a neighborhood shopping center, wherever the adult learner finds it necessary or desirable to learn. In any event, adult learners are not likely to be "aroused by the rigid, uncompromising requirements of authoritative, conventionalized institutions of learning."[41]

How might Lindeman have restated his assumptions had he updated his work in *The Meaning of Adult Education* at the end of his career? In summary, such revised assumptions can be stated as follows (with the added words in italics):

1. Education is *a process coterminous with all of* life—not a mere preparation for an unknown kind of future living;
2. adult education revolves around nonvocational *and nonacademic* ideals;
3. the approach to adult education will be via the route of situations, not subjects; and

4. the resource of highest value in adult education is the learner's experience.

Life-centered adult education of the Lindeman variety is a way of productively managing the relationship between knowledge and living.

CHAPTER 9

Danish Influence on America's Adult Education Movement

The War Against Denmark of 1864 was a nasty little conflict by nineteenth century standards. (Makers of little wars had not yet achieved that high art form that would characterize such efforts in the late twentieth century.)

So complicated was what European diplomats had long been calling the "Schleswig-Holstein question" that even those closest to the center of the controversy could not always put all of its concatenation of strands in place. Britain's Lord Palmerston commented that there had been only three men who truly understood all of the question's often obscure intricacies. The first was Albert, the prince consort, who was dead; the second was a Danish minister who had gone mad; the third was Palmerston himself, and he'd forgotten everything that he knew.[1]

But, complicated or not, Schleswig-Holstein was no laughing matter for those most directly involved. The attending turmoil set all Europe on edge, brought schism to Queen Victoria's great extended family, and stirred deep fears and animosities that ran far beyond the boundaries of the immediate contestants, Denmark and Prussia.

For a time, it appeared that all Europe might erupt in flames—an event that would be delayed until 1914. But fires of another unanticipated sort were lit by the War Against Denmark, with consequences that are still playing themselves out in the New World, as in Europe, more than a hundred years later. One of the firebrands of that long-ago war warmed the brew that eventually became the pragmatic-progressive movement in American adult education.

Two nationalistic forces collided in the Danish provinces of Schleswig and Holstein as war clouds gathered. Both provinces were duchies with vestigial feudal ties to the monarchy of Denmark. German-speaking Holstein, however, was a member of the German confederation that was emerging under the Byzantine leadership of Prussia's Chancellor, Otto von Bismarck. There were strong German, as well as Danish, ethnic roots among the population in Schleswig as well.[2]

German nationalism in Holstein carried with it a desire to promote the German language, even in the Danish-speaking areas of neighboring Schleswig, and to unite both provinces with the new Germany. Bismarck envisioned the war with Denmark as a cheap means of acquiring valuable new territory for the German Confederation (Schleswig as well as Holstein).[3]

Under this strategy, a very manageable conflict with a small and weak nation such as Denmark might become for the Iron Chancellor a sort of dress rehearsal for a larger war yet to come.[4] For it was the rickety Second Empire of Emperor Napoleon III in France that would be Bismarck's ultimate target. It was an astute plan, considered in short-range context, and would be adapted and used to the same purpose by another German Chancellor in Spain in the 1930s. Bismarck's legions in the Franco-Prussian War of 1870–71 would crush Bonapartist France in just 178 days.[5]

The Schleswig-Holstein dress rehearsal was also child's play. On February 1, 1864, Prussian troops, with their Austrian allies, crossed into Danish-held territory. The Danes fought bravely from a defense line pivoted at the fortress of Dybbøl, but the ultimate result was a Danish defeat by the two greater powers. The King of Denmark was forced to renounce all claims to the two duchies in favor of the Emperor of Austria and the King of Prussia.[6]

In the aftermath of this inglorious war, Denmark found herself economically and emotionally devastated. Her two richest provinces had been wrenched away; she had lost control also of the strategic short-cut land bridge between the Baltic and North Seas. Germany would shortly capitalize on this acquisition by building the Kiel Canal, enabling ships to bypass Danish waters altogether. There was also the usual depressing fallout of war, including an influx of refugees. Some fifty thousand Danes from North Schleswig fled their home duchy, seeking sanctuary in Denmark proper.[7] (Many of these people would later find new homes in America.)

What was left of Denmark, the northern end of the Jutland Peninsula and the scattering of islands in the opening of the Kattegat, had almost no natural resources. Much of the agricultural land was of marginal quality. With a minuscule manufacturing sector, Denmark was not a direct beneficiary of the Industrial Revolution. Located on a byway of Europe, the nation's foreign trade was small. Added to all of this was the harsh climate of northern Europe.

But nations, like individuals, can sometimes be galvanized toward growth and development as a result of crisis events. And Danes were about to show the world what they had in them. This was a nation with a great reservoir of strength—its sturdy, intelligent, hardworking people. It had, in addition, an almost larger-than-life visionary, intellectual, religious, and moral leader who saw what his nation could be. His philosophy helped the Danish people set themselves on a path that brought them, within a few short decades, riches beyond price in the wake of the military defeat.

Nikolai Frederik Severin Grundtvig (1783–1872), Denmark's Prophet of the North, is by any standard one of the outstanding men of the nineteenth century. Because he lived and worked in a small country outside the political mainstream of Europe, he is relatively unknown except in his native land and the adjoining nations in Scandinavia. Yet the life and work of this man has substantively influenced intellectual, social, political, and religious life in many nations outside his own.

As Charles DeGaulle would *become* France in the years immediately after World War II, Nikolai Grundtvig *became* Denmark in his time.[8] And like DeGaulle, he was no stranger to controversy. At one time, he was subjected to an interdict of censorship, which merely served to trigger in Grundtvig a great additional burst of creative energy.[9] To modern Danes, Grundtvig remains the symbol of national identity and lasting values.

Such a colossus was Grundtvig that even a bare-bones description of his accomplishments strains the bounds of credibility. An intensely religious man ("born-again" Christian would not be too strong a description), Grundtvig pursued with awesome vigor and insight a wide variety of intellectual journeys. He was, above all, a social philosopher and adult educator; but he was also a theologian, preacher, politician, poet, historian, composer of songs and hymns, lecturer, and teacher.[10] The only possible American comparison might be to Benjamin Franklin or Thomas Jefferson—adding generous dashes of the likes of Walt Whitman, John Dewey, Ralph Waldo Emerson, Reinhold Niebuhr, Henry Steele Commager, Stephen Collins Foster, Saul Alinsky, and Dwight L. Moody.

Grundtvig was a pastor and ultimately a titular bishop in the Danish Lutheran church, and he assertively led efforts to humanize what was then a rigid and authoritarian institution. There is still a Grundtvigian movement within the Danish church.

Grundtvig was also for a time a member of the *Rigsdag,* Denmark's Parliament. Originally a supporter of absolute monarchy, he evolved as a strong proponent of grassroots Danish democracy. He belonged to no political party, always considering himself in loyal—if contentious—opposition to the government. As a member of Parliament, he specialized in speeches aimed not so much at fellow *Rigsdag* members as at the Danish public—and in moving for votes of no confidence in whatever government was in power at the moment.[11]

As historian, Grundtvig wrote a landmark scholarly work, *Nordens Mythologi.* Later came the three-volume comprehensive *Haandbog i Verdens'–Historien.* In addition to writing these and other books, he worked feverishly to produce an avalanche of philosophical and theological essays, political tracts, lectures, song texts, translations, and sermons. Somehow, he also found time to write hymns—some fifteen hundred of them—and numerous poems.[12]

It is small wonder that relatively few of Grundtvig's writings, even in this latter day, have been translated into other languages. A Grundtvig scholar has estimated that it would take approximately one hundred fifty large volumes to accommodate all of what Grundtvig wrote, a publishing task so intimidating in scope that it has not yet been undertaken even in Denmark. There is no Danish scholar who claims to have read all of Grundtivg's collected works.[13] Even commentaries on Grundtvig's writing can become epics of their kind; a contemporary review of *Nordens Mythologi* ran for more than fifty pages.[14]

Physically robust as well as intellectually able, Nikolai Grundtvig outlived two wives. At the age of seventy-four, he married (happily) for a third time. Three years later he sired his fifth child, a daughter whom he named, with exquisite tact, Asta Marie Elizabeth, after all of his three wives—in reverse chronological order.[15]

A man of eighty-one, with a great shock of white hair and beard, at the time of his nation's great crisis period in 1864, Grundtvig was hardly a new figure on the Danish national scene. But he had not really begun to make his contribution to Danish life until he was fifty years of age—a fact that, in itself, should endear him to adult educators.[16]

After the Napoleonic Wars, Grundtvig had rallied the apathetic Danish people with a call that stands in refreshing contrast to the vengeful cries more typical of the tone of life in vanquished nations. There was work to be done, he told his countrymen, and the path toward a better day lay in the realm of education.[17]

It was but a small step to apply the same formula to the new crisis. Denmark had been beaten by those unholy allies, Prussia and Austria. So be it. Let the nation accept its temporal disaster. Inspired by Grundtvig's philosophy, Danes once again found the strength to renew their lives and rebuild their nation with resources gathered from within the spirit. In a few short decades, the Danish people worked economic, social, and political miracles to make their nation one of the small wonders of the new century.[18]

The world was impressed. So was Eduard Lindeman, who first visited Denmark in 1920 on a search for the roots of progressive Danish social legislation.[19] Hanging over the doorway in a Danish farmhouse, he saw a slogan referring to the struggle for recovery after the 1864 war: *Hvad udad tabes, det må indad vindes.* [What outwardly is lost must inwardly be gained].[20] This quotation from the Danish poet H. P. Holst, Lindeman had translated as: "What the enemy has taken from us by force from without, we must regain by education from within."[21]

These words, which refer to adult education as the prime tool for nation building, came to symbolize for him the high-minded aspirations of a remarkable people who, incidentally, had not lost *all* outwardly, after all. In 1920, the year of Lindeman's visit, 1,496 square miles of North Schleswig were returned to Denmark by Germany after a plebiscite held under a provision of the Treaty of Versailles.[22]

The glowing views of Denmark and Danish life that were presented by foreign visitors to that country in the early 1920s remind one of the wide-eyed and generally uncritical accounts submitted by foreign visitors to the Soviet Union in the 1930s and to China before the Cultural Revolution. Goody Two-Shoes seems to have coauthored many of these articles.

To Frederick C. Howe, writing in January 1921, Denmark seemed to be "quite the most valuable political exhibit in the modern world."[23] Denmark was showing the world that "the state can control the distribution of wealth and increase production as well. It can destroy monopoly and privileges of all kinds. It can put an end to poverty. It can make it possible for all people to live easily and comfortably."[24]

As if this were not enough, Denmark had "raised the standard of intelligence to a high point." It had abolished illiteracy. It had taken knowledge "out of cold storage" and made it a "practical thing." Denmark had increased the production of wealth. "And culture has lost none of its finer qualities in the process. Rather it has gained."[25] And so on.

The account of Danish life cited by Lindeman in his "Foreword" to *The Meaning of Adult Education* was that of Eugene C. Branson, a Professor of Rural Social Economics at the University of North Carolina. Branson's amusing and cleverly colloquial *Farm Life Abroad, Field Letters from Germany, Denmark and France* is another rave review of Danish life: "The fact is plainer than a pikestaff. The farmers are rich, unmistakably rich, and they have made the towns and cities rich. Everybody in Denmark is rich or feels rich, which is very nearly the same thing."[26]

For Branson, there was "nothing rotten in Denmark, or nothing I have yet discovered, not even the fish, which the Danish housewife buys alive in the market tanks and cooks with the flesh still quivering. . . No fish of any size has any chance to go stale in Denmark."[27]

Lindeman shared this belief about the absence of decay of most any kind at the gate to the Baltic. At times, this could wear down an audience. Once, as he read a paper extolling Denmark at a meeting of academics, he felt a tug at his coattails. It was Felix Frankfurter, the presiding officer, who in a very loud whisper said: "Good lord, Lindeman, isn't there anything rotten in Denmark?"[28] Lindeman's answer to this question is not recorded, but it would certainly have been no.

There is no question that Lindeman was captured—even seduced—by the Danish success story. In article after article, speech after speech, for his entire working life, he praised the model of Denmark as a society in which human beings could stand tall, grow, and be healthy and secure. In one of his first published articles, he cited the culture of Denmark as "based upon a sound economic system. Cooperative economics has been carried to such high degrees of perfection that wealth is more evenly distributed in Denmark than in any of the modern nations. There are no extremely poor and there are no extremely rich. The technique of agriculture has reached a degree of productiveness and efficiency which is comparable only to modern factories."[29]

In Denmark, not only did the people "smile frankly," but "the sea-breeze invigorates. What a contrast to Central Europe [a probable reference to Germany] where the worst of our race seems to be on top." In Denmark, "the best seems to have full sway."[30]

The truth about Denmark in the 1920s was that life for the average Dane was pleasant—if not quite paradisiacal as portrayed in some of the accounts of travelers.[31] Then, as now, Danish society set a high example that might with profit be followed by much of the rest of the world.

Grundtvig's writing about education is not gathered neatly together in a single volume. Neither does his thought about education assume the form of tight logic in any sense. To some degree, this imprecise approach was deliberate. Like Lindeman, Grundtvig had a horror of rigidity in education. He refused to contribute a structure that could calcify. Education was, after all, life—and life could not be described before it was lived.[32]

Grundtvig had long been dead when a young Eduard Lindeman first visited Denmark in 1920, but the bustling Denmark of that year was largely a creature of the nation's nineteenth century intellectual leader. The most overt manifestations of Grundtvig's influence were the Danish folk high schools (*folkehojskoler*) or people's colleges.[33] These institutions had been conceived by Grundtvig, who had also aggressively promoted the idea in a number of writings including a major book intriguingly entitled: *Lykønskning til Danmark med Det Danske Dummerhoved og Den Danske Høiskole.*[34] [In English, this means "Congratulations to Denmark on the Danish Blockhead and the Danish High School" or, as some prefer, "Congratulations to Denmark on Danish Fatheadedness and the Danish High School."] The operational character of the folk high schools, however, had largely been shaped by others, notably Christen Kold.[35]

The first folk high school, under a governing board headed by Professor Christian Flor of Kiel University, opened in the town of Rødding in North Schleswig in 1844, but it was Christen Kold's folk high school founded in 1851 at Ryslinge on the island of Funen that took firmest root in the Grundtvig tradition.[36] The folk high school movement did not, however, burst into full bloom until just after Denmark's military defeat in 1864. Some twenty-five of them were established between 1865 and 1870.[37]

Lindeman noted that the folk high schools had developed as resident institutions "appealing largely to adults who are passing through the later stages of adolescence."[38] Offering a curriculum primarily emphasizing Danish culture, these institutions stood outside the formal academic system of the Danish nation.

Frederick Howe offers a vivid account of the day-to-day functioning of Danish folk high schools at the time they were first visited by Eduard Lindeman. The methods of teaching and of study "would shock the average board of education, as they would the average parent" in America. Textbooks were seldom used. It was a "cardinal principle" to use the "spoken rather than the written word." The school day was long—extending well into the evening hours—but students worked "willingly and hard."[39]

If students did not have to pass entrance exams, neither did their teachers need formal academic qualifications in order to obtain or retain their jobs. Appointed by the principal and "selected for their ability to impart information," they had to have "personal magnetism and executive ability."

The schools did not offer vocational instruction as such, though they would assist the agricultural schools associated with them in some instances. Curricula emphasized Danish culture and effected political socialization of the people in that the objective was that of stimulating "a love of Denmark and her institutions." History, literature, singing, social science, and gymnastics were included. Subjects bearing on war and international affairs were "practically neglected"—an omission that seems curious in a curriculum designed to develop a passion toward peace.[40]

It was the folk high school, Lindeman believed, that was "the chief source of Denmark's economic and social renaissance, and hence it was that I came back from Denmark a convinced and ardent advocate of adult education." The young professor from North Carolina College for Women also concluded that there was no way to make the new Danish culture clear and meaningful "except when viewed through the lens of adult education."[41]

This progression of logic is intriguing in that it springs from an assumption that would not be accepted by most of today's adult educators, i.e., the notion that persons in late adolescence are typical adult learners. The emphasis in the folk high schools was on very young persons, from eighteen to twenty-five—those that are now referred to as "traditional," i.e., youthful, students at American postsecondary education institutions. Moreover, most of them lived in the school building, making the folk high school a residential establishment—hardly a live option for mature adults.[42]

In pre–World War II Denmark, it was usual for persons eighteen years of age and older to be admitted to the folk high schools—with some 80 percent of enrollees being between nineteen and twenty-five years of age. While 7 percent were younger than eighteen, only 13 percent, roughly today's "adult students," were more than twenty-five. Males accounted for 53 percent of enrollments, females for 47 percent.[43]

Was Lindeman on shaky ground when he built his adult education philosophical frame in part on the Danish experience with an institution that would not be serving "adults" under most current criteria? No; if his thinking—which generally paralleled that of his counterparts in Denmark—is placed in the context of the culture and the times, he was not.

In Denmark, as in the United States in the early twentieth century, postsecondary—even secondary—education was a luxury for most individuals. The typical young person acquired little more than a primary education before joining the work force or getting married and beginning a family. Such young people typically were carrying a generous share of adult responsibilities by their early teen years. It was necessary for them to earn money (or to contribute economically within a family unit) in the case of young men, or to manage or help manage a household if they were young women. Because they ordinarily carried these adult responsibilities, late teenage Danish young people in 1920 were considered adults and learned as adults within their society. Then, as now, the term "adult" did not lend itself to a simple age-range or nonstudent role definition.[44]

Neither were these Grundtvig-inspired institutions conceived as high schools, i.e., secondary schools, in the contemporary American sense. As Grundtvig used the term, it meant people's high schools that were comparable to a university or that provided instruction at what would now be called postsecondary level.

Eduard Lindeman, as well as Joseph K. Hart and other American observers, viewed the Danish folk high schools as essentially adult education institutions. But if Lindeman was impressed by the folk high schools, still he made no real effort to transplant their institutional concept to the United States. While there are some similarities to the modern American community college, there is no clear evidence that this phenomenon in post–World War II American postsecondary education has any strong links with the Danish folk high school model. More direct ties exist with just two contemporary American educational entities. One, the Highlander Folk School, is now located at New Market, Tennessee. (Its founder, Myles Horton, visited Denmark in 1931 after reading accounts of the Danish folk schools written by Joseph K. Hart, as well as Lindeman.)[45] The other, the John C. Campbell Folk School, is near Brasstown, North Carolina. (Several other attempts at direct Danish folk high school transplants to the United States and Canada foundered in the early years of the twentieth century—the victims of a mass movement toward cultural assimilation among immigrants to the New World.[46]

From the Danish folk high schools and related education enterprises derived from Grundtvig's thought, Lindeman acquired a broad range of influence upon his philosophy of adult education. In addition to the basic concept that true education is for adults as well as the young, some eight significant threads of influence can be identified as coming from Grundtvig. These concepts are: (1) education as "life," (2) adult education for everyone, (3) adult education as experience-centered rather than subject-centered, (4) the importance of interaction between teacher and learner, (5) the social and community dimensions of adult education, (6) adult education as nonvocational, (7) freedom as a prerequisite of adult education, and (8) the importance of national culture as a primary curricular base. Many of these influences, of course, overlap with those of Lindeman's roots that come from Dewey and Emerson.

Nikolai Grundtvig believed that the great need of every adult human being was to be able to cope creatively with the problems and opportunities of one's life. All around him, he found schools where one could learn reading, writing, arithmetic, the classics, the professions, but nowhere was there a "school for *life*."[47] How could there be national regeneration and continuous renewal if there were not educational programs that could help the people bring this about?

The Grundtvig-inspired folk high schools that so captivated the young Lindeman were, and are, remarkable institutions. They were conceptualized after Grundtvig had concluded that a remodeling of then-existing tradition-bound Danish schools so that they could offer a living curriculum for adults would be a near impossibility. Were they not schools for death, or "black schools," as he called them?[48] What was needed, he wrote a friend, was a body of teachers able and willing to carry out reform, and these could only be gotten by the education of the adult youth at a folk high school.[49]

Grundtvig's purpose went beyond that of supplying schooling merely to fill supposed gaps in knowledge acquired in the early years of education. Anticipating education directed at "life-stage" tasks that would not gain major impetus elsewhere until the end of the twentieth century, Grundtvig conceived of education as ideally taking place in three stages: primary, secondary, and adult education. Each was suited to the individual at a different stage of growth. With the folk high school, Grundtvig aimed at the "decisive period" of young adulthood.[50] The intention was nothing less than to strengthen young adults in their capacity to get a good start on life's road—not a predetermined path but the road of life that each person would individually choose.

In *The Meaning of Adult Education,* Lindeman adapted this idea to an American setting and affirmed that *"education is life."*[51] This meant all of life—not just the years of young adulthood targeted by Grundtvig's folk high schools. Lindeman probably did not use Grundtvig's "education *for* life" language because he wanted to avoid conveying the idea that education is "preparation for" living rather than a process coterminous with life itself. This was consonant with Grundtvig's philosophy. Grundtvig's folk high school was not to be "a house of book-learning in which people were instructed and trained in the rules by which life can be adjusted and improved." Rather, it was to be a school "alert to the demands of life and which takes life as it is."[52] In a typical refreshing departure from nineteenth century (and much of twentieth century) educational philosophy, Grundtvig conceived the objective of the "school for life" to be "a culture and enlightenment which is the affair of each individual and bears its reward in itself."[53]

Grundtvig was repelled by a teaching-learning transaction that ignored concrete experience. To him *"life* always comes from *light."* Textbooks became less important than observation of the real world—observing, for example, "a farm worked in the best possible way" or "crafts practiced in the best possible manner."[54]

What was a school for life? Like Lindeman, Grundtvig had a way of backing into a subject about which he wanted to make dramatic statements. Certainly it was *not* "a center where the rules for the governing, the improving, and the effecting of the act of recreating life are persistently taught and emphasized—beginning, of course, by dissolving life, i.e., by death." And was it not a "high German notion that life is explainable even before it is experienced, and that it must submit itself to change according to the dictum of the learned"? Wherever this "fanciful idea is incorporated into the educational structure, all such schools become workshops for dissolution and death where the worms live high at the expense of life itself." Furthermore, the school Grundtvig had in mind would *not* "give the highest priority to purely intellectual activity or to its own institutional status."[55]

So much for what a school for life was not. What, on the other hand, *would* it be? First, it would set as its "chief educational goal the task of helping to solve life's problems." Second, it would take a "realistic approach to life" and "should strive to teach about life and promote purposeful living." Moreover, there should be no nonsense about tearing down the old or wasting time "devising rules that supposedly would be followed if only we possessed another and better life."[56]

The second great influence of Grundtvig upon Eduard Lindeman was the idea that adult education is for everyone, not just for those considered "educable" in any classic sense. A democratic nation was strong if its individual citizens were strong, competent, and morally upright in their approach to citizenship. The *"common life of the people"* was an appropriate source of experience for learning; the *"unique personality"* of the individual student would also be valued and developed.[57]

If Grundtvig believed in social equity and equality of access to adult education, he was not naive as to individual differences in learning capacity and learning readiness. Folk high school planners "must remember that *everything* is not for *everybody*."[58]

The school for life was not to be a sexist institution either—at least its doors were to be open to females, a radical idea at the time. Women were "really human beings," Grundtvig had decided, and they as well as men were to have an education for life. Was not a woman "the strongest spur to culture" and worthy of an education "quite different from what it is now—worthless show"?[59] These words are especially startling considering they were written in 1807. Danish world leadership in providing educational opportunities for women has strong Grundtvigian roots.

In common with Grundtvig, Lindeman was egalitarian to the core. Adult education was for everyone—including the poor, persons with less-than-high scholastic aptitude, minorities, and women. He was certainly a feminist by the standards of his day. "Why shouldn't women do what they please?" "If women have skills, why shouldn't they express these as freely as men?"[60] "Must the educated woman choose between mutually exclusive desires; self-expression through continuance of her intellectual interests or male companionship, home and children?"[61] His belief in the inherent right of each individual to learn and to develop as a unique individual was in part derived from his exposure to the Danish educational and social experience.

Lindeman subsumed most dimensions of Grundtvig's thinking in his assumption that adult education should come "via the route of *situations*, not subjects."[62] With Grundtvig, Lindeman believed that adult education should begin—must begin—in the real world inhabited by adults.

Grundtvig was nearly alone in his time as an advocate of a free and easy interaction between teacher and learner, and, for that matter, within student instructional groups. He had serious reservations about the lecture as a teaching tool in that "no living interaction is reached between your thoughts and mine."[63]

Reaching, as he often did, for Biblical analogies, Grundtvig urged teachers to give up "gentlemenly traits" and "put on the guise of a servant." Grundtvig went so far as to begin his own lectures by addressing the audience with the phrase, "My masters."[64] He meant it.

"Reciprocal teaching" was what Grundtvig called his version of the teaching-learning transaction.[65] This was an idea that greatly appealed to Eduard Lindeman and that found its way into *The Meaning of Adult Education* and into American adult education philosophy and practice.

Grundtvig's young adult might view the world from the perspective of his or her own aspirations, but these were not to be self-centered persons. Each individual was to have a sense of oneness with the folk high school community and a sense of community responsibility.[66] By extension, this would ultimately incorporate the surrounding social environment and society.

A *"spiritual sense of a unity in multiplicity"* was to be imparted by the folk high school.[67] Herein is to be found an important wellspring of Scandinavian democratic socialism and a source, too, of Eduard Lindeman's social and political philosophy. Lindeman's chapter on adult education "As Dynamic for Collective Enterprise" in *The Meaning of Adult Education* reveals Grundtvig's influence at this source.

That adult education is to revolve around *"non-vocational* ideals," to use Lindeman's words, is an additional plank of Grundtvig's philosophical platform, borrowed and adapted for Americans.[68] While neither Grundtvig nor Lindeman intended to denigrate vocational education, their belief was that development of a vocation was secondary to the development of a creatively functioning human being.

Grundtvig expressed this idea in a letter to a friend, written in 1854: " . . . you will agree that our Danish youth not only need . . . a [folk] high school but will benefit greatly from it. This is not only true when the young people wish to become Danish legislators or Danish officials; it is true when they are to become Danish human beings *in all vocations.* [Emphasis added] For they are not to jump out of their skin but are to save it as far as possible and to live within it. In order to do this they must be more familiar with themselves, their people, and their mother tongue than our youth has been awakened, helped, and shaped to be in any school up to now."[69]

Consequently, young people should not receive a technical or vocational education, but an "education for life" that would develop a nation of adults who know how to learn.[70] The emphasis on acquiring learning skills rather than narrowly vocational preparation was another concept adapted from Grundtvig by Lindeman. Though Lindeman did not mention it, this orientation was controversial in Denmark, as it would be in the United States. Frederick Howe, who visited Denmark at about the same time Lindeman did, reported that the teaching of "practical subjects" was a debated question. Of the seventy-nine state-aided folk high schools, forty-eight taught only the Grundtvig-endorsed cultural subjects. But thirty-one schools, including some of the largest, offered courses in "agriculture, horticulture, carpentry, masonry" and similar subjects and seemed "in no danger of losing their original ideals and inspiration."[71]

The adult's freedom to learn is a theme running through all of Grundtvig's educational philosophy. For that matter, Grundtvig believed youths might have a degree of the same entitlement. Wasn't it "almost a waste of time" trying to educate boys in secondary schools? It was hard enough for a boy to "orient himself to the external world." So why shut him up in a school with desks and books? Instead, let him be outside in "God's free nature" working at farming or some trade involving healthy manual labor.[72] There was plenty of time for learning after one became an adult.

In any event, adult education should be voluntary. Grundtvig believed that the chief outcome of the compulsion to learn was that of deadening interest in subject matter, as well as in life in general. Freedom also meant freedom from examinations—either as entrance requirements or as requirements for passing courses. Grundtvig did *not* imply freedom from work or a sense of task urgency in the folk high schools; he anticipated that freedom of the spirit within a school setting would in itself be an impetus for work.[73]

Grundtvig's freedom was a condition essential for the unfolding of relevant education. A spirit of freedom—for both student and teacher—must underlie relationships between the two. A school council, with students having a majority membership, was to be consulted on all important matters.[74]

Living in freedom, as well as learning in freedom, was a topic developed by Lindeman in a full chapter of *The Meaning of Adult Education*. Grundtvig's philosophy, as well as Emerson's, jumps from every page. The contemporary adult educator who promotes self-directed learning by adults is squarely within this Grundtvig and Lindeman tradition.

Finally, there was a more subtle influence of Nikolai Grundtvig upon the thinking of Eduard Lindeman—that of national culture as the primary curricular base for adult learning. Neither Grundtvig nor Lindeman was being narrowly nationalistic in asserting that the culture of the motherland was to come first as a citizen pursued the educational road through life.

Grundtvig believed that Danish culture, *for Danes,* was the starting point in acquiring an individual world view. He was appalled at "Latinists" who insisted that in order to excel in Latin, "one must treat Danish and all of its unique expressions slightingly."[75] The national culture, including the Danish language, should be prized. And the Danish people needed to use their freedom to develop and enhance indigenous culture.[76] Lindeman appears to have borrowed this idea— perhaps unconsciously—when he enshrined Emerson and Dewey as examples of what is great and good in American culture. No one could be "fully aware of America without comprehending, in part at least, Emerson."[77]

The same concept, but with Dewey as the great American illuminator, was expressed in a 1941 speech to Pennsylvania librarians. To know and understand Dewey (and James and Peirce) "does not mean that one must condemn Kant and Hegel and Fichte, but it does mean that if you allow yourself to be influenced by the European philosophies without having taken the pains to understand the philosophy that is part and parcel of your own life and culture, you are not to be trusted as a scholar."[78]

While Lindeman was aware of Grundtvig's influence on Denmark,[79] he could not have read Grundtvig's essays and writings, since few were available in English translation until 1976 when Johannes Knudsen translated a number of them.[80] Consequently, he seldom or never quoted Grundtvig directly in articles and speeches as he was wont to do with Dewey, Emerson, and other important sources.

There may have been another reason for Lindeman's less overt philosophical tie with Grundtvig. Perhaps he did not wish to be identified with what he had chosen *not* to borrow from Grundtvig, namely the great philosopher's pervasively Christian theological edifice. Does such an omission distort Grundtvig, when his work is seen though a secular lens held by Eduard Lindeman? Is it necessary, for example, to carry forward in all educational settings, Grundtvig's emphasis on the theologically loaded concept of the "living word"? By this term, Grundtvig meant spoken words that functioned as vehicles of the spirit to engender new and active spiritual lives for listeners. Outpourings of the spirit, they were rooted in the contemporary life, as well as in the history, of the people. It was through the living word that human beings could prevail over the powers of darkness in the world and could lift themselves up toward the light. In education, the living word was most apt to be found in dialogue—in true human interaction between teacher and learner and between learner and learner. The adult learner was a seeker after living word.

The Christian overtones of these beliefs are unmistakable—which is not surprising since the teachings of Jesus were at the core of Grundtvig's philosophy. But does it follow that the curriculum in an American school for life would have to have a base in Christian doctrine if it is to claim roots in Grundtvig? The answer is no. Not even Grundtvig insisted that the education of adults be narrowly doctrinal. True education, he said, must function in freedom, not in bondage to theologians.[81] Grundtvig specifically rejected the notion of including even his most treasured Christian concepts in defining the purpose of education. Just as the church must firmly resist intrusions from the state, so must the state or the state school deflect attempts by the church to mold it.[82]

Grundtvig's dictum *"Meneske først"* meant that individuals needed to be made conscious that they are human beings—something more than animals; second, conscious also of what they must do as useful members of a community; third, conscious as well of their responsibilities in the human task of working to determine life's meaning.[83] Only then could a person be educated as a Christian.

Christianity was the flywheel of Grundtvig's life, and Grundtvig scholars are careful to admonish readers to be cautious about interpreting his educational views apart from his related views on religion. This is sound advice. but, given an understanding of the original context and of related thinking, any concept can be reprocessed—at least by a pragmatist—so that it finds a home in still another setting. At this point, the process of interpretation—and reinterpretation—begins anew.

The borrower of Grundtvig's educational ideas may with integrity harmonize them with compatible ideas from other philosophical strains. Lindeman did not need to take on Grundtvig's nineteenth century Lutheran theology any more than Emerson's transcendentalism of the same period. What Lindeman, the great synthesizer, did do was to prune the great Dane's philosophy, strip it of nationalistic and sectarian trappings that were relevant only in Denmark, and plant it with care in American soil alongside flourishing native American stock.

As is known, a bit more than that was planted in Eduard, too. It was sometime after his first visit to Denmark that he began routinely claiming Danish ancestry. The progression of this new identity can be quite clearly traced. Eduard was still German in 1912 when his first book, *College Characters,* appeared. "The circumstances of my birth caused me to be reared in an atmosphere permeated with Goethe and Schiller," the young author told his readers. In the next sentence, he spoke of "undergoing the tedious but necessary task of unlearning one language and acquiring the conventional one."[84] There is a later reference in the same article to "my Teutonic habits of speech" which had enabled him to serve as an interpreter.[85] Danes are a Teutonic people, but more commonly the word is used with references to Germans.

Dorothy Straight learned from a letter written to her by Eduard[86] that his mother used these German words to describe his joy at a gift of woolen mittens and stockings: *"Deine augen sheinen wie's himmelslicht [sic]."* Eduard was certainly of German descent by birth, and the language in his childhood home seems to have been German. But his speeches, articles, and communications with friends, beginning at about this time, were increasingly sprinkled with references to his "Danish" or "Scandinavian" antecedents. He even acquired some Danish relatives. The Danish farmer-painter first mentioned in 1926 had by 1928 been promoted to become Eduard's "cousin."[87] Denmark served a deep psychological need in Lindeman, the need to be something other than German by heritage. Eventually, the tale became so much a part of him that it must have assumed the guise of truth in his mind.

What, in summary, are the implications of Grundtvig—as interpreted by Lindeman—for the world of today?

First is the all-important assumption that education is a process coterminous with life. Adult education starts where the adult learner wants to start—and the adult learner will want to start with learning that will help him or her live life more fully and productively. Adult education is for everyone—human beings at all economic and social levels. Adult education evolves around nonvocational and nonacademic ideals. Adult learning will happen faster and with greater ease when it evolves from experience rather than subjects. Teaching and learning is a transaction between equals. Adult education has community and societal implications; it is not something that happens in a vacuum surrounding an individual. Adult learners are persons, not functions. Learners possess a high degree of personal freedom within a good learning situation. Life-based learning can best evolve from the national culture within which it will be used.

If true, all of this is profoundly good news, not only for individuals but for societies and nations. Adult education becomes not only acceptable but essential and desirable in a world that has often devalued it in the past. Middle-aged and elderly people who want to learn, in or outside of institutional settings, should be encouraged. Adult learners can rightly demand that they be full participants in the learning transaction. Adult education is not something they receive but something they acquire.

For young people and their anxious parents, there are also glad tidings. It is possible to relax a bit about the time frame in which education can be obtained. Why try to inculcate bits of knowledge into the heads of unwilling teenagers who might be better able to learn later in life? Perhaps a teenager has a right to work—or even to pause for breath before undertaking some of life's developmental tasks—as much as an adult has a right to learn.

Nations, too, can benefit from Denmark's case history. The Denmark of 1864—with its thousands of impoverished peasants and rudimentary democratic institutions—was not a very promising society if judged by standards of the budding Industrial Age. But the upwardly mobile experience of Denmark is a lesson today for such nations as Peru, Ghana, and Sri Lanka. A true learning society can lift itself up. The path upward from the "slough of despond" may be difficult, but there is a way, when societies are filled with people who want to be learners.

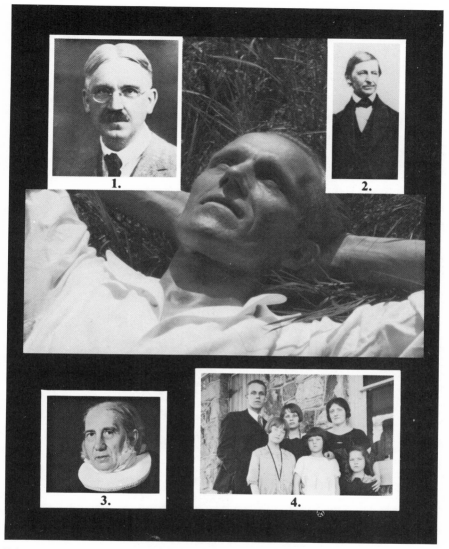

Eduard Lindeman suns himself while recuperating in Italy in 1925, the year before he wrote *The Meaning of Adult Education*. Martha Anderson, his assistant and sometime collaborator, took this photograph.

Inset Photos

1. Lindeman's friend, fellow pragmatist, and Columbia University colleague, John Dewey.

2. Ralph Waldo Emerson (1803–1882) in his role as adult educator.

3. Nikolai Frederik Severin Grundtvig (1783–1872), Danish philosopher-educator-theologian, in a portrait by C. A. Jensen circa 1847.

4. Hazel and Eduard Lindeman with daughters (left to right) Ruth, Doris, Betty, and Barbara, in passport photo, 1925. The girls don't seem too happy about being collared and scrubbed for the photographer.

Greystone, the Lindeman home in High Bridge, New Jersey. Lindeman wrote *The Meaning of Adult Education* in a few short weeks in his "crow's nest" on the third floor.

Dorothy Straight Elmhirst in a Cecil Beaton portrait, circa 1935.

Dorothy and Leonard Elmhirst (center)
with *New Republic* Editor-in-Chief
Herbert Croly and his wife, Louise, at
Dartington Hall, Devon, late 1920s.

Mary Parker Follett, with whom
Lindeman had a productive—if
tenuous—intellectual affinity during the
period when he wrote *Social Discovery*
and *The Meaning of Adult Education*.

Lindeman (left) and John Hader, with
whom he wrote *Dynamic Social Research*
(1931).

Eduard Lindeman in his prized rock garden at Greystone, circa 1929.

Eduard Lindeman at about forty years of age.

Lindeman as he appeared in later life.

CHAPTER 10

The Importance of Experience in Adult Learning

Eduard's star was in the ascendant in early 1926. He had energy aplenty, not only for dashing off *The Meaning of Adult Education* but for other major projects as well.

He began teaching a course on adult education at the New School for Social Research in March. At the New York School of Social Work Eduard started (what else?) a "small-sized revolution." Some of the older faculty members were "quite upset," but Eduard planned to persist. The curriculum had grown "without any regard for integrations" and was "a perfect hodge-podge."[1]

He felt both excited and guilty, he told Dorothy, over the great success of a speech he'd made at a dinner of the Book Publishers Association. Afterward, he was approached by someone from Dutton who asked him to write a book for their "To-day and To-Morrow series." Blanche Knopf wanted him to do something for her firm on the psychology of reading. He was to see a man from Macmillan the next week.[2]

If he was exhilarated, he was upset as well. "It seems so unfair to have these unearned privileges come merely as a result of a fifteen-minute speech when nothing but a sociable factor denies them to others who are really deserving. . . Not being a Puritan, I presume that my code tends to become much more rigid in its upper levels."

He'd met Christopher Morley at the Publishers' Dinner "and we quite fell in love with each other."[3]

There was domestic trauma—not with Hazel but with Roger Baldwin, with whom he had had a falling out over what Roger considered "a mere trifle." But Eduard had been unable to "rationalize myself out of the difficulty" with his apartment mate. He and Herbert had discussed the unspecified situation at length, and Herbert reportedly concurred that the position taken by Eduard had been "just." Eduard "believed so thoroughly in the essential purity of Roger's motives" but wondered if he'd been wrong in doing so.[4]

On August 4, with *The Meaning of Adult Education* manuscript in the hands of his publisher, Lindeman booked passage to Europe on the *George Washington*, He was being sent to Denmark as one of three American delegates to the first International Conference on Adult Education at Frederiksborg, Denmark, on August 14–17. The other two delegates were a fellow AAAE Board member, C. R. Mann, and Executive Director Morse Cartwright.[5] Afterward, he planned to go down to Geneva to hear the debates on Germany's entry to the League of Nations. Then it would be on to Devonshire for the opening of Dartington School.[6]

Lindeman was an excited participant in the Conference, but it was the host nation that again, as in 1920, captivated him. It was "the one land of earth outside my own where I seem to fit into the patterns of life without difficulty." His Danish friends, on the night of his departure, presented him with a Danish beechwood cane as a token, they said, of his understanding of the spirit of the Danish people. The cane was "a bit heavy" but the accompanying words, he told Charles Shaw, he would "carry lightly throughout life."[7]

The image of Nikolai Grundtvig's Denmark would remain a fixture in the mind of America's adult education philosopher. But Eduard Lindeman was a twentieth century man and it was pragmatism, a twentieth century philosophy, that facilitated his deepest and most penetrating analysis of adult education.

❧

The philosophy of pragmatism is identified primarily in the nineteenth and twentieth centuries with John Dewey, William Kilpatrick, Charles Sanders Peirce, and William James. However, its earlier roots can be traced still farther back through George Berkeley and David Hume to Socrates and Aristotle.

As developed by John Dewey, pragmatism is a theory of meaning. What is real to the Deweyan pragmatist is also practical.[8] And this practicality is especially manifest in performance guided by intelligence. Ideas that are true can be verified.[9] Moreover, a true idea is not static in nature. It *becomes* true to the extent that it passes each succeeding experiential test of its truth.[10] What, asks the pragmatist, are the results of each such test?[11] Ideas that cannot be verified are not necessarily false, but false ideas cannot be verified. Ideas that may be true but are resistant to verification for the moment lie in an area of limbo.

Education conceived as preparation for life is absurd to the pragmatist who is constantly evaluating ideas for their truth in light of the here and now. The collision of ideas becomes especially noticeable, according to Dewey, "when the life of adults is considered as not having meaning on its own account, but as preparatory probation for 'another life.' "[12] The essence of the life task for the pragmatist is the reconstruction of experiences in a kind of "siege of truth."[13]

For Dewey, education was "a continuous process of growth, having as its aim at every stage an added capacity of growth."[14] And "education means the enterprise of supplying the conditions which insure growth, or adequacy of life, *irrespective of age.*" [Emphasis added] "We first look with impatience," Dewey continues, "upon immaturity, regarding it as something to be got over as rapidly as possible. Then the adult formed by such educative methods looks back with impatient regret upon childhood and youth as a scene of lost opportunities and wasted powers. This ironical situation will endure till it is recognized that living has its own intrinsic quality and that the business of education is with that quality."[15]

These sentences alone, coming as they do from one of the philosophical giants of the twentieth century, assure Dewey a place among the important forebears of adult education in the United States. Dewey, however, had little time for adult education, genuine though his concern was.[16] He busied himself with other interests—notably the development and advancement of what would eventually be called "progressive education" in the childhood years. It remained for Eduard Lindeman to seize upon Dewey's ideas, integrate them with freshets coming from other philosophical sources, and apply them with potency to the field of adult education.

From Dewey, as well as Emerson, Lindeman derived his ideas about the means-ends equation. For the Deweyan pragmatist, the educational process has no end beyond itself; it is its own end.[17] The process of education becomes one of constant reconstruction and transformation, with ends viewed as *means* to still more ends.[18]

Lindeman elaborated on this theme as he criticized what he considered the folly of goal setting. It might be simple to select a goal, "an end, a truth, and thereupon mobilize all one's resources for its realization." But such a tactic wouldn't work "for, alas, goals do not remain static, awaiting our arrival." Ends also change and "at the consummation of long effort is not the object we set forth to discover but another which has been brought into existence by the means we have utilized."[19] It was not that ends were unimportant, just that means were so intimately intermingled with ends as to be inseparable. Change one factor and the other would also be changed.

The only real goal for any person was that of growth; the meaning of life emerged as a companion of struggle. "A maturing person" [Lindeman disliked the noun "maturity"] was someone "capable of meeting the changes and ordeals of experience as opportunities for further learning and growth."[20] His conception of adult education was that it was a continuing process of evaluating experiences. It was a method of awareness through which persons could become more sensitive and efficient in their efforts to discover meanings.

Adult education could not be preparation *for* life; it was a process coterminous with life itself. It proceeded not from subjects or books to experience, but from experience to subjects and books. It was not hammered in by teachers but involved intelligent interchange of facts and understanding between both parties to the teaching-learning transaction.

In the popular mind, pragmatism has often been conceived to mean that a single test may be applied to any proposition: i.e., will it work? This is a gross oversimplification—and one that greatly annoyed Lindeman. He expressed this irritation in an August 1944 letter to his friend and fellow pragmatist Max Otto, and he proposed that they organize and lead an "offensive" to answer pragmatism's "superficial critics."[21]

Lindeman spent a good bit of time doing trial runs on explicit questions to facilitate true pragmatic tests. He proposed to Otto a seven-point comprehensive pragmatic test that might be applied to any idea to determine its consequences and therefore its truth.[22]

Lindeman continued experimenting with these specific sets of pragmatic tests and developed a number of versions. In July 1950, Lindeman spoke in Buffalo on "Science, Sociology, and Philosophy of Adult Education." To his audience, he proposed these pragmatic tests: (1) Is it workable, feasible? (2) Is it specific, concrete? (3) Does it meet human needs? If so, what scientific information is available?(4) What difference will it make? To whom? (5) What are the alternatives? (6) Is room left for future experimentation? (7) How are the consequences to be tested? (8) What values are likely to be conserved?[23]

These pragmatic tests of the mature Lindeman contrast with those of the Young Turk of 1924 who had advised students to apply these tests to projects for social reform: (1) Is it honest? (2) Is it scientific? (3) Is it progressive? (4) Is it educative? (5) Is it radical, i.e., do "the technique and the assumptions upon which it is based imply recognition of the fundamental problem involved, or is it merely a makeshift means for relief?"[24]

Like its ends and means, the tests of pragmatism are inconstant.

Dewey, Otto, Lindeman, and other pragmatists considered themselves to be—and were—*social* philosophers. The reconstruction of experience, that essence of the life task for the pragmatist, may be social as well as personal, according to Dewey. In static societies, "which make the maintenance of established custom their measure of value," education of the young might be "a sort of catching up of the child with the aptitudes and resources of the adult group." But this could never obtain in a democratic society—"in progressive communities."[25] Here, education has the potential to be an agent for improving society. As such, it develops not only young people but the adult society as well.

As social philosophers, extenders of epistemology and logic to the problems of mankind, the pragmatists were set apart from the historic mainstream in philosophical inquiry. This made them targets for criticism, even contempt, within the profession. But the pragmatists could go on the attack as well. In a critical review of Bertrand Russell's work, Lindeman in 1944 commended Russell as a "brave thinker and a bold one." However, he faulted Russell for failing to furnish "a single authentic lever for action." Unless a social philosophy led to social action it was not, in Lindeman's view, complete.[26]

Not that Lindeman disparaged his more theoretical colleagues; nourishment was needed from them if applied philosophers were to keep their thinking fresh. "If practical and theoretical philosophers stopped calling each other names, they might rid their craft of certain stigmas, not the least being the charge that most philosophers practice an incestuous trade, occupying themselves chiefly with an exchange of footnotes."[27]

In applying appropriate pragmatic tests to a particular issue, the social philosopher should have as a chief aim "to keep the situation fluid until a proper sifting of evidence and an examination of relationships have been made. . . . Those who conduct an experiment should also be prepared to appraise its consequences and, if necessary, to reformulate the proposition for purposes of further experimentation."[28] He meant it when, in 1937, he told a Boston University audience: "Please don't believe what I say—the only valid answers are those you discover."[29]

Child-centered progressive education had its philosophical base deep in the pragmatism of John Dewey. A review of the basic concepts of progressive education sounds—as it should—like a comparable review of the basic concepts of Eduard Lindeman's adult education.

Progressive education, to Lindeman, was the very antithesis of orthodox or conventional education. Its underlying assumption was that learning should proceed from the child's rather than from the adult's nexus of interest.[30] Like adult education, rightly conceived, progressive education "is irrevocably humanistic in tendency. Its gaze is forward, not backward. Its faith springs from love, not hate. The sacredness of human personality stands at the very center of its modest set of presuppositions. Its ethic begins with human relations."[31] The term "progressive education" referred primarily to method. It was a way of conceiving and conducting the educative process.[32]

"All adult education," asserted Lindeman, "presumably, should be roughly classified as belonging to that school of thought which goes by the name of 'progressive education'."[33] Both classifications of education partook of bedrock pragmatic theory.[34] Among the shared concepts: the centrality of the learner's experience, learner growth as the basic aim, a process orientation rather than a goal orientation, problem emphasis rather than subject emphasis, emphasis on teacher as facilitator, and importance of a democratic setting.

By mid-century, the progressive movement in education had come under severe attack, an assault not always based upon accurate or informed understandings of Dewey's concepts and work. To Eduard Lindeman, an attack on Dewey and the progressive education movement was also an attack on himself and his work in adult education. He was at the forefront of efforts to defend Dewey.

If young people lacked "discipline and a sense of order," the critics "assume that these are defects for which . . . the progressive schools . . . must be held accountable." Noting the often emotional overtones in such outcries, he suspected this "to reveal a deeper disturbance among adults; I suspect that this new experience of being confronted with a generation of young people who refuse to be 'pushed around' is so unique that it cuts very deeply into the armor of adult egoism."[35]

But more menacing overtones, as well, were noted by progressive education's defender. The attacks were no longer "in the realm of sensible debate" but had reached a new stage of "sheer bitterness and hatred." One unnamed speaker, Lindeman noted in a 1943 address to the Progressive Education Association, had gone so far as to say in a public address that "the attack on Pearl Harbor was an application of the philosophy of pragmatism learned by Japanese in American universities, and that 'pragmatic educators are the fifth columnists in this country.' "[36] Emperor Hirohito's legions, it seemed, were marching to the drum of John Dewey.

In the same year, Lindeman noted "a strong tendency among certain American thinkers" to blame William James and John Dewey "for twentieth century decadence." The "twin evils of our time," according to this group, were "relativistic morality and progressive education."[37]

In succeeding articles and speeches covering the World War II years, Lindeman took up the defense of Dewey and progressive education. "Those who believe that true education and progress are synonymous (progressive educators)" had been "maneuvered into a defensive position." It was unfortunate that it was necessary to take time to answer the critics "since so much constructive work calls for doing." But "negativism" was in the air, "a mighty ingredient of the modern anti-rationalist movement." It needed to be squarely faced.[38]

In language reflective of its context, the war years, Lindeman called for both a defense and an offense by progressive educators. To those who said progressive educators "have no reliable set of values," the reply was to be: "This is not the primary issue; we insist that values attach primarily to individuals and not to institutions, and upon this ground we are prepared to enter upon discussion." To those who accused the progressivists of being unsure about what to teach "and then propose that they know what to teach, and this turns out to be some new variety of absolutism," then the response "with calmness and without anger" was: "Why, if absolutism is the key to teaching, did the counter-revolution against democracy originate in Germany where they surely know a great deal more absolutism than we do?"[39]

Progressivism's defender went on to urge his cohorts to demonstrate that no democracy can live without some type of progressive education. The "very essence of a democratic society" was that "it should be constantly attentive to those stirring ferments which come from dissatisfaction with what is and hence lead us forward to something better to be."[40]

Progressivism was not just something that happened in schools. The progressivist was "a person who recognizes the functional relations between ideals and action and . . . strives to establish harmony between theory and practice." To such a person, "ideals

which cannot be reduced to trial and experiment are no ideals at all."
Progressive action was synonymous with social action. Genuine progressivism was "the ability to join with one's fellows in the effort to
apply democratic means to the achievement of democratic goals."
Effective participation of this kind was even "the *sine qua non* of
democratic faith."[41]

Eduard Lindeman knew John Dewey, who was also a faculty
member at Columbia University, quite well. Though they were not
intimates, their friendship was cordial and reciprocal. They vacationed near each other in Florida.[42] Sometimes they enjoyed bird-
watching expeditions together.[43] In 1938, Dewey invited Lindeman to
visit at his cabin near Hubbards, Nova Scotia, though Eduard was
unable to accept at the time stated.[44] Lindeman was deferential as he
wrote Dewey in June of 1941 a word of thanks for "that splendid
evening at your home." He added that he'd like to see him more
frequently "but I always have the feeling that I might be intruding
upon your precious time."[45]

Most years, Lindeman would get some of Dewey's students in his
Social Philosophy course at Columbia—the usual motivation being
that they wanted to have a closer look at applied philosophy. In the
winter semester of 1930, three of Dewey's students enrolled. Eduard
wrote Dorothy and Leonard that "at times I wish I could take these
three alone and be freed from the necessity of carrying along those
who lack preparation." Lest the Elmhirsts think he had suddenly lost
his philosophical bearings, he added that he knew such an action
would constitute "an unfair selection."[46]

As the illness of the progressive education movement, as a formal
organization, was becoming terminal, Lindeman prepared one of the
most eloquent of the written memorials to John Dewey. "John Dewey
on the Doctrine of the Golden Mean" appeared in the special issue of
Progressive Education that marked the death of John Dewey on June 1,
1952. As part of this piece, Lindeman addressed the erroneous
assumption of those who used the term "progressive education" in a
derogatory sense that Dewey had been "an extreme opponent of all
subject-matter learning."[47]

The truth was that Dewey "constructed a polarization in which he
assumed that schools might be distinguished by two conflicting
emphases, one in which subject-matter teaching represents the aim of
education and the other in which the main consideration is the pupil
and his complete growth." Dewey believed that education would
"become more exciting, more valid, if subject-matter learning were
deemphasized in favor of the pupil-oriented school." In this connec-

tion, according to Lindeman, Dewey "made his most brilliant attack upon the fallacy of either-or thinking."[48]

This was not Lindeman's first public tribute to America's most powerful twentieth century philosopher. His speech at the Progressive Education Association celebration in honor of Dewey's eightieth birthday on October 20, 1939, was reprinted in *School and Society* and was repeated as a radio broadcast. Who is the "genuine educator"? In this speech, Lindeman gave an answer that survives as a classic statement of the pragmatic view of those who teach:

> . . . the genuine educator is a person (and we need not confine our search for him to educational institutions, for he exists wherever life is fresh, experimental and confident) who views intelligence as an instrument for solving human problems, who views objective reality not as an hierarchy of absolutes but rather as graded units in a series, who derives his primary enjoyments, not from the attainment of specific ends, but from methods, from the process of learning itself, who conceives of growth toward reasonableness in all affairs to be a sufficient incentive for education, who believes that freedom is a variety of experience without which growth becomes merely mechanical, who insists that whatever else education does to pupils, it must enhance their sense of personal dignity, who recognizes that we can not take our human relations for granted nor that these relations will ever be progressively improved by exhortation, in other words, who believes that we need training for good human relations. If, now, these qualities are merged into a whole, into a sort of picture of a man, an educator, there will be, not a likeness of John Dewey, since my artistry is too defective, but at least a strong resemblance to that wise man of our time in whose honor we have here foregathered.[49]

By the early 1950s, the opponents of progressive education had succeeded in stamping out most of the embers of that movement that still glowed in the nation's schools. But there was one spark of John Dewey's great fire that they did not notice and perhaps did not care about—the spark of pragmatic adult education. This was a flame that had been carefully fanned by Eduard Lindeman all during the final decades of his life. It is ironic in the extreme that so large a share of the righteous remnant of progressive educators survived by fleeing to a backwater—the marginal educational sector occupied by adult education in America.

Neither Dewey nor Lindeman would live to see the rebudding of progressive education, albeit in altered forms and under different names, in the decade of the 1960s when America once again found itself willing to experiment pragmatically.[50]

Two others of Dewey's disciples, Mary Follett and Max Otto, were the chief instruments of Lindeman's effort to operationalize pragmatism within the practice of adult education.

Herbert Croly seems to have been the first to realize that Eduard Lindeman and Mary Parker Follett were wrestling with the same intellectual problems.[51] He brought them together early in the twentieth century's third decade, and there began a period of interaction that was often trying at the interpersonal level but, at the intellectual level, productive for them both.

Follett, older than Lindeman by seventeen years and a leader of the Women's Municipal League and related organizations in Boston, had gained national attention in 1918 when her book, *The New State,* was published.[52] In this volume, she essentially proposed group organization as the key to a successful functioning of democratic entities of government. The relationship of individuals to groups, intergroup relationships, and the relationship of groups to the national government were analyzed in a way that many thought brilliant.

The New State came into Lindeman's hands in the early post–World War I years when he "sought expression in some creative channel" in response to perplexing problems attending democratic government in that turbulent, yet creative, time. In the "Preface" to his *Social Discovery,* Lindeman said that "Miss Follett's challenge to the atmosphere of fatigued futility of that period set off the 'trigger' which gave new direction and new hope to researches already partially achieved."[53]

Mary Follett studied the concept of power—its surge through the political instruments of social and governmental units. Unlike most others then (or now) studying the political process, she clearly saw the importance of adult education within a democracy. And it was on this point that her interests found intersection with those of Eduard Lindeman. Their intellectual liaison had important consequences affecting the direction taken by adult education in the United States.

It is not difficult to extract the adult education implications from Mary Follett's second book, *Creative Experience,* which came out in 1924. Her approach was that of a pragmatist, though she emphasized—and placed higher value on—the creative rather than the verifying aspects of experience. "Experience is the power-house where purposes and will, thought and ideals, are being generated." This was not to deny "that the main process of life is that of testing, verifying, comparing. To compare and to select is always the process of education. . . When you get to a situation it becomes what it was plus you; you are responding to the situation plus yourself, that is, to the relation between it and yourself."[54]

It is not possible in social situations, however, to "compare what you bring and what you find because these have already influenced each other. Not to understand this is the onlooker fallacy: you cannot see experience without being a part of it. . . Life is not a movie for us; you can never watch life because you are always *in* life." The evolving situation, "progressive integrations" and "ceaseless interweavings of new specific respondings, is the whole forward movement of existence; there is no adventure for those who stand at the counters of life and match samples."[55]

This process, which Follett had earlier called "law of the situation,"[56] is very close to the core of her thought as it relates to adult education. The process of integration, which she did not (perhaps as a true pragmatist) ever concisely define, has been described by another as "a harmonious marriage of differences which, like the nut and the screw or the parts of a watch, come together in a way that produces a new form, a new entity, a new result, made out of the old differences and yet different from any of them."[57] To integrate is to learn within a constantly changing situation.

What about verification, the pragmatic tests? For Follett, testing "in an exact sense is an impossibility" because "life never stops long enough for us to 'test,' or rather we cannot get outside life to view it." Thought and concrete experience "are always interweaving; this, not comparing, is the life-process." The life-process is "that of creating through specific response."[58]

"The people who 'learn by experience' often make great messes of their lives, that is, if they apply what they have learned from a past incident to the present, deciding from certain appearances that the circumstances are the same, forgetting that no two situations can ever be the same."[59]

"We have the choice with each fresh experience, if we do not disregard it altogether, of either pigeon-holing it to take out at some future time when a similar circumstance arises (a similar circumstance never will arise), or of integrating it with all the rest of our experience." If the experience is integrated, "then the richer human being that we are goes into the new experience; again we give ourself and always by the giving rise above the old self."[60]

Overardent apostles of the verifying process were apt to forget "the compound interest, that creating includes the increment of the increment, that it is the activity-plus with which we are chiefly concerned."[61]

In *Creative Experience,* Mary Follett also presented a view of power in a democratic society that had a magnetic attraction for Eduard

Lindeman, who made it integral with his thinking about democratic adult education. This was the concept of "power-over" as opposed to "power-with." "Power-over," Follett suggested, "is resorted to. . . because people will not wait for the slower process of education."[62]

Individuals might study "the art of persuasion" or "the method of obtaining consent," but this usually was merely a method of obtaining "power-over." In a democracy, the basic assumption in work with citizens should be that of "power-with! The validity of the 'will of the people' depends on the distinction between power-over and power-with. Otherwise, methods used to 'persuade' become hardly distinguishable from coercion. . . "[63]

Democracy had one task only—"to free the creative spirit of man."[64] It was also a method, "a scientific technique for evolving the will of the people."[65] It was "a great spiritual force evolving itself from men, utilizing each, completing his incompleteness by weaving together all in the many-membered community life which is the true Theophany."[66]

In an insightful "Appendix" to *The New State*, Mary Follett tackled "Training for New Democracy." This piece, appearing as it did in 1918, must be recognized as one of the earliest of scholarly writings on adult education in the United States. After writing of her work with youth at neighborhood centers in Boston, Miss Follett chides herself for writing "as if it were our young people who were to be educated by the group activities of the Centres, as if the young people were to have the training for democracy and the older people the exercise of democracy. Nothing could be further from my thoughts. The training for democracy can never cease while we exercise democracy. We older ones need it exactly as much as the younger ones. That education is a continuous process is a truism. It does not end with graduation day; it does not end when 'life' begins. Life and education must never be separated. We must have more life in our universities, more education in our life."[67]

She went on to quote the "successful businessman" who told her of his efforts to plan a school at his factory, not on account of what his employees might learn at the school, "but in order to make them see that their life of steady learning is just beginning and that their whole career depends on their getting this attitude." She mentions the many forms of adult education, e.g., "extension courses, continuing and night schools, correspondence schools, courses in settlements, Young Men's Christian Associations" and the like.[68]

The pragmatic continuous circle of ends was evident in her view, again from *The New State*'s "Appendix," of the process of adult education: "even if we could be 'entirely' educated . . . at any one minute, the next minute life would have set new lessons for us. . . . Adult education means largely the assimilation of new ideas; from this point of view no one can deny its necessity."[69]

The concept of creative experience was the common interest that initially induced Eduard Lindeman and Mary Follett to work together. How individuals can be helped to *reconstruct* their experience, learn from it, make it creative, was what most interested them. Beyond this, Lindeman was indebted to Mary Follett for assistance in development of his ideas about adult education as a creative instrument within the democratic political process—especially her "power-with" concept—for ideas about the freedom of individuals in "obedience to the law of one's own nature," and ideas about the truly free individual as the person who wins "freedom through fellowship."[70]

The two were, however, an odd couple, and their joint venture was wobbly from the start. The exacting, sickly, maidenly, and (to judge from her correspondence with Lindeman) severely neurotic Mary Follett did not always achieve good personal chemistry with the volatile, convivial, lusty, and often disorganized Eduard Lindeman. Though her own behavior could also be erratic,[71] the ethereal Miss Follett required personal and professional surroundings that were predictable, built upon ground that was solid—very solid. She never learned that a predictable, ordered world was not possible for friends or close associates of Eduard Lindeman.

At times, the course of events between the two could take on comic opera aspects. On one occasion, they had a whole series of massive misunderstandings with attendant hard feelings while they were supposedly cooperating in writing books on how to resolve conflicts. The irony was not lost on Mary Follett, who wrote Eduard after one skirmish asking him not to "speak again of 'throwing up your job,' for it would be too good a joke for the world, while we are teaching everyone how to resolve conflict that we cannot resolve the differences between ourselves. Let us face them and integrate them."[72] Eventually they did but only with the mediating assistance of Alfred Sheffield, who was ultimately able to inject some reason into the affair.[73]

Mary Follett never quite got over a suspicion that Lindeman would co-opt some of her ideas or be perceived as introducing them first. She worried needlessly. Lindeman had flaws, but duplicity was not one of them. By every account, he was open and generous to a fault when it came to acknowledging contributions of others. He allowed the very junior Martha Anderson and John Hader equal billing, i.e., their names listed first, in alphabetical order as true coauthors, on publications they did with him.

Lindeman was punctilious and gracious in acknowledging Mary Follett's contributions to both *Social Discovery*[74] and *The Meaning of Adult Education.*[75] In *Creative Experience,* Follett expressed appreciation for Lindeman's assistance.[76] America can be grateful that Mary Parker Follett and Eduard Lindeman persisted in their often difficult partnership. Their productive, if traumatic, collaboration enriched three landmark books of the 1920s.

Lindeman's relationship with his second important pragmatist colleague was of quite a different stripe. Max Otto was a professor of philosophy at the University of Wisconsin and one of the most popular teachers at that institution. Like Lindeman, he regarded philosophy as a base and instrumentality in the search for a better life. Critical, yet tolerant, thinking was a value he hoped to exemplify to his students and colleagues.

For much of his career, Otto was, however, a controversial figure. His course "Man and Nature," which he taught from 1910 to 1936, was essentially an examination of the influence of theories of evolution upon human self-concepts. An atheist and pacifist, he was an attractive target for religious and political figures less tolerant than he.[77]

In 1926, Lindeman had placed a quote from Max Otto (about the possibility of positively accepting "worldwide agitation" as a "search for new meanings") in *The Meaning of Adult Education.* However, their friendship did not really begin until the 1940s when both men were in their autumnal years. Max was a new kind of friend for Eduard— a friend born of a meeting of mature minds. No longer was he in need of impressing someone; no longer did he need a friend who could provide not only an audience but resources necessary to pursue his career. Max was one of the nation's best-known philosophers and was the one with whom Eduard most closely identified in the latter years of his life.[78] Eduard was a respected scholar and lecturer. The two men met as equals. Beyond their life stage and intellectual affinities, they enjoyed a sizzling chemistry of personalities. Not since Charles Shaw had Eduard found anyone whose company he so enjoyed.

The friendship was equally satisfying to Max at both the personal and professional levels. He felt the two were "together in outlook," though he felt Eduard "did a better job in the development and application of our views. Of course, you are not handicapped by being officially a philosopher!" Max may not have realized that this was, at best, a backhanded compliment to his less credentialed friend. In any event, Max was not plagued by self-doubt about their one-mindedness as to pragmatism. It seemed to him, as to Eduard, "that our philosophy has been the philosophy, and still is the philosophy, for our time."[79]

Otto also put his finger on one of the great strengths of Eduard's maturity. It dazzled him to see the volume and the quality of Eduard's work, when he put his mind to it. "Getting *things* done—well, many of us can manage that. We just put in the hours. But articles, *your* articles, are not things merely. . . You *say* something. You do say it; and believe me I happen to know that the mere saying is a job."[80] No longer was Eduard hearing from friends that his ability to write did not match his ability to speak.

Max was successful in bringing Eduard to Madison, Wisconsin's lake-laced capital city, to present a seminar in February of 1947.[81] He seems to have made a hit, not only at the university but in the Madison community. Eduard clipped from one of the local papers an editorial headed "Prof. Lindeman's Tonic for Tattered Values" and pasted it without comment in his scrapbook. He had reason to be satisfied for the writer acclaimed one of his lectures as "one of the most stimulating heard in the community in recent years." In the face of "universal pessimism," it was "a real tonic to hear a man who talks a sound, dynamic and constructive role for the future of democracy." If they wanted to "get a new grasp on the values of life which seem to be somewhat tattered and battered these days," the paper's readers were advised to hear Lindeman's second lecture on February 17.[82]

%

Eduard's friendship with Max waxed at about the same time his friendship with Dorothy began to wane. The difficulties began in September 1926 when the newly formed Dartington staff assembled for a staff development session lasting five days. Eduard Lindeman was its principal leader.[83]

Leonard had already asked Eduard to help him with the Dartington prospectus.[84] After receiving Eduard's suggestions, Leonard "recast the whole document," according to Dorothy, who added: "Leonard says he needs you at every turn."[85] Well, maybe.

Lindeman's contribution was certainly reflected in the statement of purpose for the school as set forth in the prospectus: "For us it is vital that education be conceived of as life and not merely as preparation for life."[86]

Interestingly, Lindeman recommended that the Dartington curriculum include "vocational training," though the aim would be "not professional skill but full life."[87] This is significant evidence that he did not consider *all* vocational education to be outside the realm of life-centered learning as might be construed from the most literal reading of *The Meaning of Adult Education.*

For a variety of reasons, the special training session did not go well, and at its conclusion Eduard found himself at odds with the Elmhirsts and with a key member of the Dartington School staff.[88] Consequently, Lindeman left England with a heavy heart aboard the liner *France,* sailing from Plymouth, which was just a short train ride from Totnes.

A dense fog matching Eduard's mood enveloped Plymouth as the tender bearing the boarding party set forth from the harbor. Huddled on the deck of the little vessel as it plowed the waters outside Plymouth's breakwater, Lindeman's group peered anxiously through the murky night. At last a small band of light came into view, and they were within a hundred feet of the anchored *France.* It was four o'clock in the morning.[89]

Herbert Croly was already aboard the *France,* though sound asleep at the time Eduard boarded. But the two friends made connections the next morning in the ship's dining room. They were not to rest easily; the passage to New York was rough all the way.[90]

Leonard sent Eduard his first report on progress at the school. However, Eduard lost it and his bag in a taxi and gave "only a lame account" of the opening exercises in a meeting with some of Dorothy's American friends.[91]

Eduard's friendship with the Elmhirsts was disoriented, not destroyed. Their correspondence continued, and Eduard was frequently called to Dartington as a consultant and friend. But somehow the tie had been loosened; things were never quite the same.

The bonds linking the Elmhirsts to the Lindemans were still firmly in place in 1929, however, when Eduard's always-wavering negotiations with his landlady at Greystone, Mrs. Taylor, took a strange turn. While Eduard was away, she had sent a nurseryman with a crew to take away most of the finest specimens of trees and shrubs on the place. As Eduard wrote Leonard, they had "already shipped three carloads" and were still at work.[92]

Of course the well-rooted Eduard was greatly disturbed. He and Hazel were more attached to the growing things than to the house. He had taken care of the trees and shrubs for seven years and "felt, somehow, that I had a share in them." In any case, Mrs. Taylor's unilateral action had "cancelled the bargain" as far as Eduard was concerned, and they were looking for another place to live. He was thinking of getting a smaller place and doing his own planting. Like renters everywhere, they were disturbed by the "uncertainty of living in places owned by others."[93]

If this was a hint, it worked. Eduard would not accept from Dorothy payment of a fee for his service as chairman of a committee advising Dorothy on her philanthropies in America, considering that his work, "pitifully small though it is," was a token of gratitude "for all that you have given of yourself and your means in the past."[94] But help with a mortgage for Greystone was another matter.

Dorothy instructed her New York lawyers to draw up a mortgage that would cover Eduard's requirements for the purchase of his home. He gleefully wrote Dorothy on December 15, 1929, that the deed for Greystone had arrived, "and for the first time in my life I am the owner of something!" He was especially pleased that his children would continue to enjoy the place and would be able to add to their memories of it—as, in fact, they did.[95]

CHAPTER 11

Adult Educators as Facilitators of Learning: Operationalizing Pragmatism

Helping students toward "finding things out" is more dynamic and progressive for a teacher than a method aimed at "putting things over."[1] That is the core of Lindeman's view of the role of a teacher.

One of the first windows into Lindeman's view of the teaching-learning transaction as it involved mature adult students came in a letter to Dorothy written in 1924. Lindeman was teaching at the Canadian Christian Training School on Lake Couchiching in Ontario. His course, "What the Thinkers Are Thinking," was based on such problems as expert versus experience, behaviorism versus idealism, individualism versus collectivism, and, of course, means versus ends. Each of these topics was being introduced via brief accounts of three to five persons whose works were related to the problems to be discussed. In what may be his only direct reference to Grundtvig's key concept, he wrote Dorothy that he was "striving after a form of teaching which will reveal the 'living word.'" He felt the course was going well.[2]

One of Lindeman's students was a forty-two-year-old man who had two grown daughters. Lindeman was working at his typewriter in a lakeside boathouse when the man asked if he might talk with him. "He seemed rather diffident and began by telling me that I had made him very discontented in the course of two years ago." But, as a result of this discontent, the man "had arrived at new bases of confidence in his ability to do something more than he had been doing." He had always wanted to be an artist and after finishing Lindeman's course enrolled in a Toronto night school to begin the study of art. He traveled to Europe during the summer of 1923 and came back with numerous drawings, some of which he showed to Lindeman.[3]

While a number of his "dry points were really excellent," Lindeman doubted he could become an artist, "but that doesn't matter: he has found an absorbing interest in life, a new zest." It had been exciting to learn of this experience. "I wonder," he asked Dorothy, "if the teacher's function is to precipitate discontent and to generate purposes? At any rate, it isn't to impart knowledge or merely to impart method. Whatever it is, I wish I had more of it."[4]

If he was a pioneer in informal learning for adults, Lindeman was also a teacher in a traditional academic program at the New York School of Social Work. Many of the students were mature adults— employed social workers attending the School on a part-time basis.[5] To the extent possible in this setting, he injected methods derived from the Deweyan progressive movement.

What was the view from the student side of this transaction? Malcolm Knowles never took a class from Lindeman but met former students of his who were "just rapturous about his ability to apply his principles."[6] One such student recalls that Lindeman "quite simply persuaded you to teach yourself, to learn along with him. The most courteous of listeners, he got you to analyze first what you wanted to know." He would then mention possible sources of background material that might be needed for the learning project. He might then list on the blackboard or paper some of the answers that were possible "so that you could see their relation to the problem and each other. Constantly he nudged you along till you arrived at the rest of the answers, making you aware that you were helping him toward a solution; then made sure you got full recognition for solving the problem."[7]

The subject matter content of a Lindeman course was pragmatically ambiguous. "You didn't take course from Ed. You took Lindeman," a faculty colleague recalls. The course might be called Social Philosophy, "but it didn't matter what it was called, it was still just Eduard Lindeman."[8]

So it might appear. But Professor Lindeman was engaged in something more than explaining himself. The essence of his curriculum philosophy was that the instructor should engage in discovering what adults were prepared to learn rather than determining what should be taught. The curriculum should be "derived from the impending adjustments which adults are called upon to make in any given cultural situation."[9]

Graduate seminars were informal. There would be coffee. The instructor would usually start with a provocative question.[10]

Required reading, Lindeman considered to be an "evil habit" begun in the grades and extended as "regular practice for college students." Was not Samuel Johnson right when he said " . . . what he reads as a task will do him little good"? The chief result of required reading was "that it creates a dislike for reading." Why? Because the "stimulus is always external. We learn to read, not for the purpose of reading, but in order to make a recitation, to satisfy the teacher, or to pass an examination."[11] The focus should always be on learning rather than on particular tools for learning.

Lindeman might ask for student autobiographies,[12] but he also shared certain vital aspects of his own life as a human being with his classes. The fondest memory of one student was of Lindeman coming into class one morning "rubbing his eyes—I suppose he had a sinus headache . . . and saying, 'I'm sorry, but I've been arguing with Roger Baldwin since 5:30 this morning.' " He then elaborated on what they'd been talking about. "It made you feel as a student that you were in the middle of an important life."[13]

Did the man who sometimes advocated eliminating "lectures and mass teaching"[14] ever use the lecture method himself? Yes, but only if his class were large, in which case the major portion of the course might be devoted to "straight-out lecturing of an informal variety." Discussion would be facilitated at points of student interest.[15]

No teacher satisfies everyone, and Lindeman was no exception. One student remembers her professor as a "big, burly, friendly looking man with oversized hands." He would stride into class, his arm loaded with books that would be slapped down on the desk, though they would not really be used in class. He would then proceed to "mesmerize us with his forceful, dramatic presentations of his ideas. . . I sat at his feet during that course, drinking in his wisdom. . . "[16] But the enchantment faded when she signed up for second Lindeman course. "Now he seemed more the superb showman. For me the actor had replaced the inspiring leader."[17]

Another student of the mid-1920s wrote her aunt that Lindeman's "drive and thirst for knowledge amounts almost to genius." But she noted, "No wonder he thinks we are a lazy, stupid bunch. . . "[18]

How did Lindeman evaluate students? It was not a task he enjoyed, and he experimented for a time with a simple pass-fail system.[19] By the end of his career he was using an evaluation technique that varied, depending upon whether he was working with a seminar or a large class.

In the small group or seminar, he would strive to discover what the student's gifts were. Were there "signs of special talent"? If so, Lindeman would attempt to discover some way by which the student could demonstrate such ability. The "varieties of ability" he sorted out as those of (1) keeping discussion moving without digression, (2) discovering the points of agreement in a controversial issue, (3) sharpening a conflict so that its essential features are clearly seen, (4) making use of experiences, (5) making use of reading, (6) being able to formulate a concise and meaningful report, (7) revealing values involved in issues, and (8) promoting a tolerant atmosphere in which differences may be candidly explored.[20]

He tended to disvalue the facility of "ready speech." The student who "participates less often but who says something important" usually received a rating superior to those participants "who have something to say about everything."[21]

The son of working-class immigrants had the intriguing view that it was important for the instructor to appraise a student's manners. "I presume this judgment is based upon the assumption that no matter how bright the student is, he will not be professionally successful if his manners impede his communications." Students who interrupted others or who caused others in the class to feel uncomfortable would receive lowered ratings "even when they are intellectually brilliant." The student "habitually late for class" would also find the instructor thinking less of him or her.[22] A contemporary adult educator, Jerold Apps, incorporates some of these aspects in his concept of teaching or interactive "styles."[23]

In larger classes, Lindeman found himself "reduced to a much simpler and . . . rougher form of evaluation." He started with the assumption that there were two kinds of students in the class: "those who are serious-minded, eager to learn, willing to carry their responsibilities, and equipped with a mentality capable of assimilating the basic ideas of the course" and also "a slightly inferior group consisting of persons whose comprehensions are on a lower level, who grasp most of what is discussed, who are motivated by aims other than those upon which the course is constructed, and who never make a creative contribution either in written or spoken form." This was not to infer that the latter category of students "will not make first-rate (or certainly second-rate) social workers" or that their standards would be the same in a different type of course.[24]

The first group of students would receive the School's "P–1" rating; the second group would be graded "P–2." There was also a "P–3" rating that Lindeman reserved for "those few students who seem . . . to manifest some other quality incompatible with scholarship or with professional standards."[25]

Students in Lindeman's larger classes would typically be given the choice of writing a term paper or joining small groups of four to seven students that would make a report to the class as a whole. The small groups were required to meet for a minimum of four sessions of two hours each, though the majority would meet more often. Each group had a recorder who took notes and submitted them to the instructor. Lindeman used the notes, as well as the group reports to the class, in making "evaluations which approach those of the smaller seminars." He also was "able to learn a great deal about how students appraise each other."[26]

There was, he admitted, "very little which may be called scientific or even quantitative" in his system of evaluations. If classes were smaller, "the system would become less quantitative, as seems to me proper for graduate students."[27]

Lindeman the teacher advocated a focus on situations, not subjects, in learning transactions. In the monograph "Education Through Experience," written for the Workers Education Bureau, he gave an example of how economics might be studied by working-class adults from a situation as opposed to a subject orientation.

At first, "only those facts with which the worker is familiar may be touched upon." By this was meant the "immediate facts of the worker's life, his position in industry, his role as a wage-earner." From this starting point, the economics of production and of distribution would then be approached—from a perspective of "reality—not theory."[28]

After the student discovers economics "as a functional activity, as a characteristic field of action for himself," it is possible to begin learning "how economic questions are examined and objectified." The student can then move on to read "excerpts from standard books on political economy" and learn "how definite queries are phrased, examined and rationally solved."[29]

Derived from each learner's situation is experience—the focal point of learning for the pragmatist. Minds are not "repositories into which knowledge is dumped in the hope that it can be reclaimed in the hour of need." Subject matter "disappears from the minds of students shortly after graduation. . . " Given this stark fact, of what use in programs for adults were teaching methods emphasizing rote memory? On the other hand, "if knowledge grows, it is because knowing was once a part of experiencing."[30]

What does such an approach require of the teacher of adults? It requires, first, someone who knows "a great deal about motivational psychology." There must be understanding as well of the "role played by the intellectual climate of the era, by the social environment, and by the conditions of life."[31]

The adult educator should also "be peculiarly aware of the relations between genetics (growth) and learning. An adult educator who neglects the previous crises in learning which have accompanied growth will never become thoroughly sensitized to the needs of his adult students."[32]

An adult educator must be capable of understanding the work experience of his or her students. Indeed, all experience is fodder for learning. "The teacher who does not know how to elicit experience data and put it to work in problem-solving will never become a genuine adult teacher." He did not mean to infer that adult education should not use "other types of teachers, as for example, the gifted lecturer, but its main pedagogical problem is to train teachers in the art of experience-eliciting and use."[33] No longer is the teacher the "oracle who speaks from the platform of authority, but rather the guide, the pointer-out who also participates in learning."[34] This was intended as a direct challenge to the prevailing notion that "learning is a simple device whereby knowledge is transferred from one mind to another."[35]

In Lindeman's view, the adult educator needed to "be equipped to interpret and make use of the inter- and the intra- relationships of the various disciplines of knowledge." The "basic needs of people" would never be met through specialization alone. "Acute human situations arise at those very points of wholeness from which the specialist takes his departure."[36]

Finally, the adult educator "should be familiar with the techniques of group work and must be himself a person who can participate in group activity."[37]

Beyond these objective skills was a more subtle though vitally important characteristic of the successful teacher of adults. The "revered professor" with his air of superiority, his "cultivated aloofness," and "assumed poses" would give way to the "honoured teacher" who was willing to share the aspirations and defeats of his students *and* was prepared to "learn with them."[38]

Lindeman believed the concept of teacher as facilitator could be seriously damaged by the trend toward specialization that gained strength during the 1920s and for the balance of his lifetime. It was a rare context in speeches or articles that did not give him an opportunity to attack mindless specialization or "experts."

In *The Meaning of Adult Education,* he describes the specialist "who becomes protagonist for a particularist point of view [who] labors under the *'illusion of centrality'* which keeps him and his disciples from recognizing 'that the life-process is an evolving whole of mutually interacting parts, any of which is effect as well as cause.' "[39]

Society would never be saved by "educated experts working on ignorant masses."[40] If the specialist "cuts the cord of uncertainty," the individual has in effect transferred decision to an external source. Life becomes "a chronic succession of consultations in the presence of specialists. The only meanings possible would be those purchasable from experts." And this is "precisely what any person with a grain of intellectual self-respect will refuse to do—take his meanings second-hand."[41]

Lindeman had a low opinion of the specialist as learner. He had taught at institutes "attended only by highly specialized technicians." They invariably began discussion with the assumption that "questions of value and meaning and direction had no relation to their functions." In contrast, he cited his experience with "schools of philosophy" that FDR's Secretary of Agriculture, Henry Wallace, had organized for farm leaders. How "lively and exciting" philosophy could be for those men and women who were faced with "important practical decisions."[42]

Do specialists have a function? Yes, "when they learn to integrate their functions with respect to specific problems." And integration was "not a verbal exercise but a method by which active differences interpenetrate."[43]

The function of specialists needed "re-definition." The specialist's "experience and the experience of the community must somehow interpenetrate if real progress is to result." This would be an educational process in which the expert would be "humanized" and the people "educated."[44] So tamed, a specialist might successfully function as fact-finder, fact-furnisher, arbitrator-umpire, catalyst, or integrator.[45]

Eduard Lindeman was one of the first, and certainly the most eloquent, among American adult educators to articulate the concept of teaching as the facilitation of learning. In essence, good teaching amounted to drawing out the learning skills of the individual. This could best be done by assisting the person to reconstruct experience. Lindeman was hard on those who sought to impart knowledge or information to adults, that is, to hand it out or hammer it into them.

Since they recommended the teacher as facilitator, rather than in a more directive role, Lindeman and the pragmatists set themselves apart from educators in the liberal tradition. Robert Hutchins and Eduard Lindeman might agree on outcomes as represented by Hutchins's "learning society,"[46] but their methods for getting there would be quite different.

Two extensions of his assumption that experience is the best resource for learning guided much of Lindeman's work. If learning stems from experience, then the adult years may be productive learning years because adults have experience that children lack. So, too, should experience, as a resource for learning, be injected into adult learning situations.

Lindeman as learning facilitator can be seen in his contributions to the discussion method and his recommendations relating to conference methods. The depth of his aversion to top-down educative efforts is evident in his elegant analysis of propaganda and his assignment of it to the dustbin of adult education.

"Organized talk," is Lindeman's shorthand description of discussion which he perceived as the chief instrumentality for operationalizing pragmatism.[47] It was discussion that enabled persons to exchange experience as a way of illuminating a situation. Moreover, adults were "likely to desire a participating share in their education." This could be achieved "much more advantageously through discussion than through reading, recitation and listening to lectures."[48]

Implicit in every such encounter was an adult educative opportunity. Moreover, discussion was the natural method for adult education "because adults enjoy educating each other."[49] It followed that an adult educator needed to understand the dimensions of discussion— its nature, its problems, its opportunities.

Much of Lindeman's work on the analysis of discussion was done in cooperation with Alfred Dwight Sheffield, a professor of English at Wellesley College. Lindeman probably met Sheffield, to whom he dedicated *The Meaning of Adult Education,* while doing research for his article on a fish marketing cooperative.[50] The two also worked together on The Inquiry. The tall, thin, very courtly and goateed Sheffield[51] had written *Joining in Public Discussion* in 1922. It was one of the earliest of efforts to study discussion systematically.

What should discussion be designed to do? Lindeman believed that it enabled participants to relate their knowledge (facts and information) to their emotions. It could also facilitate an "orderly exchange of experiences." It revealed the nature and significance of individual differences and indicated how such differences might become "supplementary and complementary rather than mutually exclusive." Discussion could also aid individuals in "confronting their situations more realistically." At the same time, organized discussion could help participants adapt themselves to the "process of joint problem-solving as a substitute for debating and fighting." It was a way of achieving "functional unity within a context of individual diversities."[52]

Discussion was one method for socializing learning so that those involved could be helped to bring their individual learning situations into alignment with the "living situation of actual experience." Initially, the objective of discussion was to discover why the same fact could be "interpreted with a differing shade of meaning by each member of a group."[53]

It was necessary to organize discussion so that it didn't degenerate into "mere exchange of opinion and prejudice without forwarding the real learning process." Such stagnation was almost sure to follow if "discussion procedure does not derive from dependable method. In one sense," he said, "organized discussion is to adult education what scientific method is to science."[54]

A good listener himself, Lindeman was among the first explicitly to recognize listening as an ingredient of productive discussion. He helped organize listening clinics that were sponsored by the Adult Education Council of New York City. The target clients were "people who realized that their listening capacity had deteriorated." The clinics were designed as places where such individuals could come for "reconditioning."[55]

Among the clinics' users who seemed to listen "least well" were executives and administrators. Lindeman wondered whether this might be a result of management styles that encouraged one-way communication. With no expectation of replies from employees, such persons seemed to lose nearly all ability to hear.[56]

Also poor listeners and therefore poor participants in discussion, in Lindeman's view, were "experts," who "usually experience annoyance" in discussion. The "tension would be relieved for them if someone would only turn in their direction and ask for an authoritative statement." This would be their longed-for opportunity; "their egos expand at the moment when they are able to assert their superiority. But how often they are dismayed to discover that the solution proposed with such assurance is later discarded by the group!"[57]

With the "right solution for the problem" already in their minds, the experts tended to feel that so much talk was a "waste of time and energy." But they forgot that "there is no right solution which is not essentially social in nature."[58] Doing something about a problem requires talking about it first.

Discussion groups might assume any one of four basic patterns, each of which had its appropriate uses. *Argumentative* discussion anticipated conflict and precipitated it early. In *Socratic* discussion, the leader took initiative in asking "leading" questions. *Developmental* discussion (which Lindeman favored for most experienced groups) followed a "somewhat rigorous sequence of logical steps patterned after the Dewey formula of learning." In *circular response* discussion, an attempt was made to "build resolutions of thought and conviction."[59]

The circular response discussion method, pioneered by Mary Parker Follett and further developed and advanced by Lindeman and Alfred Dwight Sheffield, was an attempt to facilitate listening in a discussion format. This technique was aimed in particular at reducing the influence of "facile talkers" who tended also to be "negativists and ineffective listeners." The ground rules for such sessions are simple. The discussion topic is started by one group member with remarks addressed to his or her immediate neighbor in the discussion circle. Each person in the group participates only in sequence with no interruptions permitted. While "A" speaks, "B" waits but is told *not* to consciously rehearse the response to be given. "B" is also told to "condition himself in such a manner as to be able to select from all 'A' has said some single element to which he will respond." The objective is to strive to build an idea by making use of what "A" has said.[60]

The leader's role in circular response discussion is primarily that of clarifier. Often the leader will restate each contribution, in this way giving time for succeeding responses. The objective is that of building an "edifice of thought in which each individual's contribution will be gradually moulded into the group product."[61]

Such discussion is orderly, but is it educative? Adult educators who try it discover that the system, while it leads to great frustrations by those who want the topic changed or who wish to talk out of turn, works admirably as a device for stimulating listening—as well as consciousness of the process of consensus development. Only one individual, i.e., the next person slated to talk, is thinking of a verbal response. Ideally, this frees up the balance of the group as listeners so that they are more likely to contribute substantively to the issue at hand.[62] Such a discussion revolves around the group situation. It is listening, as well as talking, that is facilitated.[63]

Because of his commitment to listening as a device for learning in adult education contexts, Lindeman was uncomfortable with debate in which the participant necessarily "selects his conclusion in advance and then proceeds to gather facts and opinions to prove his case." It was "victory, not enlightenment," that was the objective.[64]

Winning a debate means "excluding other points of view." In discussion, progress results from inclusions. Debate is distorted at the outset by the "naive assumption that all questions have two sides. . . " A starting assumption of discussion is that "every question has as many sides as there are interests involved and no situation is properly confronted until all relevant interests have been considered."[65]

What is the function of the discussion leader? Not one of overt leadership at all, Lindeman believed. In a 1933 article in *Progressive Education,* Lindeman summarized his view of the role of discussion leader. The first function was to "assist the group in confronting its situation." How? By stating the case, revealing issues, and sharpening conflicts. The leader was to "aid the group in sustaining relevancy and pertinency" by "relating contributions to the theme or subject" and by "pointing contributions with respect to time."[66]

To keep the discussion moving in a problem-solving direction, the leader would help the group avoid "mere debate." The leader could also see to it that all contributions are related to a problem-solving sequence that moves from "situation to involved problems," from "mass of problems to the selection of strategic problem or problems," and from "strategic problems to principles involved." From there on, the leader might guide the group in moving "from principles to possible alternatives" or solutions, "from alternatives to the formulation of experimental projects" and "from projects to the distribution of responsibilities."[67]

Summarizing the contributions of discussion participants "at points which mark advance or agreement" was the final task of a discussion leader.[68]

The discussion leader or teacher should, in Lindeman's view, function as a kind of "group-chairman." In this role, "he no longer sets problems and then casts about with various kinds of bait until he gets back his preconceived answer. . . " Neither "is he the oracle who supplies answers which students carry off in their notebooks. . . " The leader's function is "not to profess but to evoke—to draw out, not pour in. . . " The leader is an "interlocutor" of sorts—one who questions and interprets as well as a "prolocutor" who "brings all expressions before the group. . . " He or she might be a "coach" who "trains individuals for team-play" and might also be a "strategist" who "organizes parts into wholes and keeps the total action aligned with the group's purpose."[69] This view of the teaching-learning transaction as it involves the teacher is the foundation of Malcolm Knowles's articulation of the concept of andragogy.

Lindeman's great strength as a discussion leader and teacher was his skill in propounding the sort of questions that made a group try to work toward really relevant discussion.[70] Flora Thurston Allen, executive secretary of the National Council of Parent Education, recalls that Lindeman used questions of the sort that would "create something of a relationship." And he was a good listener. With this technique he had the habit of creating ad hoc discussion groups wherever he was as people flocked around him.[71] Byron Mock, a co-worker with Lindeman in the WPA, recalls Lindeman's great sensitivity in keeping discussion in organized channels. "Now we've heard one point of view," he might say, "let's hear from someone else. You had a comment, what is your thought?" When a discussion got out of hand or started to wander too much, Lindeman might redirect the effort by saying: "Now, let's summarize where we are. . . "[72]

Lindeman's view of discussion as a systematic method for arranging educative questioning, listening, and response was firmly rooted in John Dewey's pragmatism. Was it not, after all, a method for setting up a series of pragmatic tests? It was not doubt as to the verity of a fact that would cause a variety of responses from individual members of a group. Rather, such responses were reflective of efforts to test the fact against a range of each individual's thoughts and feelings.

Discussion reveals differences among a group's members. One of its objectives accordingly is to assist members of the group in discovering how much about the fact can be utilized by the collective as it seeks to advance the purposes and objectives of individuals. Discussion becomes "vital when connected with probable courses of action."[73]

The aim of discussion, by extension, is consistent with the aim of adult education, which is "to make 'arriving,' not concluding, an educative venture." Discussion will not "solve situations," but it will reveal "experimental roads to action. . . " Through discussion, the situation is recognized, the problems involved are analyzed, and relevant information and experience is sought. At this point, the discussants are ready to "envisage the consequences of various lines of action." Adult education is thus "forwarded by the group process. . . "[74]

Lindeman was well aware of the limitations of discussion methods. In remarks addressed to members of the American Country Life

Association, he noted that discussion cannot "bring new facts into existence." This is a "function of the scientific method." Neither can discussants "adequately scrutinize, test or verify all facts relevant to the problem under consideration." Again, this was the province of science. Discussion is not free of the pernicious influence of "authoritative personalities." The outcome of a discussion will not be "sharply-defined executive conclusions on which all members may subsequently act." These and other results "which are scientifically or executively derived" should not be expected.[75]

But against these imitations, he cited the numerous functions that discussion could serve. Discussion can, he said, "measure fact against fact . . . bring opposing attitudes and beliefs into comparison . . . humanize experts by exposing them to social realities . . . bring science and experience into relation . . . minimize prejudice and place a premium on intelligence . . . evaluate and test programs . . . reveal conflicting drives and motives . . . dissipate merely temperamental differences . . . lead to discrimination between facts, opinions and prejudices . . . direct research toward needed knowledge . . . suggest avenues of fresh experimentation . . . re-evaluate aims, purposes, objectives, create new unities [and] initiate new integrations on intellectual and emotional levels."[76]

The "habit of conference," Lindeman said, "is the essential quality of behavior of persons who live under democracy."[77] Conferencing is discussion's cousin, a relationship which Eduard Lindeman was among the first to identify and study systematically. The problems and opportunities of discussion were essentially a microcosm of the comparable problems and opportunities of conferencing involving larger groups.

Lindeman could be biting in his criticism of conferences and conference goers. The essence of his concern was the one-way nature of communication at conference sessions. The announced purpose of a meeting of scientists, for example, might be to exchange ideas, but this was precisely what did not tend to happen. Instead of exchanging ideas, speakers "read papers at each other. A subject is chosen, then a speaker; thereupon another subject and another speaker until the program is rounded out so as to take care of those whose 'turn' has come. The 'program manipulators' appear at this point to be reminded in some dim way that discussion has a legitimate place; whatever time is left is therefore devoted to discussion." The chairman, "watch in hand," tries to keep speakers within time limits, "but he fails." Later, he will explain to the speaker that after all, "twenty minutes was an inadequate time for the presentation of his theme." The audience will be told that the discussion "cannot take place."[78]

"If by some miracle of time or the fortunate absence of a speaker, discussion is made possible," the result is "usually fruitless." The few questions asked may either "divulge the fact that the speaker was misunderstood or that the opportunity has arrived for expressing the long-inhibited tendency toward praise or blame." Discussion, such as it is, takes place in hotel rooms and lobbies "during the brief moments between sessions."[79]

The purpose of conferencing was patently "to exchange knowledge and experience relating to specific problems." Unfortunately, Lindeman believed, "this is precisely what one rarely encounters."[80] The crux of the problem with such conferences lay in method. Reading a paper was the "poorest possible way" of furthering an understanding in a group. Effective learning could only take place when the "ideas which convey experiences are allowed to interpenetrate." How could such exchange take place? Certainly not by a simple question and answer session—or even in large conference groups, which Lindeman felt were "not amenable" to the process of learning through discussion.[81]

As in discussion, simple poor listening could be a major problem at conferences. Addressing the City Club of Portland, Oregon, Lindeman described a recent speech he had given to an unnamed group in Boston (probably an audience of librarians at Simmons College).[82] The first four questions had been "amazing." "The first three imputed to me ideas which I hadn't included in my address at all. But they all insisted they heard me say things which I'm sure I hadn't said. And the fourth imputed to me a position which was precisely the opposite of the one I had taken. . . "[83]

What, then, should conference organizers do to improve the learning potential of their sessions? They might start with the fact that delegates come to conferences with "mixed and multiple motives"—not all of them directly bearing on learning. Some conference attendees simply want opportunities to meet and talk with others. Ample time for this simple function needs to be arranged. There should also be allowance for "rest and recreation periods." Some will attend to "exploit themselves or their organizations" and opportunities for this should be provided. Privileges might also be extended "to those who come to deliver oracular pronouncements, as well as to those who feel that a conference has not been successful unless some orator has caused a vibration in the areas of their spinal columns."[84]

All of these are needs of conferees "and no disgrace is involved in this admission." Still, the "main and central purpose of a conference is to confer." Conference planning which does not "somehow arrange for an actual and free exchange of knowledge and experience represents a plot, not a plan." It might please and placate, but it will not be "a draft for educative experience."[85]

Conferring, Lindeman believed, is "itself educative." But even John Dewey's progressive educators (who included adult educators), by their behavior in planning their own conferences, all but denied and invalidated the conception of education through experience. Andragogical methods might be taught to others, but they were not being applied in conferences designed for the teachers.[86]

What should be done? Directly addressing adult educators, Lindeman had answers. Why not "make the bold assumption that adult educators need to educate themselves, that the main object in coming together in conference is, not to listen to papers which might better be printed, but to explore the ways of self-education?" Why not, for example, formulate the agenda for their upcoming conference "around problems and situations common to all forms of adult education?"[87]

Of course, a conference which began with "problems instead of pronouncements" might fail. "But why should this deter us?" Had all adult educators been "so successful in the use of traditional and non-educative conference method as to shrink from probable failure through experimentation?" Did educators "possess a special warrant to remain 'safe and sane'? And by what special grant do adult educators presume the right to preach what they fear to practice?"[88]

❆

Is there a point where the facilitation of learning crosses a boundary and becomes indoctrination? Can or should particular ideas, doctrines, or practices be propagated by assertive direction of the process of adult education?

As Herr Doktor Josef Goebbels stoked the Nazi propaganda furnace during the 1930s and early 1940s, Lindeman found himself faced with a dilemma. As perfected by the Nazis and others, propaganda was certainly effective. The whole world was listening and often acting. But was propaganda adult education? If so, was this to be the future direction taken by the movement to which he had devoted so much of his working life? As one of the organizers (and first president) of the Institute for Propaganda Analysis in 1937, he set about the task of providing Americans with a definition of propaganda and with tools for propaganda analysis.

The Institute defined propaganda as "an expression of opinion or action by individuals or groups, deliberately designed to influence opinions or actions of other individuals or groups with reference to predetermined ends." Propaganda was not adult education, Lindeman decided. The chief distinction between the two was that the propagandist attempts to "put over" a preconceived end, whereas the educator must insist "that the ends of life come about as the result of shared experience."[89] At times, adult education would even need to be employed as a "prophylactic against propaganda and misinformation."[90]

Lindeman took a hard look at propaganda—most especially the fascist version of it. While he was most concerned about the sometimes mesmerizing effect of the screaming Josef Goebbels, he was careful to identify propaganda sources closer to home. His treasured American democratic process was vulnerable to subversion from within as well as to danger from abroad. The effects of propaganda upon the nation were all too evident, and all of them were bad.

Propaganda increased *"partisanship"* to the extent that "adherents of one party can no longer see any good in the opposing party." It led to an increase in *"absolute judgements"* which, in turn, led to a "falsification of reality." It engendered *"anger, hatred* and the spirit of *bitterness."* It weakened the capacity of citizens to formulate their "own *opinions* and *judgements."* Once enlisted as partisans, people became "dependents, intellectual indigents." It weakened the capacity for *"communication,* for shared experience" as persons affected developed "blind spots for everything which does not fit comfortably into the pattern created by propaganda." Propaganda had a "poisoning effect" and increased the "tendency toward *suspicion* and *cynicism."* Finally, it produced in many individuals "a feeling or sense of *helplessness"* as individuals gave in "to flow along with the master current."[91]

The "radicals and reactionaries" frequently revealed "their underlying psychological kinship." Both stood "in the way of authentic social change because each mistakes propaganda for education." True social reformers could not pawn off "prejudices and opinions as facts" nor could they "set limits to what is to be learned. . . " "No social order worth achieving" would arrive until Americans learned to "interpret education as growth from within rather than inculcation from without."[92]

There were higher minded propagandists as well. The church intellectually had "remained far behind the general intellectual movement of our time," accepting "science and its consequences under compulsion but never in the spirit of willing cooperation. . . "

Moreover, the church "as a social institution" had been "left stranded by the rapid changes in sociological structures and process of modern communities. . . " On its "psychological side," the church remained "a propaganda medium [making] little use of newer and more valid educational methods."[93]

The nation might not be able to shut itself off from the evil of propaganda nor could it "forbid propagandists to function." But Americans could protect themselves by understanding the nature of propaganda and the instruments of the propagandists.[94]

The announced objectives of the Institute for Propaganda Analysis was that of helping Americans combat propaganda. Why then did Eduard Lindeman, the Institute's president in the fall of 1941, resign from the organization in order to "become a propagandist myself"?[95] It was a grim time in world history. Adolf Hitler, the world's chief propagandist, had crushed France and nearly all of Europe and was at the gates of Moscow. Much of London, home of the first parliament in a major nation, lay in ruins as a result of German bombing. Democracy everywhere was in danger.

It was perhaps the only time in his life that Eduard Lindeman conveniently locked up his long-held belief that good ends never resulted from bad means. Propaganda, sleazy though it might be, could be enlisted as a weapon on behalf of democracy. Lindeman's excuse that "forthright propaganda on behalf of those democratic ideals which constitute our major reason for taking the risks of war" would boost morale sounds lame through the distance of history.[96] A self-proclaimed "ardent interventionist,"[97] Eduard Lindeman was, by December of 1944, writing propaganda broadcasts aimed at an audience of intellectuals and professionals in Italy.[98] A Lindeman message to the German people was broadcast in German to Hitler's realm on D-Day, June 6, 1944.[99]

CHAPTER 12

Adult Education as the Lifeblood of Democracy

Eduard Lindeman held that democracy was fragile. It required discipline and hard work on the part of its constituents. The future of democracy depended in a genuine sense upon the intelligent use of adult education as the chief instrument of the democratic process.

"I do not see how it will be possible to secure intelligent participation in the control of our affairs unless we can produce a larger number of socially-sensitive, healthy-minded, progressive adults."[1] From this great pool would come individuals "who are to democracy what circulation of the blood is to the organism."[2] America's adult educators needed to take seriously their obligations as caretakers of the chief instrument of democracy.

Committed to the values of democracy, Lindeman was from the beginning deeply suspicious of the twin giants of fascism and communism, as the tides of these great forces gathered over the world in the decades between the two world wars. He was appalled as he heard serious debates and discussion based on the unquestioned assumption that the world would or should inevitably turn from democracy to one of these. It was a false dichotomy. The choice for America must be neither fascism nor communism. Americans should instead recommit themselves to democracy, and it was adult education that would be the lifeblood of any such effort.

In his scrapbook, Lindeman sketched out in parallel outline form his ideas as to the differences and similarities between fascism and communism. Both political systems eliminated parliamentary rule and political parties, as well as conflict and difference. Fascism furnished release for accumulated and chronic fears, worries, angers, hatreds (inferiorities), and aggressive nationalism. It attacked a class and made a show of force as affirmation of superiority. Communism, he indicated, had these same characteristics, though "with deviations." Communists, in addition, desired "ultimate peace."[3]

Fascists protected the middle class; communists protected the working class, or proletariat. Fascists substituted executive or functional government for democracy and liberalism. Communists did the same things, though they assumed that the dictatorship was temporary. Fascists protected private property and profits. Communists eliminated private property and profits. For both fascists and communists, education and related youth movements were "doctrinaire." At the end of the outline, Lindeman noted that fascists and communists had different goals, but used the same methods.[4]

Of the two ugly isms, Lindeman believed that the United States had the most to fear from fascism. As a "bourgeois nation," America would never turn in the direction of communism. The attraction of fascism, on the other hand, was quite a different matter. Had not Mussolini himself told a reporter that he found more parallels for fascism in the United States than in any other country in the world?[5]

Lindeman's aversion to fascism had grown firm during the family's stay in Italy in 1925. In a speech to the City Club of Portland, Oregon, Lindeman recalled that one of the prime arguments posed by Mussolini to the Italian people during that time had been that democracy and corruption were correlated. Corruption was supposed to be a necessary part of democracy; Mussolini would get rid of corruption in Italy by getting rid of freedom.[6]

Survey Editor Paul Kellogg delegated to Lindeman the task of editing a special issue on the topic of fascism. Lindeman recruited an impressive array of talent—including even Benito Mussolini's brother, Arnaldo, who told the *Survey*'s readers what they might expect in Italy from his brother's "superior statesmanship."[7]

On an opposite page, one of Mussolini's victims, Gaetano Salvemini, told what his life had been like under the "reign of the bludgeon."[8] It was not a pretty story. Professor Salvemini, formerly a faculty member at the University of Florence, had been charged with writing for *Non Mollare,* a clandestine and anti-Fascist news sheet.[9] After more than a month in prison, Professor Salvemini had been tried and acquitted for lack of evidence. However, he had grown weary and fearful after experiencing "continual threats and attacks upon his person and his house." He had been refused a passport by Mussolini's government, but had fled to France to join his wife. He had been deprived of his property and citizenship under a new and Fascist-inspired law.[10]

Lindeman's own written contribution to *Survey*'s special issue was an insightful and sobering article entitled "A New Challenge to the Spirit of 1776." Writing in 1927, Lindeman was chillingly prophetic as he described the "professional patriot" pretensions of the fascists. By the same token, such anti-fascists became enemies of the state. The United States had acquired a fair supply of professional patriots since the World War, Lindeman noted, and to get a picture of the problem one only had to substitute the term "un-American" for "anti-fascists." "One hundred percenters would look well in black shirts; what they lack at the moment is a gang leader and a symbol."[11] Lindeman himself would fall victim to this class of professional patriots a bit more than two decades later.

Lindeman had particular contempt for fascism's philosophical pretensions, which he thought were specious. The communists at least had a respectable philosophical base in the writings of Karl Marx. The roots of fascism, on the contrary, lay in the dark pools of history. Some of the fascists had sought to remedy their lack of sound philosophical underpinnings by attaching themselves to the philosophy of Vilfredo Pareto.

In book reviews appearing in *Survey Graphic* in 1934 and 1935, Lindeman attacked the fascist links to Pareto because he believed that philosopher deserved "a better place in the history of thought" than could be provided for him by "apologists for Fascism." "Pareto should not be appropriated, at least not all of him."[12] That philosopher, whose "basic theories of social conduct combine to illustrate how and why human beings behave non-logically" provided no rationale for a national policy in which force and coercion were self-justifying.[13]

During the 1930s fascism made fast gains at the expense of the democracies. Lindeman felt compelled to respond on behalf of democratic values. In a number of speeches and articles during the depression years, he spelled out his vision of a democracy as differentiated from a fascist dictatorship. Democracy, as he saw it, was based on "shared experience," as Dewey termed it. And the process of sharing experience was "in essence one of communication." In a dictatorship, on the contrary, experience was not the source of politics. What the dictator said became " 'truth' by declaration." The dictator was supposed to possess "unique but intuitive gifts, insights which depend, not upon his shareable experience, but rather upon his clairvoyance."[14]

In an article for *School and Home,* Lindeman wrote that "democratic behavior becomes the natural mode of life of every person who views difference as desirable. . . " Such persons would seek differences in others, would discover methods to allow these differences to interact and to become "the means of enhancing mutual powers." Differences were welcome "because freedom to express difference is one of the conditions of growth for the individual and progress for society."[15]

The essence of autocracy, as seen in the modern Fascist states, was "uniformity." The "first art" of the dictator was to "eliminate differences," to establish or impose uniform patterns upon all citizens. Success for the dictator depended upon his ability to degrade or eliminate those who did not "conform to his conception of superiority or inferiority."[16]

Germany's leader in the 1930s received somewhat less attention from Lindeman during those years than his Italian colleague, but Lindeman's disdain for the Führer and everything he stood for was total. Not until 1945, when he saw at first hand the human ruins of Europe, did the full force of Hitler's rule in Germany strike Lindeman's consciousness and send him into deep depression.

In a 1938 article for *Michigan Education Journal,* Lindeman decried the "so-called Munich Peace," and cited it as evidence that democracy had been "well nigh destroyed in Europe. . . " The totalitarian states had been the victors and the weakening European democracies had felt the full brunt of the "ruthless power of the dictators." America's moral influence in European affairs had turned out to be "unrealistic and fanciful." The Fascist states had gotten everything they wanted by "weakening democratic resistance" and without rushing into actual warfare.[17]

In the period between the two world wars, American intellectuals found it easier to oppose fascism than communism. With its straightforward totalitarian methods and its observable links with the most reactionary and brutal elements in society, fascism was an easier target.

Intellectuals tended to be more ambivalent in their attitudes toward communism. Results of the Soviet experiment were not yet in, but the preliminary indications were often encouraging—especially when seen against the backdrop of the corruption and wickedness of czarist Russia. Many intellectuals were fully open to Marxist ideas.[18]

As they surveyed what appeared to be the ruins of capitalism after

1929, Western intellectual leaders sharpened the focus of their lenses as they viewed happenings in the Union of Soviet Socialist Republics. The horrors of Stalinism were not yet fully evident. Perhaps, with its great problems inherited from the past, the Soviet Union could be excused for attempting drastic solutions. The goals of communism, in any event, were humanistic goals. Full employment, the elimination of poverty, decent housing, elimination of racial discrimination—all of these were the goals of progressive Americans, as they were the goals of Soviet Communists.

A number of intellectuals became Communists or were at least sympathetic to Marxist philosophy and aspirations. Marxism did seem to provide an explanation for the Depression. Perhaps capitalism really did carry the seeds of its own destruction. At the depth of the Depression, Amtorg, the Russian trading office in New York, was getting 350 applications a day from Americans who wanted to settle in the Soviet Union.[19]

In the 1920s and 1930s, Lindeman was free, as well as fashionable, in his use of Marxist-inspired language and symbols. "Collectivism," for example, was cited as "the road to power, the predominant reality of modern life" in *The Meaning of Adult Education*. Adult education would supply "directive energy" for collective enterprises.[20]

The Communists, however, had only contempt for *The Meaning of Adult Education* and its author. In *The Daily Worker*, the voice of the Communist Party in America, reviewer Vivian Rosen shared the generally dim view of the book taken by her capitalist colleagues. To her, Lindeman's effort was no more than "a first-rate liberal grunt, delivered after much painful effort. [She obviously had skipped the book's "Foreword," with its description of the speed with which the book had been written] . . . We are now inclined to believe," the reviewer continued, in a prefeminist vein, "the author is prepared for menopause. The change of life is upon us. . . The book is, nonetheless, true to the best traditions of *The New Republic*, which means humorless espousal of academic causes to be won by 'salvation through knowledge.' For those who believe that 'humanizing knowledge' means humanizing life, the book has its value. For those of us who believe that to be pious drivel, and that the answer to the latter lies deeper in the modern fabric of the economic, political, and social system, the book . . . is completely useless."[21]

In 1934, with the Depression near its nadir, Lindeman received cheers and applause lasting a full three minutes for a speech in which he urged Philadelphia members of the American Federation of Teachers not to "allow children to go through the schools without knowing the truth about our social order." "A new order, in which the worker may have a greater share of the products of his labor is only possible through collective organization," Lindeman told the group. "It is up to us to bring that about by education."[22]

The whole world was watching with some awe the nearly total societal transformation that was occurring within the Soviet state. Uncritical accounts of life in the Soviet Union—not all of them by doctrinaire Communists—were in plentiful supply. Lindeman's knowledge of the Soviet experiment was not obtained entirely from books. In 1932, he visited Russia.[23] The eyes with which he viewed that emerging nation were those of an American who believed his own nation's capitalistic system had broken down. Was there anything to be learned from the Russian experiment that could apply in an American setting? In common with John Dewey, he concluded it was well that the Communist experiment was being conducted in a society other than his own.

Lindeman kept his usual scrapbook-style notes of his Russian venture. They provide a generally terse account of his travels and his thoughts about his travels. About midway into his visit, Lindeman noted liabilities and assets of the Soviet Union "as seen by an outside observer." Liabilities included militarism, failure to make best use of outside technicians, too superficial training for new technicians, inability to deal with peasant psychology, too much attention to goal and not enough to quality of product, and class distinctions growing out of bureaucracy. Assets he considered to include faith, released energy, security, increasing national stability, courage, and a sense of direction.[24] He also was "frequently amazed at the sheer ineptitude of the rulers as evinced in their blundering management of their agrarian population." [Stalin was in the process of solving this problem in his own way.] But most disturbing of all to Lindeman was the Soviets' "almost childlike preoccupation with things."[25]

These, however, had not been the "most significant aspects" of newer Russian behavior patterns. On the whole, he felt most of the "observable changes in human nature" represented "a cluster of traits which would be approved by the more progressive psychologists and social scientists everywhere."[26] The "great lesson" he felt the Communists were teaching the world was "not Communism but rather the latent capacity of human nature to adapt itself to changing circumstances." If the rest of the world could demonstrate the same flexibility, improved "social and economic structures" might be the result.[27]

Lindeman had a characteristically tolerant and open view toward Marxism and the incipient Marxist experiment in the Soviet Union.

But any chance that communism had to win a convert in Eduard Lindeman crashed upon the hard rocks of ends that were supposed to justify means. In the battle of bedrock philosophy, it was Ralph Waldo Emerson and not Karl Marx who would win. "The great evil of communism," he told the Illinois Summer Educational Conference at Urbana in 1951, "does not rest in its economic theory. It seduces people into believing that a good end can be achieved by an evil means which is contradictory not only to morality, but to science as well."[28]

Two years earlier, Lindeman had elaborated on the same theme in an elegant speech that later appeared as an essay in a book called *Defense of Democracy*. Defendants of "so-called Eastern or Russian democracy" might declare "that any action is democratic if it is in the interest of all the people." As inheritors of "Western democracy," Americans must insist, on the contrary, "that the action must also be taken *by* the people and must be a function *of* the people."[29]

Why must Americans hold "so stubbornly that democracy is both means and ends, method and goal?"[30] Means must be in harmony with ends because "science teaches that we become what we do." To anticipate good results from faulty methods was "an unscientific belief." Moral reasoning in a democracy was "based on the assumption that those who violate the principle of compatibility between means and ends sooner or later become so careless concerning their means that they finally take on the pattern of conspiratorial behavior. Those who do not test their means as well as their ends become manipulators." Ends, no matter how good, could not be achieved "through the instrumentality of means that are in themselves a denial of the ends proposed." This incongruity, he continued, represented one of the most tragic aspects of the Soviet state. "It is utterly unthinkable that the Soviet Union will ever achieve the lofty goals the leaders so loudly proclaim if they continue to utilize brutal, non-humane, and tyrannical means."[31]

"It is necessary," Lenin wrote, "to agree to any and every sacrifice . . . to resort to all sorts of devices, maneuvers and illegal methods, to evasion and subterfuge. . . "[32] Few words could more completely contradict everything Eduard Lindeman stood for, and it pained him to see American Communists adopting Lenin's advice. As chairman of the Committee on Academic Freedom of the American Civil Liberties Union, Lindeman had attended meetings to see that professors trapped in "one of our witch hunts" in New York State received fair hearings or trials. One day he listened as a young professor of sociology in a city college was caught in three perjuries in a half hour. Convinced the man was lying, the troubled Lindeman consulted John

Dewey, who had his own ugly experiences with duplicitous Communists as a member of Local No. 5 of the American Federation of Teachers. Lindeman explained the situation to Dewey. The man was living under three names, one at the school where he taught, another at the apartment house where he lived, and still another in his Communist cell. Lindeman had been placed in the position of trying to defend a person who was lying, whose "whole life had become a conspiracy."[33]

Dewey listened, looked out the window of his office for a long time, and puffed on a cigarette. Finally he turned and, with a wistful smile, said, "Well, Eduard, it has taken us a long time, hasn't it, to realize that people who tell lies will never make a better world."[34]

Lindeman's position on the right of Communists to teach was consistent with that of John Dewey. In June 1949, he put his thoughts to Dewey as he wrote "to say how happy I am over your letter to the [*New York Times*] on Communists as Teachers." As chairman of the Commission on Academic Freedom of the ACLU he had been "striving to sustain the position which you have now so clearly stated. . . " There had been times when he'd felt "extremely lonely," he told Dewey, but Dewey's letter had given him "renewed courage."[35]

Five days later, in a letter to Max Otto, Lindeman mentioned Dewey's letter to *The Times* on the subject of Communists as teachers. "He says they're not fit to teach but an attempt to suppress them is a much worse disease." That, he said, was his position as well.[36]

With every cell in his body, Eduard Lindeman believed in the values of American democracy, but for all of his life he was deeply troubled about the companionship of American democracy with capitalism. Somehow, capitalism was a corrupting influence, an unsuitable economic companion for the pure maiden that was democracy.

He, of course, rejected the fascist alternative out of hand. He had been open to Marxism but soon discovered that here, too, was a sullied and deceitful suitor for the hand of democracy. Couldn't there be something better for America than an economic system that tended to reward greed and avarice?

The full promise of democracy would not be realized until its concepts had been extended in a real way to the economic and social spheres, as well as to the political life of America.[37] Toward the end of his life, Lindeman made his peace with the somewhat tamed version of capitalism that had evolved in the nation. But it was after a long philosophical struggle.

Early in his career, Lindeman wrote a short piece which revealed his developing concern that Americans must "act upon the faith that the persons who produce our goods are more important than the goods."[38] Later, Lindeman's words became sharper: "There is still time to bring about a fusion between ethics and industry, but the time may come, and sooner than those deluded by temporary lulls of prosperity and fitful revivals of capitalism are aware, when the new social ethics can be erected only upon the sacrificial altar of human lives, or not at all."[39] He meant revolution.

Lindeman was becoming more discouraged about the possibilities of putting a more humane face on capitalism. "Present industrial organization" did not seem to him to provide employment "to either women or men on terms which will be best suited for the development of their personalities." The industrial machine was driven by the profit motive, and "something bordering on a psychological and spiritual revolution must take place among those possessing economic power before this formula is reversed."[40] This was a deep-seated belief that was even then feeding his interest in the new concept of adult education.

In 1927 Lindeman saw the United States as possessing "the most virile, convinced and resourceful capitalist rulership which the world has ever seen—not a dictatorship, but a whole culture which starves not merely the unions but all liberalizing groups and movements." But the young critic of capitalism was still not Marxist. "I do not believe in economic determinism." He did believe in "the determinism which results from the cooperative thinking of human minds."[41]

Lindeman was less than sanguine in those years about the "insidious defenses of capitalism." He labeled profit sharing, for example, as "sure poison to the co-operative movement." It merely "accentuates and distributes bad habits."[42]

Lindeman's and other criticisms of American capitalism had few serious hearers among the general public during the 1920s. Warren Harding's "normalcy"—as extended through the administration of Calvin Coolidge—was a goal in itself for many. But with the crash of 1929 came quite a different intellectual climate. With crisis came opportunity. The temper and mood of the nation, for the first time in years, was encouraging for those who favored fundamental social and economic change. To Eduard Lindeman, it looked as if democratic change would be possible "without waiting for the rise of a revolutionary proletariat."[43]

Was Lindeman's brand of democracy possible at all in a capitalist society? The question was posed directly to Lindeman after a 1938 speech on "The Labor Movement" before the Northern California

Chapter of the American Association of Social Workers. His answer was a curious blend of no and yes to the question. If the questioner meant by "a capitalist society" one "such as we now have, organized in the fashion we have, working against public control of its processes [and] the organization of workers, insisting on determining its own profits, insisting upon the importance of the iron laws of wages, etc., . . . then, of course, the answer is 'No.' That kind of capitalism stands almost at the opposite of democracy." But he hedged. If the word "capitalism" were used "in the more technical sense, I don't see how we can have any economy which is not based upon some conception of what capital is and the use of capital." Unless the structure of capitalism could be "thoroughly remodeled in terms of human nature," however, it would "become and remain an enemy of democracy. That is my definition . . . of democracy—a society dedicated to satisfying all basic human needs."[44]

Lindeman made no special truce with capitalism during the years of World War II. In 1942, he reacted to a *Fortune* magazine monograph about "democratic power" that ended with this sentence: "That power must be strong enough and wise enough to give confidence in the future on the part of investors and entrepreneurs." Not so, said Lindeman, in a radio talk. "The peace which is to come and which we hopefully believe will endure must first of all inspire confidence, not in investors and entrepreneurs, but in the people. . . Investors will be safe if the people are safe. . . And, it cannot be assumed that the people will be secure if the world first of all is made safe for investors."[45]

In his scrapbook for 1945, Lindeman mused about what should be the attributes of the economy for a democratic society. A democratic economy would first be "pluralistic," not "totalitaristic," allowing a variety of economic enterprise. It would be "planned," but this would be a joint enterprise in which all "enterprisers" would participate— not just the government. It would be a "guaranteed economy" with government assuming responsibility for its stability. Finally, the "authority of the guarantee" would have to be "constitutionally clear." There could be no ambiguity. Lindeman thought a constitutional amendment might be required. Such a "plural economy" could not succeed, Lindeman thought, unless supported by "a form of economic morality" which "would probably have to be inaugurated through statutes."[46]

One of the last entries in his scrapbook—written just before his death in 1953—reveals the full extent of Lindeman's compromised peace with capitalism. It was a compromise born of his belief that there was a fundamental "incompatibility between Communism and Democracy." Communism, the philosopher noted, stemmed from the philosophies of Kant, Fichte, Hegel, and Marx. Democracy, on the other hand, came from Locke, Hume, Mill, and Jefferson. In the aggregate, these represented two "antithetical conceptions of human nature and the universe and morality."[47]

The totalitarians say: "We will give you welfare and security if you will abandon freedom." The "*Earlier* Capitalist" [emphasis added] had said: "We will give you your freedom provided you don't ask for security." The "New Democracies" were saying: "We believe it is possible to provide both freedom and welfare." If this could be done, Lindeman noted, the nation would have found "the real answer to the Communist challenge." "And we must," he said, "strive to find the answer. . . "[48]

What was this democracy so aggressively defended by the author of *The Meaning of Adult Education,* and by what sort of logic could adult education become its chief instrumentality? Lindeman's democratic compass pointed at all times to a north represented by Ralph Waldo Emerson.

In an apparently unpublished manuscript prepared in 1931, Lindeman set down his reasons for believing that "Emerson needs to be reinterpreted for our age. . . " Why? First, because he was present at the beginning of the nation's "mechanized, material culture and observed its elements with keenness of insight. . . " Second, because he "ranged over such wide expanses of intellectual territory."[49]

Because of the breadth, as well as the depth, of Emerson's work, Lindeman was convinced "we shall never quite get rid of him. When energies ebb and faiths waver we shall turn his pages over, not so much to find answers as to rediscover his modes of inquiry, his methods of belief, and his arts of affirmation. In times of distress Emerson will again become a contemporary thinker."[50] At every point in his life, Lindeman would turn to Emerson for refreshment. He told Max Otto in a letter written the year before his death: "I never grow weary of drawing from his well. Always it comes up fresh and clean."[51]

It was no simple task, however, to provide reinterpretation of Emerson for a quite different age from the one in which the Sage of Concord had lived. He had not formulated a philosophical system as such. "Besides, he utilized rationalistic procedures which are not wholly congenial to those of us who have been trained in the modern scientific disciplines." Nor was he consistent or a believer in consistency's virtue. There were "hazards," then, for the Emerson interpreter, who "must expand, project, and fill in with his own notions in order to make use of Emerson as a ferment, as a stimulator of reflection."[52]

Eduard Lindeman did not shrink from the task of making a "ferment" of Waldo Emerson. He filled his scrapbooks with Emerson quotes, Emerson analyses, Emerson ideas, Emerson "preoccupations," a giant glossary of Emersonia, clippings about Emerson—including one in which Emerson is compared with Sigmund Freud[53]—and lists of books about Emerson. One scrapbook running from 1933 to 1939 is almost exclusively devoted to Emerson materials. There are, in addition, outlines for the numerous articles and books about Emerson that were written or planned for writing by Lindeman.

Lindeman produced "Emerson's Pragmatic Mood" for *American Scholar* in January of 1947. Here he put Emerson to the means-ends test. There could be no surer test of a philosopher's "incorruptibility" than in his treatment of the problem of means and ends. "Failure to come to grips with the means-ends question leads to opportunism. Denial of the necessary relation of consonance between ends and means is an invitation to conspiracy. Individuals who have not resolved the means-ends issue are not to be trusted, and when statecraft operates on the assumption that ends justify the means the consequences are tragic."[54]

Did Emerson pass the test? "I doubt if anyone has yet uttered wiser words about this ancient and perplexing problem than those found in this crisp sentence of his: 'Cause and effect, means and ends, seed and fruit, cannot be severed; for the effect already blooms in the cause, the end pre-exists in the means, the fruit in the seed.' We become what we do. *The end pre-exists in the means.*" Could there any longer be any doubt concerning "Emerson's pragmatic mood?"[55]

Emerson as the "radical democrat" that he called himself held particular appeal for Lindeman. By this Emerson meant that his concern was rooted in those basic values upon which the ideal of democracy rests. Because he devoted himself to fundamental democratic issues, Lindeman believed that Emerson "will continue to serve as America's conscience so long as Democracy remains our professed way of life."[56]

Democratic government might be surfacely inefficient and, with its separation of powers into executive, legislative, and judicial branches might at times be the cause of "confusion and impediment." However, this was "one of the costs of freedom." With Emerson, Lindeman believed: "Democracy is like a raft. It never sinks but you're always getting your feet wet."[57]

If Emerson was primary in articulating democracy, Lindeman believed him also to be the first American to devote himself "to what is now called adult education." The enlightenment of adults was his objective "wherever a few earnest people gathered for the purpose of enlightening their minds"—in the School of Philosophy at Concord, at mechanics institutes, at the various centers of Boston.[58]

In a manuscript (apparently unpublished), Lindeman summarized Emerson's philosophy of education. "Knowing," to Emerson, "is not in and of itself important. Education consists of skillfulness in making use of knowledge." Emerson "was not deeply concerned over subject-matter itself and believed that the child with sharp sense-perceptions would be better educated than one whose mind was filled with other people's knowledge. He did not respect neutrality in persons. The pupil with the best chance to learn . . . was the pupil with a bias, a tendenciousness. His optimism regarding the learning potentialities of individuals might have been tempered had he lived to know intelligence tests and measurements, but he believed that once the knack of learning had been acquired, all essential learning was thereby made possible."[59]

For a number of the central concepts of his philosophy of adult education, Lindeman drew upon the resources of Emerson. Education is—or should be—lifelong. This is a thoroughly Emersonian concept. In Emerson's *Journal* appear these words: "But it is plain that the adults' education should be undertaken. When our Republic, O Plato! shall begin, the education shall not end with the youth, but shall be as vigorously continued in maturity."[60]

Lindeman made a point of including two additional quotes about adult education in his *Emerson: Basic Selections:* "I see with joy the Irish emigrants landing at Boston, at New York, and say to myself, There they go—to school,"[61] and also: "It seems to me sometimes we get our education a little too quick in this country."[62]

From Emerson, as well, came some of the roots for Lindeman's belief that the approach to adult education will be via the route of situations. "The one condition coupled with the gift of truth is in its use. That man shall be learned who reduceth his learning to practice."[63] "Education," Emerson said, "aims to make the man prevail over the circumstances."[64]

Finally, Emerson's thought influenced Lindeman as he assigned the learner's experience as the resource of highest value in adult education. "Man is great," said Emerson, "not in his goals, but in his transition from state to state."[65]

Emerson was as unhappy as Lindeman about the evils of authoritative teaching and rigid pedagogical formulas. Emerson's *Journal:* "It seems the Law has touched the business of Education with the point of its pen and instantly it has frozen stiff in the universal congelation of society. . . We are shut up in schools and college recitation rooms for ten or fifteen years, and come out at last with a bellyful of words and do not know a thing. . . Far better was the Roman rule to teach a boy nothing that he could not learn standing."[66]

As for the teaching-learning transaction, Emerson developed the ideas that would later be embedded by Lindeman in his foundations for adult education. "The teacher," thought Emerson, "should be the pupil; now, for the most part, they are *Earth's* diameters wide of each other." In a recommendation since generally ignored by faculty search and screen committees, he suggested that a college professor be selected by setting all the candidates loose on a miscellaneous gang of young men taken largely from the street. "He who could get the ear of these youths after a certain number of hours, or of the greatest number of these youths, should be professor. Let him see if he could interest these rowdy boys in the meaning of a list of words."[67] It was a test Eduard Lindeman could certainly have passed.

Lindeman was fond of retelling Emerson's story of the young teacher in Concord who had invited Emerson to observe one of his teaching sessions. Afterward, the young man asked Emerson for his reactions. "It was all wrong," the great man replied. "But surely, Mr. Emerson, everything I did couldn't have been wrong! If so, how do you explain it?" responded the young man. Emerson's dry answer: "So far as I could see, what you have been doing this morning is to strive to make all of your pupils into little you's, and one of you is enough."[68]

The democratic idea in America could be thought of as "ways of living which stem from democratic experience and which appear in the character of disciplines." This idea of the "disciplines of democracy" was especially important because of Lindeman's convictions that a consideration of disciplines would bring "the democratic situation into the sphere of science" where it could be taught and that it should be possible to find "workable means for including democracy within our education system."[69]

What were Lindeman's democratic disciplines? The exact titles varied from article to article and from speech to speech. By the end of his life, he tended to include in one form or another as "democratic disciplines" (1) creative use of diversity, (2) means consonant with ends, (3) partial functioning of ideals, (4) majority rule, (5) emotional sanctions, and (6) humor.

"Democratic experience appears to have demonstrated the fact that diversity is superior to uniformity," Lindeman told an audience in 1951. *E Pluribus Unum* (through diversity towards unity) brings results, "when measured by humane standards."[70] It was a theme familiar in many of his talks. The unity promised by democracy would never be achieved through uniformity. There would instead be movement toward unity brought about through the creative use of diversity.

Democracy fared poorly, Lindeman believed, "at the hands of the egalitarians, the levelers. Individuals are not equals striving for sameness; they are inequals striving for an equal opportunity to express their differences."[71]

Lindeman's second democratic discipline was that means, so far as possible, must be consonant with ends. In the era of rampant totalitarianism, Lindeman found it necessary to challenge the slogan that ends justify the means. It was "validated by both science and morality" that democratic goals could never be attained through undemocratic means. Good human experience "cannot emanate from a relationship in which one person commands the other obeys; from situations in which one person or one group chooses the ends and thereupon uses others as the means." Further, end-gaining individuals who excessively concentrate on goals "are likely to become careless respecting their means."[72]

Since perfectionism and democracy were "incompatibles," Lindeman cautioned Americans to expect that democratic solutions would always be partial, never complete.[73] "You have to accept the rules of imperfection. There isn't going to be any utopia. We're not going to have a perfect society, and you're not going to be perfect individuals in it."[74]

The rule of partial functioning of ideals, when practiced by citizens in a democracy, was also in itself a safeguard against absolutism and its inevitable corollary of authoritarian persecution. Individuals "who know that the most they can hope for is a partial operation of their ideals" will not be attracted to the totalitarian alternatives.[75]

The principle of majority rule, Lindeman believed, "furnishes a sound working basis for conducting human affairs."[76] But majorities shouldn't be followed because they were necessarily right on a particular issue. On the contrary, in the long-term perspective of history, Lindeman thought it might be easier to demonstrate that minorities were more likely than majorities to be right. "But we follow the majority. Why? Because it's the only way to keep the game going." Refuse to follow the majority and the democratic game stops.

The likely result: "some kind of arbitrary dictatorial rule. And so we take our partial imperfect results from imperfect majorities continuing the experiment and that's what makes it democratic."[77]

Lindeman referred to the rule of emotional sanctions as "the belief that decisions which must be taken when all the relevant facts are not available should be tested according to one's integrity of feeling."[78] Believers in democracy would sometimes need to learn to use "emotional sanctions" when, "as so often happens, the relevant facts are not there, or if there, are not to be trusted."[79] An affective, as well as cognitive, rationale could serve as a form of validation for at least one pragmatist.

Lindeman earnestly believed that there is a correlation between humor and the democratic experience. He allowed, in the gray cold Korean War days of 1952, that "it looks now as though the grim and the aggressive are going to inherit the earth. . . " But he was optimistic. "I believe that ultimately the world will belong to those who are able to see life as a kind of drama. Sometimes a drama in which the outcome is sheer tragedy and sometimes it's a kind of melodrama without much sense and sometimes it's sheer comedy, nonsense. . . But there is a relationship between nonsense and sense which is a continuant and I'm now talking about genuine humor, the humor which comes out of life and out of experience."[80]

Education was also the "only instrument for social change which a democracy may safely use." Given a crisis, there might be some acceptable "short cuts" but only in the realization that these would be "Deviations from Principle."[81]

Lindeman took into account, and accepted, the role of the pressure group in a democratic society. He saw no need for such entities to be "furtive." The right to petition the government was, after all, guaranteed by the Constitution as a means of "checking upon government officialdom. . . " It was possible to use the collective strength of such groups to "break down barriers of unreasonableness" and make public administrators "less arbitrary."[82]

In a letter to the editor of *American Scholar* in 1945, Lindeman was critical of a prior article in the publication that had apparently ignored the possible contribution of adult education to the resolution of "Group Tensions in Postwar America." "There is no solution for the difficult task of maintaining a democratic society save through *adult* education." There would otherwise not be enough responsible citizens "who will know what kind of a world it is in which they live and make decisions." When such responsible citizens "begin to recognize their responsibility for adult education, both for themselves and their fellows, then we may be able to shatter that absurd convention which regards education for a profession as dignified and acceptable whereas education for human relations is considered to be a luxury."[83]

CHAPTER 13

Bursting Institutional Boundaries: Reaching Out to Adult Learners

Eduard Lindeman prophesied that education was "about to leap over the boundaries of academic institution and make itself integral with life and living."[1]

He was skeptical about the ability of any existing educational institutions to serve adults. With most adults already organized in ways suited to their individual lives, Lindeman saw the difficulties in organizing them still again for specifically educational purposes.[2] For examples of such problems, he had only to look around him.

The "plain truth of the matter" was that the "vast educational establishment" was engaged in training students in "methods for securing personal advantages." As a result, it had roots in "that variety of individualism" which had brought the entire world to the disaster of the Great Depression. Sorely missing were educated persons who possessed "social feeling."[3]

Colleges and universities were a major part of the problem. Their programs of adult education, as orphans, led an existence that was "fitful and precarious."[4] This was a disaster, perhaps especially for persons desiring continuing education in the professions. Nothing went out of fashion more rapidly than professional training. In the fast-moving world of 1928, Eduard Lindeman noted that scientific facts were being "revealed much more rapidly than they can be assimilated." The professional person who regarded education as "completed" after leaving graduate school would "find himself outdated before he has had time to apply what has been learned."[5]

Musing in his scrapbook in 1946, Lindeman pondered a speech he was about to make on the potential benefits to adult education of university sponsorship. Shouldn't the topic be reversed? "What contribution might adult education make to the universities?"[6]

He was not impressed either by lyceums and chautauquas of the "commercialized, profit making" variety. They "sacrificed independence" whenever it interfered with income.[7] Some counterpart to Aristotle's academy and Emerson's lyceum was needed.[8]

Why not an army of some "three thousand well trained adult educators (one for each county) who were prepared to go forth into the highways and byways organizing small groups in which neighbors talk to neighbors. . . " The result would be "an awakened self-confidence" that would bring America back to essential democratic tradition.[9] Obviously, Lindeman did not consider the Cooperative Extension Service, which many would describe in almost exactly the same words, as qualifying for this role.

Lindeman devoted less time to the need for reform of institutional mechanisms for adult education than to other concerns. However, he made substantive contributions in a number of areas involving outreach by institutions and agencies already serving American adults in other capacities. At traditional academic institutions, courses might be available "for those adults who desire to round out an academic background by accumulating credits in subjects which they deem important."[10] But for "expanding their personalities and illuminating their lives," some type of wide collaboration between "all agencies of enlightenment" would be required.[11]

Lindeman focused his efforts on the learning outreach efforts of the most basic of American institutions—churches, labor unions, parent education organizations, service clubs, women's groups, wherever Americans banded together. He was also an assertive pioneer in the successful effort to introduce a simple, but controversial, new package for adult education—the paperback book. From his base at the New York (later Columbia University) School of Social Work, he nurtured the adult education dimension of the social work profession.

Although he was not in his middle and later years a conventionally religious man, Eduard Lindeman spent many hours throughout his life in churches. He was in great demand as a consultant by church groups—Quakers, Unitarians, the more liberal main-line denominations. His emphasis in these efforts was always counter to authoritarian traditions within institutionalized Christianity. Religious truth could not be "expounded; it must be discovered."[12] Often he struck at instrumental, as well as theological, sore spots.

"Is Preaching a Valid Method?" This was the title question of an article Lindeman wrote for *Homiletic Review,* a journal for ministers, in 1926. He began with the assumption that the aim of preaching was "to influence human behavior." It could "not be justified on lesser grounds." Given this assumption, Lindeman developed the idea that preaching was largely ineffective as an adult education method.[13]

First, it was "not congenial to a democratic atmosphere," nor was it a "participating method." The preacher "by virtue of traditionalism, ornamentation, and the conditions of effective oratory inevitably sets barriers between himself and his audience. He 'has his way,' but the audience has no opportunity of contributing to the performance." The situation was analagous to "arguing a case with both judge and jury absent."[14]

In addition, preaching was "an awkward . . . instrument for an age which has set forth on the adventurous journey of life with the assumption that it can do without external authorities." The church, he wrote, had been slow in adjusting itself to this fact and was perhaps incapable of making the necessary adjustment. The problem was that the roots of the church lay "deep in the soil in which autocracy also grew. . . Much of its internal mechanism, many of its institutional traits, and the bulk of its theological and philosophical assumptions belong inherently to the Middle Ages and before." The church had "never made graceful adjustments to change." True, it had "often been pulled backwards after resistance became useless," but this was not adjusting; it was "rather capitulating, admitting defeat, and each successive failure of this sort has weakened the base and undermined the prestige of the Church." It was perhaps "too late to propose such minor changes as new techniques for ministers," but this did not dissuade Lindeman from doing exactly that in the remainder of his article.[15]

As a method for influencing conduct, preaching was "unscientific." Its appeal was based on "an abandoned concept of authority and a questionable method of teaching." Human beings did not learn by being told; they learned by doing. Persuasion came "by the consequences of our behavior, not by the sounds which enter our ears. . . If the sermon could be used as part of a joint inquiry in which both preacher and parishioner participated in equal terms, it might still be considered as a fruitful and valid means for influencing behavior."[16]

The "forum method" to supplement preaching might also be tried though in Lindeman's view the chances of success with it were "not too promising. . . The mood for learning, i.e., joint learning, is rarely present in forum audiences." "Smart and inadequate answers to smart and inadequate questions" were the usual criteria for most successful forum performances. No subject got thorough discussion, conclusions were still individually derived, and net results too often were "ego-satisfactions" merely.[17]

What, then, should a minister do? He "must somehow discover a method which will set up a synthetic process involving both his expertness and the congregation's experience." But this would not be possible with large groups. Large congregations, like large classes, inhibited the learning process. "If religion is to be influential in the on going adjustments of life, problems must be considered in particular, not in general." Satisfactory conclusions would depend upon continuing attention to the same problem, and for this purpose "small, flexible and fluid groups"—similar to those of the early church—were essential.[18]

The editor of *Homiletic Review* asked his readers to react to "Professor Lindeman's indictment of preaching," but none of them did.[19] At least, no letters on the subject were printed in subsequent issues. Was this because Lindeman's recommendations that churches experiment with smaller groups and interactive preaching were too far ahead of their time to be considered of much practical interest by most clergymen? Most of them would not try such innovations for another three decades or more.

In church, as in other places where adults were to learn, educational democracy was to prevail. Sermons, speeches, and "external forms of authority" were to be replaced by adult education with plenty of emphasis on discussion and exchange of experience. Specialists were to be put "in their proper place: they should be 'on tap' but never 'on top.' "[20]

If Lindeman was disaffected by preaching as an adult education method, he was well aware of the spell that could be cast by evangelistic preachers. In 1936, a fascinated Lindeman heard Aimee Semple McPherson preach at Angelus Temple in Los Angeles. Most of the notes he later made in his scrapbook had to do with the audience rather than with the spotlighted speaker. Most were elderly women, not too well dressed but neat. The working class and also farmers predominated. A fat lady across the aisle from Lindeman "looked and moved as if she might 'throw a fit' any moment." All in the audience appeared to him to be leading "starved lives." Young people had "queer looks" in their eyes.[21]

The congregation sang, shouted, and clapped "like children."

They were invited, men especially, to pray at a watchtower from 9 P.M. to 6 A.M. If they were unemployed, God would help them find a job. Except for the childlike singing, Lindeman found the performance as a whole "disgustingly emotional, 'sexy' in the worst repressed sense." It had been a mixture of "evangelism, sex, money, and simple primitive rhythm."[22] Evangelistic preaching might be outreach, but it was not adult education.

It was in his work with the Workers Education Bureau of America, where he served for a time as director of research, that Lindeman first used the European term "andragogy." As always, he was resistant to educational programs that did not start with the learner. "The intelligent worker," Lindeman believed, "does not study merely to adjust himself *to* industry; he proposes also to call forth from industry some adjustments on behalf of his enlarging and evolving needs, desires, and aspirations."[23] This was not a view looked upon with much understanding or sympathy by employers in the 1920s.

The same principle applied in parent education, another of Lindeman's adult education ventures. The learning potentialities of family life he termed "prodigious. . . " Individual differences—those irritants, even destroyers, of family life—could "be not merely recognized, but utilized. . . " So could "tensions, frictions and conflicts . . . when we come to appreciate the manifold ways in which differences may be recombined, resolved into new meanings."[24] He was cool to anticipatory parent education, emphasizing that the best time for parents to learn how to be parents would be *after* the fact of parenthood.[25]

He was remarkably ahead of his time in his view of parental roles within the family. Writing in prefeminist 1932, Lindeman noted that the American father "may feel that his obligation to finance the family enslaves him [and] implies the loss of certain kinds of freedom which men are likely to cherish." But what if the mother should work to share the income-generation burden? Lindeman's answer must have stunned fathers—and mothers, too—in that Depression year. "It might . . . be assumed that a more equitable sharing of family responsibilities would follow in cases where both mother and father contributed to family income." It was up to adult educators to "somehow find inviting ways of enlisting the father's intelligent interest in the growth of the child from infancy onward." The approach that was "clear-cut and obvious" was "one which utilizes or assimilates other vital interests of the father in the learning process."[26]

It is small wonder that Lindeman's obituary in the journal *Child Study* noted that "when he was speaking [on parent education at meetings sponsored by the Child Study Association Board] a 'standing room only' audience was assured."[27]

It is difficult in the media-washed latter half of the twentieth century to understand a society in which something as simple as the construction of the cover used for a book could be in any sense controversial. As paperbacks began capturing public imagination in the late 1930s, Eduard Lindeman saw them as a new mechanism for facilitating adult education. The opposition critics worried that the paperback, which had been nearly synonymous with trash in literature, was unsuitable as a container for better writing. In his account of "the paperbacking of America" Kenneth C. Davis describes Eduard Lindeman as a pioneer advocate for the paperback.[28] He served as a member of an editorial board appointed to advise the publisher of the Penguin and Pelican lines.[29] Lindeman and his friend Charles Shaw were appointed to the screening committee of New American Library.[30]

"There is real hope," Eduard said, "for a culture that makes it as easy to buy a book as it does a pack of cigarettes."[31]

Eduard Lindeman's contributions to the field of adult education should not obscure his comparable gifts to the profession of social work—a subject given detailed examination in 1958 by Gisela Konopka.[32] Though he never considered himself a social worker, and in fact always felt himself to be something of an outsider in the profession, the bulk of Lindeman's professional time was spent as professor in a school of social work. Much of his practice as learning facilitator came in his capacity as teacher of social workers and would-be social workers.

Lindeman admonished social workers in 1934 that a goal of "rehabilitating unadjusted individuals" could not become a unifying principle for social work. Such a narrow concept of adjustment would mean helping people adjust to an inequitable and unjust status quo. Rather, professional social workers should be "skilled in conditioning human behavior" and at the same time "devoted to the aim of releasing the potentialities of individuals by means which relate them to a changing and dynamic society."[33]

Social workers needed an awareness of the same democratic values that guided enlightened adult educators. And there were the democratic disciplines, basic rules of conduct, that must be applied if democratic values were not to become "mere slogans and thereby meaningless."[34]

Social work should gladly form a partnership with science but should remain aware that science was a language of "what is," not necessarily of "what should be." Social work should not seek to indoctrinate individuals but to train them in the power of criticism. The professional social worker should not hesitate to engage in social action in pursuit of democratic aspirations.[35]

In 1953, just a few weeks after Lindeman's death, Nathan E. Cohen presented a paper on the meaning of the teachings and philosophy of Eduard Lindeman for social work at the meeting of the National Conference of Social Work in Cleveland.[36] With very little adaptation, this presentation could have served as a summary of Lindeman's contributions to the field of adult education. That was understandable. Was not the social worker, like the adult educator, "viewed as the person in the community who turns all human experience into grist for his educational mill"?[37]

An endowed Eduard C. Lindeman Professorial Chair in Social Philosophy honors the memory of Lindeman at the Columbia University School of Social Work.

CHAPTER 14

Adult Education and National Crisis

The Chinese, as they were developing their written language, may have been the first to articulate the concept that crisis might include components of opportunity as well as danger. It was a linkage to be tested by America in the 1930s and early 1940s as the nation confronted two massive challenges to its existence as a democracy, the Great Depression and World War II. Throughout all of this decade and a half, Eduard Lindeman tried to help Americans discover the role of adult education as a weapon of national survival.

By February of 1928 Roger Baldwin, just back from Russia, was again rooming with Lindeman at the apartment on Minetta Lane, but their arrangement would be temporary. Roger was scheduled to go to prison in Paterson, New Jersey, in late May. "You may remember," Eduard wrote the Elmhirsts, "that he is under sentence for six months for reading the Declaration of Independence from the court house steps. . . " Actually, it was a bit more complicated than that. The ACLU's founder had in fact asked the Paterson police to book him so that he could share the fate of members of the striking Associated Silk Workers union whom he had advised to read the Bill of Rights at city hall.[1]

In the meantime, Roger was entertaining himself and pleasing his roommate by "playing the piano beautifully." Lindeman would read his favorite poems and Baldwin would "compose the most delicate and fitting airs." While spending time in jail during World War I for failure to comply with the draft act, Roger had been entranced when an old lilac bush in the jailyard had burst into bloom. As far as Eduard could tell, Roger's only objection to returning to jail was that it would remove him from an enjoyment of spring in the outside world.[2]

By the fall of 1929, John Hader was spending considerable time with Lindeman at Greystone, driving over from the rural home he and Mathilda had acquired some twenty miles away. Often, Hader would stay overnight. The men ordinarily worked in Eduard's third floor crow's nest. They had decided to publish their research, most of it done under Inquiry sponsorship, in book form.[3]

The book was shaping up nicely, Eduard wrote Dorothy, "as a sort of continuation of *Social Discovery*." Success, he hoped, might be built upon earlier success. The working title for what would eventually be published as *Dynamic Social Research* was "Techniques for Co-operative Research." The two men knew they had good material. It was just a matter of getting it organized and presented in a way that would be useful.[4] What the two researcher-writers had not counted on was an apparently unrelated event that would occur on Wall Street in New York on October 24, 1929, even as they busied themselves with their project in Greystone's generous attic. It was an event that would not ignore them.

By 1931, when *Dynamic Social Research* was released by its publisher, the United States economy was in tatters. With more than six million unemployed, fear gripped the national psyche.[5] The nation was perhaps in need of dynamic social research, but it was hardly in the mood to read about it. The book hit with a thud and was unnoticed even by potential reviewers. John Hader remembers receiving only one $80 royalty check from the American publisher. There was eventually an even smaller return from the British version. The Haders took all of the money they had, some $500, and bought gold.[6]

More than fifty years would pass before Lindeman and Hader received credit for the work represented in *Dynamic Social Research*. In 1984, Charles D. Wrege and Sakae Hata produced a paper at a meeting of the Academy of Management stating that the work of Lindeman and Hader "represents one of the earliest studies of the interaction process in small groups." Previously, these researchers said, such efforts had been traced back only to the work of J. L. Moreno (1934), Kurt Lewin (1939), and R. F. Bales (1949).[7]

As the Depression deepened, it dragged Lindeman's mood with it. The extent of his concern is revealed by the evidence that his faith in democracy itself was being shaken. President Hoover's financial reconstruction bill had "restored some degree of confidence, especially in banking circles," but to Eduard, this seemed "an artificial remedy" for a much deeper disease. With the nation's four largest cities—New York, Philadelphia, Detroit, and Chicago—"bankrupt and unable to meet current expenses," municipal budgets were "now in the hands of bankers. . . ."[8] It was small wonder that the air was full of easy talk about revolution.

Incredibly, considering the suggestion came from the most democratic of men, Eduard believed that the "next logical step" would be "some mild form of dictatorship which will enable the government to operate by executive proclamation." He felt, however, that this could not come until after the approaching elections. "Coolidge is, of course, the only person the people would entrust with this power." Nonetheless, he believed, correctly as it turned out, that Hoover would be renominated by the Republicans. His prediction for the candidate of the Democrats: Al Smith. Newton Baker, he felt, could not be nominated because of his League of Nations and World Court convictions.[9]

Eduard had a good view of the Depression from his office window at the School of Social Work. Across the street was the relief employment office, where long lines of people formed each morning at daybreak in the hope of securing work.[10]

Was it partly the national mood of despair that caused so many Americans to respond enthusiastically to the sometimes discomforting, but still basically positive, messages of Eduard Lindeman the lecturer? He wrote Dorothy in early 1933 that he'd just returned from California, where he had lectured for five evenings for the State Educational Association on the general theme "Education in a Time of World Crisis." The audiences had been splendid, both in numbers and in quality of response. There had been three thousand at the first lecture and after that a steady attendance of four thousand. On the last night, Eduard had been kept on stage for three hours after the lecture, just answering questions. Especially satisfying to Lindeman was the fact that the local Chamber of Commerce and Better American Federation "were not quite so mean to me as they were on my former visit when the latter organization had interfered and tried to have me 'deported'. . . ."[11]

Eduard Lindeman had dramatic platform presence though he was not always an eloquent speaker in the usual sense of the term. He knew the techniques for reading and connecting with his audience. He varied the volume and tone of his voice, ranging from loud ringing statements to just above a whisper. Typically, he'd work from his current scrapbook—which might have been updated on a train that very afternoon. He would mark the desired places in the scrapbook with note cards.[12]

His message to each audience was essentially synthesis. There would be new syntheses constructed of old ideas. For every audience, the synthesis would be different, though certain subject-matter elements—the means-ends equation, democracy, and values questions—cropped up in almost every talk. Often he would begin with a statement about "confusions" which he would then proceed to analyze and clear up.[13] He spoke with conviction; he generally had the rapt attention of his listeners.

With the philosopher's traditional prerogative, Lindeman spoke on almost anything with authority. In 1928, at the Springfield, Massachusetts, Foreign Policy Association meeting, he debated J. Alfred Spender, an English journalist. Their topic: "Is Neutrality Possible?"[14] A Wallingford, Connecticut, audience may have been engrossed as it heard the visiting philosopher expound on "Courtship and Finding a Mate," in 1947.[15] In 1937, an audience in Washington, D.C., learned something from Lindeman about the Spanish Civil War.[16]

His first post–Pearl Harbor speech, in January 1942, was on "Civil Liberties in Time of War" to a meeting of the ACLU.[17] "What Makes Education Liberal?" was heard in Illinois on Charter Day 1946 at Rockford College (which had given Lindeman an honorary degree).[18]

His first recorded lecture on adult education, "Adult Education: A Creative Opportunity for Librarians," was delivered at the Southeastern Library Association meeting in Asheville, North Carolina, on October 16, 1924.[19] His last such talk may have been to a Convocation of the Board of Regents of the State of New York in Albany on October 26, 1951. The theme of the Adult Education Session where Lindeman gave the address was "Citizen Participation in Education."[20] There were many similar talks in the years between.

In his career as a lecturer, Lindeman helped Americans to ask the right questions. He also helped them in formulating answers, and his answers, even in a latter day, have the ring of truth. Thousands of Americans understood more about their country and about themselves because Eduard Lindeman went among them.

As she contemplated Eduard's growing fame, Dorothy must have taken some satisfaction in the results of her aid to this man. By helping him initially, she had launched a dynamic proponent for progressive change into the world, and that was always her basic objective.

Dorothy's solution to her earlier dilemma regarding continued salary support for Eduard was brilliantly imaginative. In essence, she stopped giving him money except for specific projects, though she continued paying Martha Anderson's salary so that Eduard would have reliable and essential administrative backup. But, as she did this, she put Eduard in charge of helping her give money away for causes in America.

Eduard was appointed chair of the advisory committee that would become the forerunner of the William C. Whitney Foundation. Other members (as of 1935) were Louise Croly, Ruth Morgan, George Soule, Vinton Lindley, and Anna Bogue.[21] Their task was that of investigating requests for money and advising Dorothy as to the decisions she should make. The committee's emphasis areas, which reflect Eduard's influence, were (1) experimental learning and (2) social education.[22]

As she reassessed her commitment to Eduard and others, Dorothy Elmhirst took a hard look at The Inquiry. For some nine years, The Inquiry had been a game of musical money for America's social reformers, and Dorothy was playing the piano. In 1929, the Inquirers were still in their chronic state of indecision as to what should be the future direction of the group. Lindeman, in a letter to Dorothy, may have been less than helpful when he expressed the belief that there "seem to be valid reasons for living up to our oft-repeated promises to come to a close." But then, "there seem to be also good reasons for going on."[23]

His suggestion for the future was essentially that The Inquiry should graduate from life to a kind of living death. Why not stop at the end of the year, Eduard proposed, but then "reorganize on a more modest scale, or . . . wait two or three years to learn whether or not the whole idea should be revived."[24]

Eduard wondered whether he was correct in thinking that the decision about whether or not to continue Dorothy's support "will be largely in the hands of our committee next year." If Dorothy did choose to pass the responsibility "to those of us who are on the ground," Eduard told her he would be presented with a difficult problem. Ned Carter, The Inquiry's harassed chief executive, wanted very much to continue in that role, "but I'm not at all sure that it would be good, even for him." Eduard concluded a long yes-no paragraph with what seems to have been a no. He felt "rather strongly that a great deal of clarification might result in a bold decision to bring just one organization voluntarily to an end."[25] In faraway Devon, Dorothy must have read this paragraph a number of times. What did he mean, really?

Dorothy's decision was that The Inquiry had served its purpose; her financial support was to be gradually withdrawn. Ned Carter began the slow process of liquidation. By early 1930, the task was almost complete. Carter asked Lindeman to edit a volume which would aim to evaluate the totality of the group's work. After some hesitancy—he rather dreaded this "most difficult task"—Lindeman accepted.[26] He produced a monograph that is the best surviving record of activity that left a permanent mark on American thought about adult education and a number of related subjects.[27]

Like many another organization with noble aims and supported by noble people, The Inquiry foundered upon the shoals of terminal chaos. It lacked the kind of cohesiveness that could bring stability. Its mission had never been much more than the pursuit of whatever causes its most assertive members viewed as important and timely. Given the talents, values, and pragmatic philosophy of its adherents, this was not necessarily a flaw. The thinkers had been thinking, and in due time the nation would benefit. From a latter-day perspective, a case can be made that Dorothy Straight Elmhirst got her money's worth.

With Dorothy's financial backing, Lindeman also produced in this period one of the first studies of organized philanthropy. But Eduard wasn't happy with the book since he had lost a battle with its publisher. They "damn them, finally dictated its form," so it was a reference book. "And, they are, no doubt, right!" the author told Charles Shaw, by now at Swarthmore. In any event, all the statistical tables were in and much of Eduard's prose was out.[28] Entitled *Wealth and Culture* and released in 1936, the book enjoyed quite a good sale—much better than expected in that Depression year. It got generally excellent reviews—far better and far more in number than *The Meaning of Adult Education* had garnered in 1926.[29]

By any standard, Eduard Lindeman was a success at his chosen work as his country entered one of its great crisis periods. But there were flaws, as his friends and colleagues knew. In a sentence, he spread himself too thin. Eduard Lindeman was a man who said yes to almost everything. His intentions were good, but the result at times could be greatly frustrating to those who had a right to expect a better response.[30]

The record carries scars that Eduard inflicted on himself and others because he was a poor manager of his time. Deadlines and even entire meetings might be missed. Tasks would be done late or would be unfinished altogether. His offices—at Greystone and in Manhattan—were strewn with years of old paper. The man who so often asked for—and received—the best from others could be incapable of delivering the best of himself simply because he had allowed himself to acquire a superhuman agenda.[31]

Eduard's habitual inattention to the details inherent in effective management of a task could drive Max Otto, his best friend in latter years, to near distraction.[32] Dorothy Elmhirst must also have become irritated when she heard criticism of Eduard's casual management of her American advisory committee from Louise Croly, among others.[33] Dorothy was forgiving—for a time. Eventually, even her store of patience wore thin—though she left no direct public record of it.

Interviewed after Dorothy's death, and Eduard's, Leonard Elmhirst underlined Eduard's importance in the life of his wife, but said that ultimately she had grown tired of his habitual disorganization. He was "always being bailed out."[34] By this he meant that commitments—such as that of doing the research and writing for what eventually became *Wealth and Culture*—could be prolonged for an eternity with attendant expense and annoyance for Dorothy.

Still, Eduard's capacity for work was gargantuan. In the Lindeman papers is a letter from a publisher for whom Lindeman was reviewing books. It begins: "I am ever so appreciative of your cooperation in sending us in so promptly your review of the ten volumes sent you last week."[35]

※

Times might be bad as the new year opened in 1933, but Eduard's fundamental mood of optimism remained unchanged though "superficially I am anything but hopeful, particularly about the immediate future." He believed—quite correctly as it turned out—that upcoming 1933 would be "our hardest year . . . we may have accommodated ourselves to a pain economy, and we shall keep people from starving." But in reaching this "level of subsistence," he felt the nation had lost something very precious—faith in itself. He was haunted by the fear that America would not grasp its "present opportunity to reorganize society and that therefore we shall drop down to an even lower level of mediocrity and uncreativeness. . . What is now needed is courage to experiment, and there we are timid, weak, hesitant, and filled with fears."[36]

Lindeman's flirtation with a "mild dictatorship" incarnate in a resurrected Calvin Coolidge presidency was short-lived as he joined millions of other Americans in enthusiastic support of a new president, Franklin Delano Roosevelt. He had direct ties to the New Deal through Roosevelt's chief lieutenant, Harry Hopkins, whom he knew through social work circles. In November of 1935 Lindeman accepted an offer of a job as director of the Department for Community Organization for Leisure, a division in the newly organized Works Progress Administration (WPA).[37] The core of the job was that of supervising the WPA's educational and recreational projects that were designed to put people to work at projects that would benefit local communities.[38]

There were some "perks" to the job, not least of which was occasional access to FDR himself. Lindeman became well acquainted with Eleanor Roosevelt as well and their paths crossed with fair regularity—often when they shared a speakers' platform.[39]

Eduard's empire, which he headed from his base in Washington, included some thirty-three thousand souls, all of them at work on "leisure time projects" and another thirty-nine thousand in the various arts.[40] Though he didn't enjoy "bossing," Eduard was now definitely a boss.[41]

One of Lindeman's adult education responsibilities was that of supervising the training operations of the National Youth Administration (NYA) at the national level. This meant developing training programs for both the agency's employees and local volunteers. Among Eduard's employees, hired in 1935, was a young Harvard graduate, Malcolm Knowles. Knowles remembers Lindeman helping him in 1936 to develop such programs through the Boston Recreation Training Institute. Lindeman's influence lingers in some of the course titles: "Recreation Philosophy, Organization, and Administration," "Forum and Discussion Group Leadership," and "Leadership Through a Neighborhood Approach." There was heavy emphasis on training instructors in use of experiential methods of instruction, especially discussion methods.[42]

Lindeman's collision with the ponderous civil service machinery began on the day he and Hopkins decided that his project would be called "Community Organization for Leisure." When that title was sent to the Treasury Department, the official in charge "very promptly sent it back and said there was no such language in the Government, they had never heard of such words and did not see how they could draw checks on the United States Treasury in the interest of such a project. . . ."[43]

Lindeman fell back to a more acceptable title, "Recreation and Leisure," but that led to further difficulty because Treasury insisted that a sharp distinction be made between "what was recreation and what was education." In an impish moment, Eduard wrote what was intended as an internal office memorandum, in which he said that "the easiest way to distinguish between recreation and education is this: if the chairs are fastened to the floor, it is education; if the chairs are movable, it is recreation."[44]

A legal advisor in the department—he was a man "wholly without humor," Eduard said—thought the definitions were serious and incorporated them into a procedure which was sent over to the Treasury Department. Eduard was now in great difficulty. " . . . I had to go over finally and apologize and get the definition extracted from Treasury literature."[45] (Contemporary educators may ruefully recognize the parallel between this episode and latter-day federal government insistence upon hours of classroom "seat time" as a criterion for determining whether veterans may qualify for financial aid for educational programs.)

If he was, to use his own words, "lacking in the essential gifts" necessary as an administrator, Lindeman as a WPA executive had ample opportunity to work as an adult educator.[46] His objective was always that of helping Americans work toward a democratization of the economic and social sectors that would be comparable to the democratized political sector in the United States. It was the lag in these second and third democratizations that created so many of society's problems.[47]

Though Lindeman would stay on with the WPA until 1938, he was never really happy in the job and was grossly miscast as a bureaucrat. He wrote Charles Shaw that his life was almost all action but with little sense of direction. Of course, he had wanted the experience of working with "a huge governmental mechanism" and it had been "grand discipline," but the satisfactions of the inner life were meager. "One's private life disappears the moment one enters the government service, and as I grow older it seems to me that significance attaches primarily to thought and not action."[48]

Just before resigning from government work, Lindeman wrote Marion Beers, a close friend, in a mood of despondency. "The bells no longer ring for the New Deal, at least I don't hear them, and I can't afford to stay long where there are no bells."[49]

His friendship with Hopkins, who was by this time Roosevelt's closest advisor, had cooled. Eduard and other colleagues from the past blamed it on Hopkins's second wife, wealthy socialite Louise Macy, whom they felt had led their friend in the direction of high society and away from his roots in social work.[50] It was with sadness, but also relief, that Eduard left Washington—a city he had once described as "unwholesome."[51]

❦

One of Lindeman's most sustained intellectual efforts during the latter portion of the era between the two World Wars was in the interest of adult education that could make possible a durable world peace.

Lindeman's interest in adult education as an instrumentality for assuring world peace gained momentum in 1926 when he went to Geneva to observe the League of Nations Disarmament Conference. He had a press ticket to the Assembly because of his connections with *The New Republic*.[52]

Lindeman agreed with Newton Baker, member of the Permanent Court of Arbitration at The Hague, when he announced that he would not favor leading the United States into the League of Nations except as the result of a longtime educational procedure. "When Mr. Baker affirms that there is a valid and an invalid method for bringing this country at last into The League, and that the former is based upon education and the latter upon coercion, he postulates a most significant principle. He views education, and particularly adult education apparently, as an alternative for force and coercion in the affairs of government."[53]

All of Lindeman's many messages to Americans and to the world about peace carry the assumption that adult education is vital within any effort at peacemaking or peacekeeping. A speech in 1942 before the National Peace Conference illustrates the views of a mature Eduard Lindeman on this subject.

In the midst of World War II, what should peaceloving Americans do that would prevent recurrence of the horrors of war? The basic problem was "how to bring about a genuine intellectual and moral conviction on behalf of world government that will withstand the tensions of crisis." Obviously, crisis would be ongoing even in the presence of world government and "some kind of basic security."[54]

Three alternatives, "all of them inadequate," presented themselves. The "Quaker testimony, which refuses to engage in all acts of war and all acts accompanying war, will not stand up in the face of total war." Neither would "Christian exhortation [be] sufficient for those dealing with functional problems."

Training youth so that "on reaching adulthood they will have pre-disposed attitudes" in the direction of peace "and behave accordingly is also impractical. . . ." Youth need to adjust themselves to an adult world. Unless "some corresponding change is made among adults there will not be enough liberals to bring about a liberal change."[55]

Needed: a "fourth alternative—some form of adult education with a practical conviction with respect to world government which would become deep-seated among opinion-making adults." The conference goers then listened as their speaker described who in particular should be educated for peace, what set of values was predicted, and what devices would be most likely to succeed.[56]

Who should be educated? Lindeman identified six groups as potentially "most influential": (1) business and professional men—"an important group, who are often cut off from opportunities for discussion and other methods of informal education"; (2) farmers, in part because they had disproportionate influence in the policy-making Senate; (3) trade unions, where the task would be formidable "because we have no background of experience in this field"; (4) religious bodies; (5) women in organized groups; and (6) organized consumer groups.[57]

What values would guide an adult education "mass movement" for peace? First, "order is better than chaos." This needed to be taught in "some new way in order to make a genuine intellectual as well as moral conviction since the behavior of the United States in the past twenty years falls short in the light of this value." Second, the "value of sacrifice." There might be dispute on this point from those who said that advantages to the individual and the nation, not sacrifice, should be emphasized "if we want the United States to enter into a world order. . . " Lindeman had more confidence in his fellow Americans, whom he believed would "accept some sacrifice in order to get a far-off gain, something even in the nature of atonement because of our large share in the responsibility for the course of world events."[58]

In 1939, after Hitler invaded Poland and caused Britain and France to declare war, Lindeman experienced "terrifying days" as he contemplated what lay ahead. He wrote the Elmhirsts, who were much on his mind, that he would "do whatever is needed" in spite of his continuing belief that "war is more futile now than ever." It was a world in which "logic no longer suffices. . . " It was a "pathological world," a world gripped by "a collective form of psychosis," and "only those who are prepared to view it as a sickness can find out what they have to do."[59]

Communists in Western countries, some of them, had been seriously disoriented by Stalin's pact with Hitler under which Poland had been divided between the two dictators. Others dutifully accepted the aggressive Soviet act and followed the Party line. American Communists, Lindeman told the Elmhirsts, were "behaving very badly" but had been effective nonetheless "in influencing the opinion of large bodies of youth, even those who have no sympathies with communism per se. Their present line in the colleges is to annoy the liberal teachers and to placate the conservatives." Lindeman had been "getting plenty of annoyance this semester. I simply cannot understand the logical processes which lead them to their so-called 'lines' of conduct." Toward some of the young Stalinists, he felt "a sense of pity." It was not uncommon, he said, to hear American Jewish Communists speak as if they hoped for a Hitler victory. "It makes no sense."[60] Indeed it didn't.

The Elmhirsts were having their own experience with communism. Dorothy's son, Michael Straight, had joined many of Britain's brightest young people in Marxist-led activities. Eduard wrote Leonard that Michael's "venture to the Left interests me very much." But the people who really worried him were the "middle-aged who go Communist all-of-a-sudden; the effect is startling, like religious conversion, and on the whole, so I believe, unwholesome." He presumed "our groping experiments to bring a better economic society into existence must be given labels and names, but I'm much more interested in the methods than the labels."[61] Michael would wait until 1983 to tell the world the spellbinding story of his bruising "venture to the Left," as Lindeman termed it.[62]

As the war became a disaster for the European democracies, the most peaceloving citizens took alarm. In once tranquil Devonshire, Dorothy took up rifle practice.[63] Nazi parachutists would not land at Dartington if she could help it.

Lindeman found himself driven away from any position that could accommodate the aims of Adolf Hitler. On August 13, 1941, a full four months in advance of Pearl Harbor, Lindeman received a letter from Bruce Bliven informing him of *The New Republic*'s plan to publish an editorial urging the nation to make an "immediate declaration of war"—a decision which was implemented in the publication's August 23 issue.[64]

In his response, Lindeman told Bliven he thought he understood something of the "anguish" undergone by the editors in taking such a position. "Ever since the fall of France I have also been moving steadily in this direction, not by reason of any predilection of my own, but solely by the logic of events." It was "a terrifying decision to make," but not to make it was "to reduce us as individuals and as a people to the level of sordidness." He "reluctantly but without any further reservations on the side of realism" agreed with the decision. He added that he believed FDR was hesitating "only because he is distrustful of the nation's unity and morale."[65]

Lindeman was always careful to separate his views about war from his views of conflict, which he perceived as healthy—and ripe with educative potential. "The dream of life minus strains, tensions, and conflicts is exactly that, a dream." The problem for the individual was not that of escaping conflict but rather that of "making certain that the conflicts which do engage our attention and energies move onward to higher planes."[66] "Jesus did not say 'blessed are they who run away from conflicts' [but] 'blessed are the peace-makers.' "[67]

It might even be true that the "best learning comes also from conflict." He told the Pennsylvania League of Women Voters that their organization "may be educative in an even higher degree when at election time it devotes itself to the precipitation of vital differences in issues, and to the cultivation of civic participation."[68]

Lindeman's views of adult education as the remedy—or more accurately the preventive medicine—for a nation in crisis were an extension of the brief note in *The Meaning of Adult Education* about political upheaval. If adults approached education "with the end-in-view that their new knowledge is to be the instrument of a probable future revolution, they will almost certainly defeat the very purposes of learning." But revolutions "are essential only when the true learning process has broken down. . . We revolt when we can no longer think or when we are assured that thinking has lost its efficacy. Revolution is the last resort of a society which has lost faith in intelligence."[69]

CHAPTER **15**

How Firm a Foundation? Adult Education for a Postwar World

For more than two hours, beginning at about 1:00 A.M., they came—hundreds of migrating birds. Their intended destination was Central and South America, but they got no farther than New York. One by one they slammed with dull thumps into stone, steel, and glass of the upper reaches of the Empire State Building.

Soon the sidewalks along Thirty-third and Thirty-fourth Streets and along Fifth Avenue were covered with them—some twelve species, eleven of them warblers, the other a red-eyed vireo. Many fell to setbacks or ledges of the building. Some dropped to the streets where they were run over by cars. The air around the building was filled with the sounds of mangled and dying birds still chirping.

Pedestrians, moved by the plight of those alive and injured on the sidewalks, tried to nurse them on the spot. Others picked up birds and took them to nearby restaurants or to their homes in the vain hope that food would revive them. A number of the still living birds were transported to an animal hospital.

It was a dense fog in the Hudson Valley that had caused the tragedy, according to the general curator of the Bronx Zoo. The birds had lost a sense of direction and so were drawn by the bright lights of the Empire State.

It was September 12, 1948, when Eduard Lindeman—the avid amateur ornithologist—clipped the account of this tragedy of the natural world from *The New York Times*. He pasted it in his scrapbook; alongside it he pasted another news item labeled "The New Turn in History" which was an excerpted paragraph from Arnold Toynbee's *Civilization on Trial*. It was Toynbee's explanation of the efforts across species "to create a new manifestation of life . . . " Such an effort "never succeeds at the first attempt . . . It wins its ultimate successes through a process of trial and error. . . " The "failure of previous experiments" did not necessarily doom subsequent experiments to fail in exactly the same way. On the contrary, it "actually offers them their opportunity of achieving success through the wisdom that can be gained from suffering." Western civilization might "commit social suicide. But we are not doomed to make history repeat itself; it is open to us, through our own efforts, to give history . . . some new and unprecedented turn."[1]

Adolf Hitler was dead; his Nazi thugs were dead or imprisoned. But Joseph Stalin was alive and posing an ominous threat to Western democracy. Eduard Lindeman was entering the last years of his life. Physically, he was failing. More and more time was being spent in hospitals or at home in bed. The years since World War II had not always been kind. The very foundations upon which he had built his life were being put to the most rigorous tests.

Lindeman's faith in adult education was severely shaken in the year immediately following the cessation of hostilities in Europe. In September 1945 he became one of the first American civilians to visit defeated Germany, in his role of consultant for education to the British Army.

He saw thousands of Germans without seeing even one smile. Along the roads were "empty, homeless people," many of them with pushcarts.[2] On October 21, Lindeman's party passed Camp Belsen, then mostly burned over, though the smell of decomposed human flesh could still be detected up to one-fourth mile away. Little boys with sticks were poking around in the remains of the camp. It was a "grisly, gruesome sight."[3]

Lindeman did not quickly shake off the horror of what he saw in Germany. On January 3, 1946, he spoke and answered questions on a radio broadcast of "America's Town Meeting of the Air." The other panel members: Gregor Ziemer, former head of the American School in Berlin; Leo Cherne, executive secretary of the Research Institute of America; and the "dean of American commentators," H. V. Kaltenborn.[4]

In his remarks on "Town Meeting," Lindeman cited Germany as the example of what happened when a modern nation "eliminates its sensitive and its humane leaders." In that event, "the degenerates come to the top and control." He had seen Camp Belsen, "that most efficient human slaughtering house." He had "looked into the faces of the officers of that camp as they were being tried at the Court House in Luneburg." He had "heard their shocking testimony . . . "[5]

To de-Nazify Germany, "we should stop placing faith in so-called good Germans." When he had landed in Germany, he looked for these good people and he found them, "but they are a whining, defeated, and a discouraged lot. They have lived in darkness for too long."[6]

To de-Nazify Germany it would also be necessary to "stop trying to teach democracy directly." There was no "soil in the German mind" in which democratic ideas could grow. "They look upon such teaching as nothing more than propaganda and consequently intensify their resistances."[7]

Lindeman published two articles about his 1945 visit to a prostrated Germany. "Death of a German Generation" appeared in *The New Republic*. "Inside the German Mind" was in *Saturday Review of Literature*. Both articles reveal his deep pessimism about the future of the German people.

To his readers in *The New Republic* he said he had "found not the slightest shred of evidence that Germans feel any sense of responsibility for the present world chaos." The ordinary Germans believed, he said, that Great Britain had started the war. Germans had merely fought a war of defense. [8]

The "materials and qualities" with which to create a genuine sort of community did not exist in present-day Germany. Hitler had "thoroughly destroyed the Germany which was . . . and [had] well-nigh achieved his boast of destroying Europe as well." The "utter physical destruction of the German cities" was nothing when compared to the "spiritual desolation" of the people. Through "hatred of themselves," the German people had "at least realized their collective death-wish . . . The corruption and degradation of living Germans is complete." If this was a "harsh judgment," Lindeman said, "so it is meant to be." [9]

Lindeman essentially wrote off the value of adult education as a tool of German reconstruction. The older generation of Germans was hopeless. It was the young, when they had "reached a level of liberal understanding," who should be given responsibility for the nation. But the older Germans were not to be entrusted with the task of teaching the young. " . . . German teachers equipped for this fateful task simply do not exist." New teachers would have to be trained, and while their "reconditioning" was in progress, teachers should be recruited from "other regions, especially from neutral countries." [10]

In the meantime, the armies of occupation could disarm the German nation. Technicians could help restore industrial and agricultural activity. But these were "simple tasks" alongside the more "difficult undertaking" which was that of making room for Germans "who will have no need of fear or hate or envy." This was the giant task, the task requiring the "highest sort of competence available . . . " The qualities needed were "those of an educator." [11]

Eduard Lindeman did not live to see the full economic and even moral resurrection of democratic West Germany. It would have been a pleasant surprise. The adult education instrumentalities, if any, of this feat are as yet unrecorded.

⁕

In 1949, Eduard and Hazel went to India, where Eduard had an appointment as visiting professor at the University of Delhi. En route, they would be visiting in England. There had been a long silence between the once warm friends, as Eduard noted in his letter to Dorothy and Leonard Elmhirst on June 15. Knowing "how deeply both of you have been in India in the past," he thought he and Hazel "might perhaps see you on the way." If that should be impractical, Eduard hoped that Leonard "might wish to send me some advice about India and perhaps suggest a few people I ought to see." [12]

It was Leonard, not Dorothy, who replied with a brief and overly correct letter. He and Dorothy were to be at the International Conference of Agricultural Economists at Stresa in Italy in early September when the Lindemans would be passing through. However, he was to be in India himself in November and December and hoped to see them then. He said he had a brother there "who is head of the Air Force." Other than that, he did not know many Indians in Delhi, "except the Premier." [13]

As he invariably did while traveling in foreign countries, Lindeman jotted in his scrapbook some of the more interesting questions asked him by various audiences. Former Vice President Henry Wallace was challenging Harry Truman for the Democratic Presidential nomination that year. This fact triggered a barrage of questions from students at Indian universitites. Is Henry Wallace to be compared with Gandhi? Have you ever been close enough to him to be able to touch him? Will the wicked millionaires who conspired against him ever be tried and punished? [14]

Other questions were equally distinctive. Is it not true that your moral geniuses, Emerson, Thoreau, and Ingersoll are now regarded as imbeciles? Is it not true that American culture begins with seeing half-naked Hollywood stars? In communist countries there is security of food. Nobody starves. In democracies there is never a moment when somebody does not die of starvation. So, what is wrong with communism? [15]

Before leaving India, the Lindemans were invited with seventeen others to dine with Prime Minister Jawaharlal Nehru. Another American, the Nobel prize physicist Arthur Compton, was also there. [16]

As the time drew near for his retirement, Eduard found himself passing through "most peculiar moods," a sort of disengagement. Issues which seemed important to his colleagues left him completely uninterested. In spirit, he'd already left the School of Social Work. Only when teaching did he feel at home. "What a funny profession this teaching business is," he told Max. [17]

In his mid-sixties, Lindeman was not really old. He still possessed a commanding presence. Yet his physical deterioration was by now marked. He had the pallor associated with nephritis in its terminal stages. His blue eyes were sunken in their sockets. He looked ill, and he was. [18]

In the last three years of his life, Lindeman was hospitalized five times. [19] Still, as a veteran of serious illness, he understood that there were "compensations." In 1950, he wrote Charles Shaw, who was recovering from an operation, "There is something deeply humanizing about an operation, at least so it was with me . . . " [20] Often he would feel as though he were "walking across a narrow bridge, not too sturdy. Now and then the bridge would shake and tremble and I wasn't quite sure that I'd reach the other side. Then there came a time when the going became smoother and I could actually see the other shore, and knew I'd make it." He knew that Charles, with his "sinewy and wiry constitution," would soon be "better than ever, if that's possible." [21]

By this time, their family grown, Eduard and Hazel had left Greystone. Home in those days was an apartment at 235 East Twenty-second Street in lower Manhattan. [22] Near Gramercy Park, it was a cozy, pleasant place—filled from time to time with happy sounds of grandchildren.

Eduard officially retired from the faculty of the School of Social Work on September 30, 1950. [23] The couple's retirement home would remain New York—certainly not Florida, where so many of their peers in age were trekking. Though he and Hazel vacationed there every year beginning in the late 1930s,[24] Eduard grew to hate "that monstrosity called Florida. . . What I mean," he told one of his audiences, "is that they have ruined the natural beauty of the state. It used to be a paradise for the naturalist, but that is almost finished now, and if they keep on they will ruin it completely." [25]

What worried him also was the aggregation of thousands of aimless, querulous, old people who presented something less than an inspiring vision of adult learning in retirement years. "I have never seen such awful people in my life. Miami just gives you a nightmare; there are people with leisure and with no sense of dignity at all." He had listened to them talk while sitting in the parks at Daytona Beach and in St. Petersburg. It was "tragic . . . They talk mostly about other people they hate [and] a great deal about their diseases . . . " [26]

And how they crowded meetings. At one of these, a forum, Eduard spoke. It was a bright Sunday afternoon and the crowd numbered about five thousand. "Most of them should have been outdoors . . . " They came to the forums not to learn, just to fight. The "smart young people" who directed the question periods at the forums were a "new breed and a very disagreeable breed to me. If you do not precipitate a fight they will precipitate one. They think it is not a successful meeting unless they have everybody fighting." [27] This was not Eduard's idea of adult education for senior citizens.

Eduard could, and often did, incite insurrections, but how he did hate a nasty little fight. It seemed as if the whole world was filled with "snarling contentiousness." As he wrote Max, people "seem to want terribly to hurt each other." Eduard felt as if he were living on "a small island called Humane surrounded by a sea called Hate." Max should forgive the awkward figure of speech. His friend was grasping for "a simile with sharp edges." [28]

His retirement, though it seemed a "queer experience" at times, got off to a good start. Eduard settled in for a semester of teaching as visiting professor at the University of Kansas City in the fall of 1950. The undergraduates in his classes were a different breed from the students he'd been used to in New York. He found them eager, on the whole intellectually honest, but unsophisticated. Their backgrounds were "meager," but what they lacked in a general orientation, they seemed to make up in willingness to work. He found it necessary to revise his materials, but he assesssed that as a good thing for him. [29]

Hazel was taken in and kept busy by the faculty wives. She was having a good time. It was a sociable community and the two dined out frequently. [30]

Lindeman published two books during his brief retirement years. *The Democratic Way of Life*, coauthored with T. V. Smith, came out in February 1951. Eduard told Charles Shaw he wasn't very happy about it. He was pleased, however, that his edition of *Plutarch's Lives* was selling well. "You never can tell what this here crazy American public will buy." He had recently lectured at Stevens College in Columbia, Missouri, on "The Cultural Contribution of Low Cost Books." [31]

Given his array of interests and his professional stature, the latter years of Lindeman's life could have been good ones. But fate had plans that were less than benign for Eduard in these years. His health was precarious, and he was forever having to withdraw from or change plans on that account. But his most distressing crisis was to be professional, not physical. The state of Wisconsin had produced one of Eduard's best friends; it would also produce a mortal enemy. Lindeman, the democratic man, in his last years was to become one of Joseph McCarthy's indirect victims.

In the pleasant and clean little city of Eau Claire in northwestern Wisconsin, Lindeman encountered an incident that heralded something of what lay ahead. The local Roman Catholic hierarchy objected to the presence on a local platform of an "atheistic Communist" who favored birth control. There was an aggressively hostile clique in his audience. Lindeman could handle tough and even sharply worded questions, but these were mean-spirited and threatening opponents. [32] Eduard was soon to learn more about the growing McCarthy phenomenon.

The Civic Federation of Dallas is one of the oldest adult education councils in the nation. [33] Its programs, including open forums, adult classes, and a library, were already well established by the time Lindeman first participated as a speaker and teacher at the Federation in 1932. He became one of the Federation's most popular outside speakers and became great friends with many on the board and staff of the organization, especially with Elmer Scott, the organization's founder and executive secretary. [34]

When he was scheduled to speak or work with the Civic Federation of Dallas, Lindeman would frequently accept invitations to speak to other groups in Texas as part of the visit. There had been many such arrangements during the two decades of the 1930s and 1940s. A similar visit to Texas was scheduled by Lindeman in the fall of 1951. But it soon became apparent that this would not be just another pleasant visit to well-known and friendly territory. In fact, it was not going to be a visit at all.

Lindeman was scheduled to speak first before the Rotary Club in Orange, Texas. There would then be a needed day of rest (he had been seriously ill), [35] followed by an appearance at the Texas State Teachers Association (TSTA) meeting at the Rice Hotel in Houston.

He was to participate as part of a panel presentation on "Citizenship and the Three R's." [36]

But Houston's American Legion Post No. 52 and other groups had differing plans for the TSTA conference than were then being discussed by Eduard Lindeman and the panel's moderator. A letter signed by William H. Dalton of Houston was being distributed among Texas school administrators and newspapers. It began with this sentence: "Why should Texas Teachers be addressed by Communist Fronters and intellectuals with Socialist leanings?" The writer went on to accuse two speakers for the upcoming TSTA conference as possessing "actual Communist Front records as revealed by official files . . . " A third speaker, Eduard Lindeman, was described as a "controversial educator who is a notorious advocate of 'Progressive Education' which is the entering wedge of Socialism in our school systems." There were a multitude of other charges. [37]

"Most all of the speakers selected to address the T.S.T.A. convention," Dalton's letter continued, "belong to the 'Progressive' school of academic thought, a system which is concerned mainly with stressing the social attitudes, social living, and social outlooks. The tools used to change the American concept of education are 'workshops' which stress human relations, propaganda for World Government and the Welfare State." [38]

Even adult education got a pasting: "Under the new educational concept adults as well as children must come under the control of the school. Originality is suppressed, leadership is advocated only when necessary and FOLLOWSHIP is accepted procedure." [39]

What could readers of the letter do? They could "PROTEST" to TSTA's president and executive secretary. They could also "PROTEST" to "your local school superintendent" and finally, they could "PROTEST" through "your local newspaper." [40] And PROTEST they did.

The pressure quickly built, especially upon the TSTA's president, Dr. Mortimer Brown, who was superintendent of schools at El Paso. Early in November, he sent Lindeman a telegram: "Due to circumstances that have arisen a readjustment of the program has been made . . . " [41] Circumstances, indeed. Lindeman's invitation to speak was summarily cancelled.

The *Dallas Morning News*, for one, was gleeful. In an editorial entitled "They Will Not Speak," the paper commended American Legion Post No. 52 for their action. The writer cited Lindeman as "well known in New Deal activities, including a prominent post with Works Progress Administration." Lindeman had "associated himself with a wide range of organizations and activities, some of which are certainly on the list of subversives . . . As a man who has lent his name right and left, let us say, his absence from the Houston program is not a cause for great public regret." [42]

Among friends who learned of the cancellation, there was warm support. Elmer Scott declared himself "terrified" in a letter to Mortimer Brown. For this letter, Scott had fashioned a unique letterhead: "THIS IS AMERICA—*NOT* RUSSIA." [43] Another supporter, Laura Brannin, wrote the *Morning News* itself, pronouncing them guilty of "a shocking piece of character assassination."

What was the truth about Lindeman's "subversive activities"? A detailed response to the American Legion refuting the charges against both Lindeman and another panelist, Ethel Alpenfels, was prepared—apparently by Elmer Scott or the ACLU.[44] But Lindeman's best defense against what became a cumulative nation-wide attack on him by the American Legion came in a letter written in February 1953 just before his death. Addressed to Joe R. Hoffer, executive secretary of the National Conference of Social Work, Lindeman (then the NCSW president) responded to an American Legion article, apparently accusing him of being a Communist, that had been sent to Hoffer by a Legion member in California. Referring to the sender of the article, Lindeman wrote Hoffer, "You might tell him this:

> I was the first president of the Americans for Democratic Action of New York State. As you know, this organization came into existence in order to exclude Communists from liberal political action. It was and is definitely anti-Communist in every respect. I have been since its organization a board member of Friends of Democracy which is also, as you know, dedicated to the struggle against totalitarian systems of both the Left and the Right. I have been for years a director of the American Civil Liberties Union which was the first large national, liberal organization to exclude Communists. In other words, I have always been opposed to Communism.
>
> In order to make matters more explicit, I shall now state my chief reasons for being an anti-Communist: (1) on philosophical grounds I belong to the American tradition of pragmatism of which William James and John Dewey were the chief exponents. This philosophy is experimental and non-authoritarian and is definitely opposed to the dogmatic German philosophy of Hegel, out of which Marxism arose. (2) On moral grounds I am opposed to Communism because it teaches the immoral doctrine that good ends may be achieved through the use of evil means; it practises conspiracy and falsehood and thus, through the employment of such means, produces gross immorality; (3) I am a believer in cultural pluralism while Communism advocates cultural uniformity. I believe in

diversity because I believe in freedom . . . (4) I believe in what may be called the Judeo-Christian ethic which is founded upon the conception of human brotherhood and love. Communism, on the contrary, preaches hate and conflict. There are many other reasons for opposing this malevolent movement which has perverted so many millions but the above are fundamental.

There are various ways of conducting the struggle against Communism and I have chosen my way. It is not that of the witch-hunter who confuses the situation by calling people who are liberals Communists. I am extremely careful to avoid betraying our basic American tradition of freedom. My loyalty to the Bill of Rights is unwavering. On that account I tolerate a wide range of free expression, even of ideas which are repugnant to me. My sentiment was beautifully expressed . . . by Adlai Stevenson in his Jefferson-Jackson Day dinner speech when he said: 'Our farms and factories may give us our living. But the Bill of Rights gives us our life. Whoever lays rough hands upon it lays rough hands upon you and me. Whoever profanes its spirit diminishes our inheritance and beclouds our title to greatness as a people.' " [45]

In concluding this letter—among the last as well as the most eloquent that he ever wrote—Lindeman said that he was "of course deeply disturbed by this new attack upon me and I do hope you will not be made to suffer on my account."

The foundations still held. With this statement Lindeman laid on the line the bulwarks of his life.

There had been other unpleasantness. In 1952, McCarthy's local legions tried to prevent him from fulfilling a teaching commitment at Lewis and Clark College in Portland, Oregon. The charges were the usual—atheism, socialism, and even progressive education. The college president wanted to cave in, though the faculty did not—and ultimately Lindeman was allowed to proceed. But his heart was no longer in it; it was a struggle to get through the sessions. [46]

There were others, however, who did not share in the national mood of madness. For its twentieth anniversary celebration in 1953, the New York Adult Education Council collected letters of tribute from individuals and organizations that had some adult education tie with Lindeman. Many of the tributes paid him are more substantive than would be usual to satisfy ordinary standards of courtesy. Some thirty-eight of them were in the form of letters from adult education–related organizations ranging from the Department of the Army in Washington to the Young Women's Christian Association National Board. [47]

Writing for the Women's Trade Union League, Rose Schneiderman wished "we had a million like you." Her fellow unionist David

Dubinsky, president of the International Ladies' Garment Workers Union, congratulated Eduard for being "just the opposite of the polysyllabic professor" in making his contribution to workers' education. Moreover, he was "not misled by the dangerous Stalinist illusions of short cuts to progress by dictatorship."

"You are the very best listener I know," Bessie Sharp of the New York Adult Education Council told Eduard. "Your participation in Association on American Indian Affairs leadership for some fifteen years was one of the cornerstones on which this citizens movement built its strength to serve the American Indian minority," said Alexander Lesser, executive director of the association on American Indian Affairs.

The letter signed by Paul Essert, Wilbur Hallenbeck, and Ralph Spence, all of Teachers College at Columbia University, was addressed to Dr. Eduard C. Lindeman, "Adult Education Father."

These messages came in just the nick of time, for Eduard would soon enter the land of dust and shadows. The specter of death that had stalked Eduard Lindeman for so many years found its quarry on April 13, 1953. He had been deathly ill for months, but from his bed in Harkness Pavilion of New York's Columbia Presbyterian Medical Center, he fought back at Joseph McCarthy. Among his last words to family members were these: "This is a beautiful country. Don't let the demagogues spoil it. Promise me you won't." [48]

It was at about 4:30 A.M., just as dawn was breaking, that Eduard Lindeman's tortured body released his impassioned spirit. [49]

CHAPTER 16

Eduard Lindeman's Agenda for Lifelong Education in America

Dorothy Elmhirst's friend Ruth Morgan entertained a "mixed group" of about twenty at dinner in her New York home on March 14, 1929. Eduard Lindeman was one of them. Each guest was asked to tell what he or she thought the next social revolution would be like. [1]

For Bruno Lasker, it would be the revolt of the consumers. Chester Rowell said an industrialized China would precipitate the next great world change. Lindeman had a bit of difficulty in deciding what level of change to select, so he mentioned three: (1) "the rise of urbanism, or the decline of rural culture in western civilization," (2) "the consequences of the quantum and relativity theories, or rather the new implications of science—which seem to point toward a universe far less ordered than we had all along been led to expect," and (3) "the new conception of education and its ultimate results." [2]

The new concept of education that he meant was life-centered adult education spanning a lifetime, as he had described in *The Meaning of Adult Education*. Lindeman's prescience with respect to developing concepts in a world he would not live to see is almost instantly recognizable to anyone who reads such later twentieth century books as *Megatrends* by John Naisbitt and *Future Shock* and *The Third Wave*, both by Alvin Toffler.

The "reconceptualized" education that Naisbitt describes sounds very much like the adult education that Lindeman outlined in 1926. Like Lindeman, Naisbitt starts with a base in pragmatism, with Mary Parker Follett's law of the situation. When the situation changes, so must the individual change and adapt. Of course, the process of reconceptualization must itself be constant. [3]

Toffler's "third wave" also involves a reconceptualized education. More learning is expected to occur outside the classroom. There will be no more "rigid age segregation." "Education will become more interspersed and interwoven with work, and more spread out over a lifetime." [4]

Toffler, too, identifies a trend toward education outside the classroom and a need to "combine learning with work, political struggle, community service, and even play." [5]

Toffler's third wave workers are not narrowly vocational either, that is, trained for "highly repetitive work." On the contrary, they need to be capable of "discretion and resourcefulness rather than rote responses." [6]

Lindeman abhorred runaway specialization, the coronation of the expert. Toffler's third wave citizens will have to "think like generalists, not specialists." [7]

Adult education at its best begins with a situation, not a subject—a Lindeman axiom and a building block for Toffler as well. Asserts Lindeman: "There is no lasting, satisfying method of adjustment [to contemporary culture] which is not at bottom a form of education." [8] Toffler's version of this idea: So much effort goes into teaching such courses as "the structure of government or the structure of the amoeba. But how much effort goes into studying the structure of everyday life—the way time is allocated, the personal uses of money, the places to go for help in a society exploding with complexity?" [9]

Lindeman shared with both futurists a view of adult education as an instrument for adjustment to the new world, of shortening "cultural lag," which he defined as "the distance between our technological advances and our cultural values." Unless this were done, a progressive society could not be sustained because it would be burdened with a large group of people who were "unequipped for change." [10]

No one can remain contemporary by relying on what was learned in the years of youth. But Lindeman defined learning as something more than an adjustment to the present. There was always a "futuristic factor in true learning." [11]

There were three components, really, those of "exploring the past, living the present and preparing for future contingencies." "The accelerated tempo of modern life" [these words were penned in 1926] demanded more concentration on "future contingencies." An individual, while engaged in "solving the contemporary problem" looks ahead "in the direction of the imminent situation. We are engaged in a continuing rehearsal for a drama in which we know we are destined to play a part, but a drama which has not yet been written. To the extent that a bare outline of the 'plot' is discernable, we can conduct our rehearsal in an atmosphere of realism." [12]

Lindeman and his fellow pragmatists were among the first to develop ideas of education based on the assumption that modern society was inherently unstable—in a condition of constant transformation. In this environment, it was not enough to find ways to disseminate knowledge. The crucial task was that of finding ways of "releasing intelligence," of helping individuals acquire the capacity for understanding change and integrating it in the pragmatic sense. [13] Learning how to learn became explicit as the pathway for persons in search of their full human potential.

Charlotte Demorest, quintessential volunteer and later director of the board members in the Education Department of the Federation of Protestant Welfare Agencies, was one of the first to call Eduard Lindeman "the father of adult education in the U.S.A." [14] The label is overly broad. It implies a more extensive influence over the whole realm of adult education than Eduard Lindeman has had.

What can be said without question is that Lindeman was the earliest major conceptualizer of the progressive-pragmatic tradition in American adult education. Taking John Dewey's ideas about education, Lindeman added generous doses of Waldo Emerson and Nikolai Grundtvig to synthesize Deweyan progressive education for application to adults. It is this tradition that is still mainstream within the world of adult education in the United States in the latter days of the twentieth century.

Eduard Lindeman's work has received international recognition as well. Lindeman's *The Meaning of Adult Education*, though it had been out of print for more than three decades, was selected in 1960 as the first in a series of books issued in response to the "Montreal Declaration" on adult education at the UNESCO World Conference on Adult Education. Lindeman's little volume was selected because it "breathes the same spirit and illuminates the same theses as does the Montreal Declaration." [15] In his preface to the new edition, J. Roby Kidd noted that the "capital of ideas" operative in adult education was "*universal* but it became common currency through the voice and writing of Lindeman." [16]

Lindeman's particular genius was that of synthesizing. He lived, as Ordway Tead has said, "in the House of the *Interpreter*." [17] Lindeman did not have original ideas of the sort that flowed from an Emerson, Grundtvig, or Dewey, but he was unexcelled as an adapter and polisher of ideas that spilled out of these philosophical giants. Eduard Lindeman was one of the first Americans to think systematically and extensively about adult education. There were, of course, gaps and occasional tangles in his thoughts and his logic. But upon Lindeman's foundations many others have found sure footing.

Lindeman also deserves credit for his work in bringing Americans to a qualitative and fresh conception of the whole learning process. Moreover, he urged them toward a *conscious* recognition of the entire learning system experienced by human beings. There was traditional school-based learning, but there was also an informal learning system. Though this system clearly existed, it was grossly underused as society encouraged and rewarded only formal subject-based learning. Learning directed toward the highest aspirations of individuals as human beings was thereby ignored or even devalued. Lindeman made a substantive contribution when he made explicit that which was too often implicit in the minds of work of others.

Taking Lindeman seriously means taking a leap of faith. Lindeman's faith was that a society will be happier, more prosperous, and more productive if its individuals are free to learn on their individual agendas and on their own terms. And they *can* do it on their own, thank you, with sensitive instructional guidance provided by persons who function more as learning facilitators than as traditional teachers.

Lindeman's chief disciple and advocate in contemporary America is Malcolm Knowles. Taking Lindeman's four most basic assumptions about adult education, Knowles adapted them as building blocks for his own work, though he stated them differently (and perhaps more clearly from a contemporary perspective). Knowles has also extended Lindeman's philosophy as the foundation for making institution-based programs more suitable for learning by mature adults.

Lindeman said essentially that (1) education is a process coterminous with life, (2) adult education revolves around nonvocational and nonacademic ideals, (3) the approach to education should be via the route of situations, not subjects, and (4) the resource of highest value in adult education is the learner's experience.

Knowles's version, as stated in *Andragogy in Action*, is that (1) the adult learner is "self-directing," (2) "adults enter into an educational activity with both a greater volume and a different quality of experience from youth," (3) "adults become ready to learn when they experience a need to know or do something in order to perform more effectively in some aspect of their lives," (4) adults "enter an educational activity with a life-centered, task-centered, or problem-centered orientation to learning," and (5) "the more potent motivators" for adults are "internal—self-esteem, recognition, better quality of life, greater self-confidence, self-actualization, and the like." [18]

Near the end of his career, Eduard Lindeman was still in the process of deciding just what adult education was. He chose the odd setting of a propaganda broadcast to Nazi Germany to bring the world up to date on his latest thinking on the subject. There was, he said, a "cluster of confused conceptions" in the United States with respect to the definition of adult education. For many, adult education meant "an opportunity to acquire as an adult the education one should have enjoyed as a child." Others thought of adult education as "a discipline for foreign-born citizens who are at the moment being Americanized." Still others regarded "all forms of informal vocational training on the part of adults as adult education." [19]

Lindeman told his German audience that some order was coming out of the conceptual chaos. "At any rate, when one now hears the term used by educators it appears that they mean something quite specific and distinct from other varieties of education. They mean learning for those adults who are free to choose what it is they wish to learn; learning for adults who no longer care about academic credits but who are anxious to understand the world in which they live; learning for adults who realize that they cannot be good citizens in the present world unless their education is continued throughout life; learning for adults who wish to engage in social action but who also insist that such action should be based upon knowledge and reason." [20]

In short, Lindeman was still defining adult education as life-centered, rather than subject-centered, learning. And its meaning was still pragmatically imprecise.

If he was inexact—deliberately so—with definitions, Lindeman was not comfortable, either, with goals. He was actively hostile to development of goals except as linked to methods given equal, even superior, importance. There was "but one supreme and constant goal" that could guide the educator, namely "the *harmonious development of personality*, 'the nurture of the human spirit,'" growth for the individual. There might be "many subsiding goals" enjoying a short-term span of attention, but it was "a grievous error to confuse these minor strivings with the major purpose of education." [21]

At this juncture, Lindeman's philosophy becomes a problem for behaviorists in the tradition of B. F. Skinner and others oriented toward programmed instruction and design. They tend to be critical of Lindeman's generalities and what is perceived as inattention to the details of instructional design. They might fault, also, Lindeman's unwillingness to prescribe more directive efforts by the adult educator.

To accept Lindeman's progressive-pragmatic philosophy, therefore, one must make a leap of faith in the direction of assigning value to the *process*, or means, of learning that is at least comparable to the value given to the ends of learning. To the pragmatist, the self-actualizing individual multiplied by millions would make a better America. It is not just what is being learned that is important; it is the learning of it that is socially, as well as individually, desirable.

Accordingly, Lindeman never issued an "agenda for lifelong education" and would hardly have approved of any extension of his philosophy toward development of fixed or terminal goals. It is possible, however, to extract from his work the precipitate that constitutes guidelines—or at least a kind of checklist—for today's educators who wish their practice to follow the Lindeman tradition. The guidelines are proposed with the underlying assumption that Lindeman's principles can be applied to improve the existing school-based learning system, as well as to strengthen the informal life-driven learning that was the focus of what Lindeman called "adult education."

Boiled down to its essentials, the agenda can be stated as it affects respectively (1) the adult learner, (2) the curriculum, (3) the teaching-learning transaction, (4) the institutions and agencies of adult education, and (5) the public policy governing education. Often the words can be Lindeman's own.

About the adult learner:

1. *Life-centered adult learning opportunities of every type should be available and easily accessible to every citizen in a democracy.* This includes fully employed adults, the elderly, women, minorities, everyone. Whatever is "dormant in the humblest individual must be sought out, released and put to useful tasks. Every individual normal life must not only count for something but must become thoroughly cognizant of the fact that he or she counts." [22]

2. *All learners or prospective learners have the right to participate in determining the content and method of learning.* Adult education is undertaken *with* the learner; it is not something done *to* or *for* an individual.

3. *Adult education should develop, as well as serve, continuing learners.* Learning how to learn and to continue learning is as important as learning a particular subject matter. "An educated person," Lindeman said, "is one to whom a valid learning method has become so natural and congenial that he applies educational method to all the affairs of his experience." [23]

4. *Ease of access to adult learning opportunities should be the right of every citizen.* Lindeman would be pleased at efforts to improve access—late afternoon and evening classes, weekend colleges, external or extended degrees, off-campus programs, independent study programs, education through television or other electronic means.

About curriculum:

1. *Value distinctions between credit and noncredit programming should be removed.* Credit and noncredit programs may be different, but the quality of programs in either category should be measured in terms of performance in meeting the needs of adult clients. Adult educators should be "alert to discover what activities give joy to particular students [and] be on the watch to uncover temperamental hobbies, pursuits which may seem ludicrous to others but which to the doer bring peculiar satisfactions. Indeed, adult education will have justified itself if it does nothing more than make adults happier in their hours of leisure." [24]

2. *Life situations should be tapped as the starting point for adult learning.* Crisis situations, or "tensions" as Lindeman termed them, are in reality educational opportunities. [25] Adults should be approached about learning opportunities that are related to their life stage problems and opportunities—marriage, parenthood, divorce, occupational changes, midlife crises, etc. The beginning point for such efforts on the part of the learner would be: What sort of a situation is this which confronts me? [26]

3. *Societal problems should trigger associated adult education programs.* Lindeman said adult educators working through small groups should begin "where the people's worries begin . . . [27] Unemployment, racial tensions, environmental pollution—every type of problem should be attacked with relevant adult learning programs. The task of the adult educator is to see that citizens participate intelligently in problem-resolution endeavors associated with those factors in modern life around which their activities circulate.

4. *Adult educators should build into their programs components designed to serve the values of democracy.* True adult learning cannot be accom-

plished in the absence of freedom. Freedom requires democracy. Therefore a kind of tithe for the support of democracy should be offered by the adult education enterprise.

5. *Subject-based educational programs should be modified or adapted to better serve the needs of adults.* Lindeman would approve of individualized majors, external degrees, contract learning, credit for prior life or work learning.

6. *Social action programs should have adult education components.* Behavioral change is the objective of social action movements. Behavioral change can come through adult education. Any group of individuals organized under democratic conditions should feel free to use adult education as an instrument to further its objectives.

7. *Vocational education should be designed around needs that the learner believes to be important.* Lindeman is unjustly accused of denigrating vocational education. He instead urged that vocational instruction not be imposed from above; here, too, the teaching-learning transaction should be democratic territory.

8. *Adult learning programs beginning with the assumption that learning should follow from life, rather than subject-matter, orientation should be instituted.* Americans have been so indoctrinated with the subject-first approach that is is hard for them even to understand an approach that is life-centered. Subject-matter learning need not, and should not, be denigrated, but a parallel approach with equal resources should be tried.

9. *Process is part of curriculum.* As Malcolm Knowles has pointed out, learning is "more efficient if guided by a process structure (e.g., learning plan) than by a content structure (e.g., course outline)." [28]

About the teaching-learning transaction:

1. *Experience-rooted learning is the essence of a teaching-learning transaction involving an adult; experience should be employed in every possible way in learning situations of adults.* The teacher must be an expert at the task of identifying relevant experience that will be useful in the learning situation.

2. *Resources, in and out of traditional education setting, should be identified and used to facilitate learning.* In a sense, this is a corollary of the foregoing statement bearing on the learner's experience. Human and physical resources that inhabit the learner's world can be employed as instruments to facilitate new understandings.

3. *Good questions from a teacher are better than facile answers.* Lindeman cast his teaching within a constantly interrogative context.

Growth can be facilitated by teaching methods that emphasize continuous inquiry.

4. *Programs that recognize the validity of experience-based learning should be encouraged and supported.* Lindeman would undoubtedly be excited by the efforts of Morris Keeton and others to develop protocols for systematically assessing and recognizing the educational value of prior experiential learning in higher education and other settings.

5. *The teaching-learning transaction should be considered democratic territory.* [29] Adult learners have rights and responsibilities that are comparable and reciprocal to those of the instructor or learning facilitator. The traditional conception of "teacher" is abjured and replaced by the concept of the teacher who is learning facilitator or consultant. The learner's experience counts as much as the teacher's knowledge. Both are "exchangeable at par." [30]

6. *Individualized instructional arrangements should be encouraged.* Learning contracts are sound conceptually. So are independent learning arrangements. Lectures are not ruled out, but the main task of the teacher is that of teaching "the art of experience-eliciting and use." [31] And the intended audience would "reserve the right to select both him and his subject." [32]

7. *The lecture system of instruction should be deemphasized in favor of more interactive methods.* The lecture will find its principal use where an audience is known to have little prior knowledge of the subject being presented. Even then, lectures should be followed (or interrupted) by questions and discussion.

8. *Wherever possible, arrangements should be made for adult learners to have lively interchanges with fellow learners.* In one sense, discussion is to adult education what the scientific method is to science. Also, individuals enjoy the opportunity to educate each other. [33]

9. *The methods of evaluation in programs of learning toward self-actualization must be internal, not externally imposed.* Adult learners need to learn how to evaluate their own success or failure. Grades, examinations, and related evaluation associated with school-based programs should not be used in programs where learning is undertaken because it bears a specific relation to one's life. [34]

10. *Volunteers are a valuable resource in adult education programs and should be used where possible.* Without their use, adult education will "tend to become less democratic in goals and methods." Some examples of good volunteers for various purposes: "the college graduate with skills once used but no longer in use . . . the college graduate with no professional skills . . . the prestige person who is over-used . . . the person who actually knows how his community

operates, the nature of its 'plot' . . . " [35] Adult education can often begin in a community through an institute designed to train board members and other volunteers.

11. *Adult educators should use the democratic political process as a vehicle for facilitating education of the electorate.* Lindeman believed in adult educators and citizens working within the political parties of their choice. He was also intrigued with the potential educational value of third political parties. The "function of a third party is to educate the electorate; it serves its function well if it helps to clarify those muddled issues which the older parties have avoided or reduced to degrading compromises; it serves its purpose well if it gives the older parties a lesson in good sportsmanship and political decency; and finally, it serves its purposes well if it succeeds in polling a vote sufficiently large to serve as a warning to the public officials that the people are awake, that they do not propose to allow blind allegiance to party to lead them to the betrayal of their country." [36]

12. *Andragogical concepts should be built into existing formal systems of education that serve adults.* Any program serving adults, whether school-based or not, will be improved if it incorporates methods tailored to the learning styles of adults.

About institutions and agencies of education:

1. *Institutional policy should recognize the links between theory and practice.* Adult education theory should guide and enlighten practice. Practice should be allowed to refine theory. The policies of adult education institutions and agencies should not lead to rigid separation of theory from practice.

2. *Institutional arrangements should facilitate adult learning.* Classes should be held at night, on weekends, and at other times convenient for prospective adult clients. Educational institutions should carefully review their policies respecting registration, admission, student government—all facilities and services—to see that there is no discrimination against adults.

3. *Institutions or organizations not having education as a chief interest should nonetheless explore starting or improving an educational arm.* Since human beings can and do learn everywhere—on the job and at play as well as in traditional educational settings—every institution in society is a potential learning resource. Lindeman was a pioneer in urging libraries to assume an active role in programs of adult education. Libraries, he said, "will never become potent centers of learning until more space is provided for human beings than for

books." The library ought to have rooms "where small groups of people might meet for discussion classes, not lectures." Knowledge was most likely to become assimilated "if it is sought at the time when actually needed to solve a problem." If adults could study in an environment of books, "the information which books contain might enter consciousness in normal and permanent fashion." [37] It follows that librarians should be classified as educators of adults.

4. *Nonacademic institutions "aiming to meet the needs of adults who seek to learn, not for the purpose of capturing 'credits' but for the sake of expanding their personalities and illuminating their lives . . . ought to multiply."* Lindeman cited the New School for Social Research in New York as a good example of this approach—though he cautioned that even such "new" institutions might become "dull and stereotyped." The "genius" of adult education lies in "a wide collaboration between all agencies of enlightenment." [38]

5. *Adult education institutions and agencies should take seriously their responsibility for providing adult learning and programs bearing on community development.* Lindeman once proposed the idea of a "democracy clinic" sponsored by an adult education program in each community. Its purpose would be that of formulating "a series of tests or criteria which would be applied in relation to every proposed community project." It would be staffed by a group of trained persons plus an equal group of "laymen." [39]

6. *Adult education councils representing agencies and institutions for which adult education is either a whole or a partial function should play the "gad-fly" role in prodding "public and private agencies to do more adult education."* Such organizations should also act as "pressures" on administrative and legislative bodies for the purpose of securing more adequate financial support for adult education." [40] There should, in short, be an adult education lobby.

7. *Organize adult learning where adults are.* Most adults are already organized in many ways and may not need further organization around an institutional base. The best adult education sponsor may not be an institution at all. Voluntary organizations, committees, discussion groups of all kinds may present learning opportunities that are unrealized. [41]

About public policy governing education:

1. *Adult learning should be voluntary.* [42] Adults learn best what they want to learn and are ready to learn. Forced adult education, like forced democracy, is a contradiction in terms.

2. *The formal, credit-based system of education should not be emphasized at*

the expense of noncredit adult education. Public policy should reward adult learning of every kind. A learning society is a happy, healthy society.

3. *Public policy should encourage learning for its own sake or learning aimed at flexible, learner-identified goals.* There should be reexamination of educational policies that identify "success" solely in terms of achievement of narrow, rigidly defined, or terminal objectives.

4. *Public policy should encourage development of adult education arms of many types of organizations and institutions.* Adult learning should be facilitated through employers, clubs, museums, libraries, every type of societal group entity.

5. *Public policy should explicitly recognize adult education as the chief instrument of democracy.* A democratic government cannot safely assume that democratic values will prevail in the absence of a healthy system of adult learning that facilitates the democratic process itself.

6. *The national government should encourage the development of curricula and programs designed to promote learning associated with world peace.* It is possible, as well as essential, for citizens to learn how to make a just, orderly, and peaceful world—to bring about a genuine intellectual and moral conviction on behalf of world government that would withstand the tensions of crisis. "The only reliable instrument for establishing confidence among nations is adult education." [43]

7. *Adult education should be explicitly identified as an essential component of programs aimed at conflict resolution.* Lindeman identified racial tensions, for example, as a problem that might be resolved with "a minimum of violence and a maximum of reasonable understanding" through adult education. [44]

What is the status of Lindeman's agenda for lifelong education vis-à-vis the agendas of the educators of today? Are they aware of it? If so, is it relevant for them now?

Certainly it is easier than it used to be for adults to secure learning opportunities in the realm of *noncredit* programs. Life-centered adult learning has blossomed in a host of ad hoc, as well as institutional, settings. American adults, at least those who reside in fair-sized cities, who want to learn something that will enable them to live a richer, fuller life can probably find the opportunities.

Mainstream educators, however, are still likely to dismiss such programs as "non-college-level" or "noncredit," with the emphasis always upon what they are *not* by definition. There is less inclination in such circles to explore and appreciate the life-centered values that may be at the very core of such educational endeavors. This attitude is reflected in public policies that subsidize or otherwise encourage credit course programming while ignoring or even discouraging development of life-centered courses and programs at public institutions. Such policies may also have produced an environment in which low-quality life-centered programs become the standard.

Lindeman's agenda is also evident wherever agencies and institutions not having education as a primary responsibility have taken responsibility for adult education. In Lindeman's day—and with his encouragement—this direction was being taken by public libraries. Today a host of providers—including businesses, employers, clubs, associations, churches, the military, and various governmental units—directly or indirectly sponsor educational opportunities of all kinds. It is not always necessary to "go to school" to advance one's education.

Lindeman's concept of the teacher as facilitator of learning, rather than imparter of knowledge, is being brought into clear focus by two contemporary phenomena. First, teachers are finding it impossible to impart information in any significant way from a knowledge base that is increasing at an explosive rate. Second, the task of information storage and disbursement is being taken over by machines. Through programmed or mediated instruction, students can now acquire information without directly consulting a teacher.

What the assortment of machines cannot do is provide an environment that is supportive and encouraging beyond what is possible in a purely mechanistic sense. This role remains in the domain of the teacher. Increasingly, the role of the teacher in situations involving adults is becoming that of helping the student learn how to learn.

Eduard Lindeman did not, in any specific way, propose that his adult education ideas be applied to traditional subject-based degree programs. He might be pleasantly surprised that his ideas about adults as learners have made incursions, however modest, into traditional degree programs at some American postsecondary education institutions. No longer is it virtually impossible for adults to acquire postsecondary education while holding jobs and managing family responsibilities. At a few institutions there are degree programs especially designed for mature adults.

Change has, however, been slow in coming and uneven in its progress through the sclerotic channels of institutionalized education. More classes may now be taught in late afternoon and evening hours, but often the instructional approach to the new adult learners differs not at all from what is given to learners in the traditional eighteen-to-twenty-five-year age range. Problem-solving learning and teaching situations that truly take into account the advantages of adult learner experience are all too rare.

There is a further great glaring gap—and one that would deeply trouble Eduard Lindeman. That is the lack of recognition of adult education as the chief instrument, the lifeblood, of democracy. The promise of America, Lindeman believed, is that of "progress toward freedom by means of education." But this is a fragile thrust in the face of antidemocratic forces if the adult education dimension of the educational enterprise is not recognized and nurtured. [45]

Whatever else might be said about the democratic way of life, Lindeman believed that "democracy and education are inseparable. Where the people are consulted, where the governed are also the governors, the people must be informed." American citizens must be educated to realize their responsibilities and duties. "The price they must pay for the freedom democracy grants is informed citizenship." [46]

The future of democracy, he said, depended in a genuine sense upon adult education. The key word of democracy was participation. It was the task of the educator to see that citizens' participation in decision making was intelligent. The government of a democracy had a responsibility to provide opportunities to learn how to participate intelligently. Consequently education, *including adult education,* should be tax supported.[47]

Lindeman's audiences were invariably reminded of their democratic responsibilities, but they were never left with the idea that democratic practice was easy. "Democracy is neither a goal nor a gift. On the contrary, it is an exceedingly difficult mode of life that emerges as a result of certain kinds of experience and which places upon its participants an unusual form of responsibility." [48]

It was the responsibility of adult educators "to understand the causes and consequences of confusion among citizens . . . " It was also the function of adult educators "to aid the citizen in dispelling his confusions and in preparing him for a high level of participation in public affairs." [49] In his own time, Lindeman was not sanguine about the ability of existing adult education programs to accomplish this task. He was "profoundly dissatisfied" with most of them, which did not "seem to be directed toward the increase of social feeling nor toward joint problem-solving." [50]

It follows that Lindeman would be comparably disturbed at the lack of a strong social action commitment among large numbers of American adult educators. To him, adult education was "not merely education of adults," it was "learning associated with social purposes." Wherever adult education had been "utilized as an instrument for social change, as in the Scandinavian countries," learning had "invariably been accompanied by a redirection of social aims and values." [51]

It was the "complete objective of adult education . . . to synchronize the democratic and the learning process." The adult learner was "not merely engaged in the pursuit of knowledge: he is experimenting with himself; he is testing his incentives in the light of knowledge; he is, in short, changing his habits, learning to live on behalf of new motivations." [52]

If the Lindeman agenda is to be taken seriously and its promise fulfilled, who will take on the job? Are contemporary adult education programs any better fitted for task at hand than were their forebears?

For nearly all of its history in the United States the adult education movement has been marginal as compared with the largely school-based elementary, secondary, and higher education enterprise. Adult educators generally have been consigned to peripheral roles. There are a number of reasons for this, but most of them stem from two notions that are thoroughly ingrained in the American psyche. These are that (1) education is for the young and (2) the only education that is worth anything is school-based.

But events are overtaking the traditional purveyors and spokespersons for institutionalized American education. Already, more than a third of college students in the United States are twenty-five years of age or older. [53]

These new learners are demanding opportunities that meet their educational needs as adults. They want educational opportunities that can lead to career change. They want job retraining when their jobs disappear because of societal or economic change. Displaced housewives want educational help as they enter the labor market. It is *life situation* change that is bringing this great demand. Eduard Lindeman's adult education that begins with situations rather than subjects exerts a powerful appeal to this new generation.

Reduced to its most common denominator, the Lindeman agenda spells out a society that values learning for its own sake. Learning itself is a national treasure. It follows that the person who learns will be highly valued by the nation.

It is good news for a society when an individual wishes to learn something—provided it's not Burglary 101. Such learning would not need to be "job related." Such an arrangement already exists in the agreement negotiated by the Norwegian employers association and trade unions in that country. All jobs under its provisions must include both opportunities for continued learning and must be "compatible with a desirable *future*, irrespective of prospects for promotion." [54] In the United States, the Ford Motor Company's recent agreement with the United Auto Workers for a life-centered learning program supported by the company bears watching. In philosophy, it is consistent with Lindeman's ideals.

Eduard Lindeman was a social philosopher—a breed he characterized as generally caring about human beings. Such persons strove to include "factual material taken from the social sciences as basic components" of their thought, and sought "appropriate avenues for social change." There was "nothing inherently incongruous in the social philosopher who is also a social actionist." In fact, it was "practically impossible to play the role of social philosopher without assuming at times the hazards of social action." [55] Facts, values, and actions needed somehow to be blended. He was always irked at the idea that theory was somehow separate from—even opposed to—practice. For him, philosophy was the most practical of subjects.

During his lifetime, Eduard Lindeman wrote or edited some 12 books and approximately 406 journal articles. He also gave dozens of speeches each year. A review of this prodigious outpouring reveals the existence of eight basic themes or ideas about or affecting adult education. These are as follows: (1) adult education is a process coterminous with life, (2) experience is the most potent resource for learning, (3) means in education are related to and are as important as ends, (4) diversity among individuals in a learning situation may be a source of strength, (5) adult education is the chief instrument of the democratic process, (6) the scientific method is applicable in problem-solving associated with adult learning, (7) adult education has important social action dimensions, and (8) mindless specialization is antithetical to humanistic adult education endeavors. These themes still occupy the attention of thoughtful Americans, and the proposals that Lindeman advanced within each of the categories have stood well the tests of time.

What might happen—if Lindeman's dream of lifelong education for all Americans were implemented—if any man or woman could learn or try to learn anything, any way, at almost any time—if schools were only a part of the resources available for such learning—if gratification of each individual's educational aspirations, no matter how idiosyncratic, were an unquestioned right of any individual in the society?

And what if there were systematic attention to these concerns—as evidenced by societal commitment of resources and rewards comparable to those now lavished on a school-based, credentialized, youth-oriented system? Would it work? Would it make a better world?

No one knows. It's never been tried.

Notes

Short forms for some author/title references have been used; e.g., the short form used for Eduard Lindeman's *The Meaning of Adult Education* is "Lindeman, *The Meaning*, 1961." A more complete reference incorporating the repository is given for those unpublished materials that do not fit such general headings as "Scrapbooks" or "letters" between two major figures in the narrative.

ABBREVIATIONS OF ARCHIVAL REFERENCES

AHC/MSU: Archives and Historical Collections, Michigan State University, East Lansing, Michigan.

BLC/SWHA/UM: Betty Leonard Collection, Social Welfare History Archives, University of Minnesota, Minneapolis.

DHT: Dartington Hall Trust, Totnes, Devon, England.

DWSEP/OL/CU: Dorothy Whitney Straight Elmhirst Papers, John M. Olin Library, Cornell University, Ithaca, New York.

ECL/SWHA/UM: Eduard Christian Lindeman Collection, Social Welfare History Archives, University of Minnesota, Minneapolis.

ECL/RBML/CU: Eduard C. Lindeman Papers, Rare Book and Manuscript Library/ Columbia University, New York.

MOP/WSHS: Max Otto Papers, Wisconsin State Historical Society, Madison, Wisconsin.

Chapter 1. *A Fresh Hope Is Astir*

1. Lindeman, *The Meaning* (1961) 4–5.
2. Lindeman, *The Meaning* (1961) xxx.
3. Eduard Lindeman to Charles Shaw, August 1926.
4. Lindeman, *The Meaning* (1961) 3.
5. Lindeman, *The Meaning* (1961) 19.
6. Lindeman, *Rotary* (1935) 378.
7. Lindeman, *The Meaning* (1961) 35.
8. Lindeman, "Evaluating" (1953) 18.
9. Lindeman, *The Meaning* (1961) 4–7.
10. Lindeman, "Radical Democrat," (1942) 5.
11. Ilsley, "Relevance," in *Proceedings* (1983) 125 [as cited by Brookfield, "Contribution" (1984) 186].

Chapter 2. *Understanding America's Adult Learning Movement at Its Roots*

1. Cross, *Adults As Learners* (1981) 255–260.
2. Patten, "University Extension" (1894) 265.
3. Lawton, "Extension's Apologia" (1895) 87.
4. Sheats "Bridge" in Dave, *Reflections* (1975) 21–26.
5. Stubblefield, "Emerging Paradigms" (1985) 64.
6. Hesburgh, Miller, and Wharton, *Lifelong Learning* (1973) 7.
7. Higher Education Act of 1965, Title I, Part B, Section 132.
8. Cross, "Learning Needs" (1980) 5–6 [unpublished].
9. Lindeman, review of Yeaxlee, *Spiritual Values* (1926) 96.
10. Yeaxlee, *Lifelong Education* (1929) 27.
11. Yeaxlee was greatly ahead of his time in his examination of terms. In *Lifelong Education* (London: Cassell and Co., Ltd., 1929), he noted that the term "educare" was used by Latin scholars to describe the process of mental growth (page 28). This term has enjoyed fleeting use in the late twentieth century, usually as an alternative to lifelong learning or lifelong education. Also in *Lifelong Education* (on page 51), Yeaxlee used the term "lifelong learning," far ahead of its general use elsewhere.
12. *Dictionary of Scientific Biography* (1975) 504.
13. Carelli, "Foreword," in Dave, *Foundations* (1976) 9.
14. Dave, *Foundations* (1976) 51–52.
15. Lindeman, *The Meaning* (1961) 109.
16. Lindeman, *The Meaning* (1961) 38.
17. Lindeman, *The Meaning* (1961) 105.
18. Annual Report AAAE (1926–1927) 4.
19. Lindeman, "Experience" (1926) 546.
20. Lindeman, "Meaning of Adult Learning" (1929) 37.
21. Lindeman, *Encyclopedia of Social Sciences* (1930) 463–464.
22. Lindeman to Michigan Council, 11 November 1947.
23. Lindeman, "After Lyceums" (1927) 246.
24. Houle, *Patterns* (1984) 55.
25. Lindeman, "Scrapbook 1944 and early 1945" (The quote is from Thoreau, *Walden*, 110).
26. Hart, *Adult Education* (1927) 168.
27. *Encyclopedia of American History* (1982).
28. Landon, *Lake Huron* (1944) 148.
29. Additional and significant pieces of the puzzle of Eduard Lindeman's childhood and youth have been located by Betty Lindeman Leonard who is assembling them as part of a forthcoming biography of her father.
30. Roger Baldwin, interview with Betty Leonard; Eleanor Von Erffa, interview with author.
31. Malcolm Knowles, interview with author.
32. Eleanor Von Erffa, interview with author; Flora Thurston Allen, interview with Betty Leonard.
33. Fedör Dostoevsky, *Notes from Underground*, as cited in Alfred Kazin, "The Self as History: Reflections on Autobiography," in *Telling Lives: The Biographer's Art*, ed. Marc Pachter (Washington: New Republic Books/National Portrait Gallery, 1979) 74.
34. Eduard C. Lindeman to Dorothy Straight, 10 September 1925.
35. Flora Thurston Allen, interview with Betty Leonard.

36. Lindeman, "Vacations" (1944) 16–18.
37. Lindeman, "Recreation" (1923) 211.
38. Frank Karelsen, interview with Betty Leonard.
39. *New York Times*, 23 August 1950.
40. Gessner, *Democratic Man* (1956) 18.
41. William Collins, interview with Betty Leonard.
42. Sally Ringe Goldmark, interview with Betty Leonard.
43. Lord, *Agrarian Revival* (1939) 35.
44. Beal, *Michigan Agricultural* (1915) 105.
45. *Wolverine* (1910).
46. Lord, *Agrarian Revival* (1939) 35.
47. Beal, *Michigan Agricultural* (1915) 103.
48. Kuhn, *Michigan State* (1955) 240–241.
49. Kuhn, *Michigan* (1955) 238.
50. *New York Times*, 23 August 1950.
51. Flora Thurston Allen, interview with Betty Leonard.
52. Gessner, *Democratic Man* (1956) 22.
53. *Wolverine* (1911).
54. *Wolverine* (1911).
55. *Wolverine* (1910).
56. *Holcad*, 23 November 1909.
57. *Holcad*, 27 January 1910.
58. *Holcad*, 10 April 1911.
59. *Holcad*, 9 January 1911.
60. *Holcad*, 5 June 1911.
61. *Holcad*, 19 September 1910.
62. *Holcad*, 20 March 1911.
63. *Holcad*, 22 May 1911.
64. *Holcad*, 27 February 1911.
65. *Holcad*, 20 February 1911.
66. *Holcad*, 5 June 1911.
67. Patterson, Commencement Address (1911).
68. *Wolverine* (1908).
69. *Holcad*, 24 March 1910.
70. *Holcad*, 23 November 1909 and 6 February 1911.
71. Lindemann, *College Characters* (1912).
72. Konopka, *Eduard C. Lindeman* (1958) 24.
73. Lindeman, *Boys' and Girls' Clubs* (1919).
74. Eduard Lindeman to Charles Shaw, 22 June 1926.
75. Herbert Croly to Eduard Lindeman, 17 November 1927.
76. Wells, *Treasury of Names* (1946).

Chapter 3. *Young Man in a Hurry*

1. Kuhn, *Michigan State* (1955) 153.
2. *Jubilee Wolverine*, Class of 1908, unpaged.
3. Beal, *Michigan Agricultural* (1915) 426.
4. Gessner, *Democratic Man* (1956) 21.
5. *Holcad*, 27 April 1909.
6. *Holcad*, 25 May 1909, and Betty Leonard, conversation with author.

7. *Holcad*, 3 October 1910.

8. *Holcad*, 30 January 1911.

9. *Holcad*, 23 October 1911.

10. Konopka, *Eduard C. Lindeman* (1958) 26.

11. Gessner, *Democratic Man* (1956) 22.

12. Lindemann, *College Characters* (1912) 12.

13. Lindemann, *College Characters* (1912) 46–47.

14. Gessner, *Democratic Man* (1956) 22.

15. Ruth O'Neil, conversation with author.

16. *Lansing State Journal*, 30 August 1912.

17. King, *Mustard Tree* (1964) 7.

18. King, *Mustard Tree* (1964) 19.

19. Fran Garlieb, letter to author, 17 June 1983.

20. Fran Garlieb, letter to author, 17 June 1983.

21. *M.A.C. Directory*, 1914–1915.

22. Kuhn, *Michigan State* (1955) 242.

23. Kuhn, *Michigan State* (1955) 242.

24. *55th Annual Report*, 89.

25. Lindeman, *Boys' and Girls' Clubs* (1919) 7.

26. *57th Annual Report*, 172.

27. Lindeman, "Legislature" (1915) 163.

28. *58th Annual Report*, 159.

29. Lindeman, "Rural Culture" (1924) 329.

30. Lindeman, "Rural Culture" (1924) 329.

31. Betty Leonard, conversation with author.

32. *Detroit News*, 17 October 1932.

33. *Detroit News*, 17 October 1932.

34. Content in this and the succeeding descriptive paragraphs relating to the personality and appearance of Eduard Lindeman is drawn (unless otherwise indicated) from the author's interviews with John Hader, Mathilda Hader, Herbert Hunsaker, Malcolm Knowles, Michael Straight, Stephen Gessner, and letters from (and conversations with) Betty Leonard; from Betty Leonard's interviews with Susan Pettis, Hester Turner, Bradley Buell, and Marion Beers; from Miriam Stewart's interview with Martha Anderson; from Alexander Charters's interview with Wilbur Hallenbeck; from a letter from Robert Hollowell to Eduard Lindeman, 15 December, 1931; and from Demorest, "Mountain in the Molehill," 18–20.

35. Eduard Lindeman to Charles Shaw, 22 January 1926.

36. Bradley Buell, interview with Betty Leonard.

37. Bonaro Overstreet, interview with author.

38. John Hader, interview with author.

39. *Association College Bulletin*, August 1919, 5.

40. *Association College Bulletin*, December 1918, 19.

41. *Association College Bulletin*, August 1919, 5.

42. *Association College Bulletin*, December 1919, 11.

43. Eduard Lindeman to Harriet McGraw, 7 July 1919.

44. Eduard Lindeman to Harriet McGraw, 15 July 1919.

45. Eduard Lindeman to Harriet McGraw, 15 July 1919.

46. Eduard Lindeman to Harriet McGraw, 25 July 1919.

47. Eduard Lindeman to Harriet McGraw, 25 July 1919.

48. Eduard Lindeman to Harriet McGraw [August 1919?].
49. Eduard Lindeman to Harriet McGraw [August 1919?].
50. Eduard Lindeman to Harriet McGraw [August 1919?].
51. Eduard Lindeman to Harriet McGraw [August 1919?].
52. Eduard Lindeman to Harriet McGraw [August 1919?].
53. Eduard Lindeman to Harriet McGraw [August 1919?].
54. Eduard Lindeman to Harriet McGraw [August 1919?].
55. Eduard Lindeman to Harriet McGraw [August 1919?].
56. Eduard Lindeman to Harriet McGraw, 21 July 1919.
57. Konopka, *Eduard C. Lindeman* (1958) 31.
58. Gessner, *Democratic Man* (1956) 24, and undated manuscript fragment in "E.C. Lindeman Manuscripts, A–I," Box 12, ECL/RBML/CU.

Chapter 4. *Another World*

1. Levy, *Herbert Croly* (1985) 5.
2. Levy, *Herbert Croly* (1985) 11.
3. Young, *The Elmhirsts* (1982) 54.
4. Leonard Elmhirst, "Croly Correspondence," DWE Gen. 2, DHT.
5. Roger Baldwin, interview with Betty Leonard.
6. Bliven, September 1947, DWSEP/DMUA/CU.
7. Levy, *Herbert Croly* (1985) 293–299.
8. Lindeman, "Cooperation in Tobacco" (1922) 44–45.
9. Herbert Croly to Dorothy Elmhirst, 23 June 1924.
10. Levy, *Herbert Croly* (1985) 278, 281; Eduard Lindeman to Dorothy Elmhirst, 24 November 1928.
11. Eduard C. Lindeman to Dorothy and Leonard Elmhirst, 24 November 1928.
12. Abrahams, review of *Herbert Croly*, *Washington Post* (1985).
13. Swanberg, *Whitney Heiress* (1980) 3.
14. Adams, *Henry Adams* (1961) 347–348.
15. Swanberg, *Whitney Heiress* (1980) 5.
16. Swanberg, *Whitney Heiress* (1980) 186.
17. Swanberg, *Whitney Heiress* (1980) 217.
18. Swanberg, *Whitney Heiress* (1980) 234.
19. Nicholls, *Ultra-Fashionable Peerage* (1904) 11–19.
20. Young, *The Elmhirsts* (1982) 46–47.
21. Michael Straight, interview with author.
22. Swanberg, *Whitney Heiress* (1980) 327.
23. Michael Straight, interview with author.
24. Young, *The Elmhirsts* (1982) 195.
25. Young, *The Elmhirsts* (1982) 45.
26. Straight, *After Long Silence* (1983) 20.
27. Croly, *Willard Straight* (1924) 409–411.
28. Swanberg, *Whitney Heiress* (1980) 341.
29. Swanberg, *Whitney Heiress* (1980) 342.
30. Young, *The Elmhirsts* (1982) 55.
31. Levy, *Herbert Croly* (1985) 212.
32. Swanberg, *Whitney Heiress* (1980) 469–470.
33. Swanberg, *Whitney Heiress* (1980) 447.
34. Swanberg, *Whitney Heiress* (1980) 144, 226; Betty Leonard, conversation with author.

35. Swanberg, *Whitney Heiress* (1980) 227–228.
36. Swanberg, *Whitney Heiress* (1980) 223.
37. Robert L. Johnston to author, 12 May 1983.
38. Michael Straight, interview with author.
39. Swanberg, *Whitney Heiress* (1980) 392.
40. Michael Straight, interview with author.
41. Mary Bride Nicholson, conversation with author.
42. Swanberg, *Whitney Heiress* (1980) 277.
43. Swanberg, *Whitney Heiress* (1980) 450.
44. Dorothy Straight to Leonard Elmhirst, 24 September 1921.
45. Dorothy Straight to Eduard Lindeman, 11 September [1924?].
46. Michael Straight, interview with author.
47. Michael Straight, interview with author.
48. Betty Leonard, conversation with author.
49. Michael Straight, interview with author.
50. Anna Bogue to Leonard Elmhirst, 8 June 1929.
51. Michael Straight, interview with author.
52. Herbert Croly to Dorothy Straight, 23 June 1924.
53. Herbert Croly to Dorothy Straight, 23 June 1924.
54. Konopka, *Eduard C. Lindeman* (1958) 32.
55. Eduard Lindeman to Dorothy Straight, 19 July 1922.
56. Malcolm Knowles, interview with author.
57. Harrington, "Function of the Kidney" (1971) 19–22.
58. Betty Leonard, conversation with author.

Chapter 5. *The Social Action Dimension of Adult Education*

1. Lindeman, "Meaning of Adult Learning" (1929) 37.
2. Lindeman, *The Meaning* (1961) 101.
3. Lindeman, *The Meaning* (1961) 104.
4. Lindeman, "Sociology" (1945) 10.
5. Lindeman, "Sociology" (1945) 10.
6. Lindeman, *The Meaning* (1961) 105.
7. John Hader, interview with author.
8. Lindeman, *Social Education* (1933) 207–226.
9. Lindeman, *Social Education* (1933) 183.
10. Lindeman, *Social Education* (1933) xix.
11. John Hader, interview with author.
12. Lindeman, *Social Education* (1933) 28.
13. Lindeman, "Evolution" (undated, unpublished) 7.
14. Lindeman, "Evolution" (undated, unpublished) 1–2.
15. Levy, *Herbert Croly* (1985) 244, 248.
16. Chambers, *Seedtime of Reform* (1963) 133.
17. Chambers, *Seedtime of Reform* (1963) 105.
18. Lindeman, "Inquiry Principles" (1929) 101.
19. Lindeman, "Inquiry Principles" (1929) 101.
20. Lindeman, "Inquiry Principles" (1929) 101.
21. Lindeman, "Inquiry Principles" (1929) 101–102.
22. Lindeman, "Inquiry Principles" (1929) 102.
23. Lindeman, "Inquiry Principles" (1929) 102.

24. Lindeman, "Inquiry Principles" (1929) 102–103.
25. Lindeman, "Inquiry Principles" (1929) 103.
26. Herbert Croly to Dorothy Straight, 18 November 1924.
27. Leonard Croly to Dorothy Straight, 9 July 1924.
28. Leonard Croly to Eduard Lindeman, 3 November 1926.
29. Michael Straight, interview with author.
30. Levy, *Herbert Croly* (1985) 202–203.
31. Herbert Croly to Eduard Lindeman, 21 February 1927.
32. Levy, *Herbert Croly* (1985) 199; Herbert Croly to Eduard Lindeman, 25 January 1927 and 21 February 1927.
33. Lindeman, "Adult Education" (1928) 26.
34. Lindeman, "Adult Education" (1928) 26.
35. Lindeman, "Adult Education" (1928) 27.
36. Lindeman, "Adult Education" (1928) 27.
37. Lindeman, "Adult Education" (1928) 27.
38. Lindeman, "Adult Education" (1928) 27.
39. Lindeman, "Adult Education" (1928) 28.
40. Lindeman, "Adult Education" (1928) 28.
41. Lindeman, "Adult Education" (1928) 28.
42. Lindeman, "Adult Education" (1928) 28.
43. Lindeman, "Adult Education" (1928) 29.
44. Lindeman, *Social Education* (1933).
45. Lindeman, *Social Education* (1933) xv.
46. Lindeman, *Social Education* (1933) xvi.
47. Lindeman, *Social Education* (1933) 195.
48. Lindeman, *Social Education* (1933) 200.
49. John Hader, interview with author.
50. John Hader, interview with author.
51. John Hader, interview with author.
52. John Hader, interview with author.
53. John Hader, interview with author.
54. John Hader, interview with author.
55. John Hader, interview with author.
56. John Hader, interview with author.
57. John Hader, interview with author.
58. Eduard Lindeman to Dorothy Elmhirst, 2 January 1933.
59. Chambers, *Seedtime of Reform* (1963) xi.
60. Chambers, *Paul U. Kellogg* (1971) 44–45.
61. Bradley Buell, interview with Betty Leonard.
62. Eduard Lindeman to Dorothy Straight, 5 July 1924.
63. Eduard Lindeman to Dorothy Straight, 5 July 1924.
64. "Farmers and Tradespeople," 28 June 1924.
65. "Farmers and Tradespeople," 28 June 1924.
66. Eduard Lindeman to Dorothy Straight, 5 July 1924.
67. Eduard Lindeman to Dorothy Straight, 5 July 1924.
68. Eduard Lindeman to Dorothy Straight, 5 July 1985.
69. Eduard Lindeman to Dorothy Straight, 5 July 1924.
70. Betty Leonard, conversations with author.
71. Betty Leonard, conversations with author.
72. Betty Leonard, conversations with author.

73. Betty Leonard, conversations with author.
74. Betty Leonard, conversations with author.
75. "Scrapbook (1932–1933)," 10.
76. Lamson, *Roger Baldwin* (1976) 10; Betty Leonard, interview with author.
77. Roger Baldwin, interview with Betty Leonard.
78. Betty Leonard, interview with author.
79. Betty Leonard, conversations with author; Stephen Gessner, interview with author; Michael Straight, interview with author.
80. Louise Croly to Dorothy Elmhirst, 25 September 1927.
81. Louise Croly to Dorothy Elmhirst, 25 September 1927.
82. Louise Croly to Dorothy Elmhirst, 25 September 1927.
83. Louise Croly to Dorothy Elmhirst, 25 September 1927; Betty Leonard, conversations with author.
84. Louise Croly to Dorothy Elmhirst, 25 September 1927.
85. Betty Leonard, conversations with author.
86. Roger Baldwin, interview with Betty Leonard.
87. *Wolverine*, Class of 1911.
88. Mathilda Hader, interview with author.
89. Stephen Gessner, interview with author.
90. Betty Leonard, conversations with author.
91. Betty Leonard, conversations with author.
92. Eduard Lindeman to Dorothy Straight, 14 December 1923.
93. Eduard Lindeman to Dorothy Straight, 14 December 1923.
94. Eduard Lindeman to Dorothy Straight, 14 December 1923.
95. Eduard Lindeman to Dorothy Straight, 14 December 1923.
96. Eduard Lindeman to Dorothy Straight, 14 December 1923.
97. Eduard Lindeman to Dorothy Straight, 9 April 1924.
98. Dorothy Straight to Eduard Lindeman, "Xmas night" [1924?].
99. Dorothy Straight to Eduard Lindeman, 11 September [1924?].
100. Dorothy Straight to Eduard Lindeman ["Christmas night"].
101. Dorothy Straight to Eduard Lindeman, 11 July [1924?].
102. Eduard Lindeman to Dorothy Elmhirst, 18 May 1930.
103. Eduard Lindeman to Dorothy Elmhirst, 18 May 1930.
104. Dorothy Straight to Eduard Lindeman, 23 September [1924?].
105. Dorothy Elmhirst to Eduard Lindeman, 11 September [1924?].
106. Dorothy Straight to Eduard Lindeman, 14 July [1924?].
107. Dorothy Straight to Eduard Lindeman, 11 September [1924].
108. Dorothy Straight to Leonard Elmhirst, 5 March 1922 and 24 October 1924.

Chapter 6. *1925: The Turning Point*

1. Straight, *After Long Silence* (1983) 29–30.
2. Young, *The Elmhirsts* (1982) 62–63.
3. Young, *The Elmhirsts* (1982) 17.
4. Bonham Carter and Curry, *Dartington Hall* (1970) 19–20.
5. Dorothy Straight to Leonard Elmhirst, 20 October 1924.
6. Leonard Elmhirst to Eduard Lindeman, 7 January 1924.
7. Leonard Elmhirst to Eduard Lindeman, 7 January 1924.
8. Leonard Elmhirst to Eduard Lindeman, 7 January 1924.
9. Leonard Elmhirst to Dorothy Straight, 16 August 1924.

10. Dorothy Straight to Leonard Elmhirst, 19 November 1924.
11. Dorothy Straight to Leonard Elmhirst, 19 November 1924.
12. Leonard Elmhirst to Eduard Lindeman, 6 May 1927.
13. Straight, *After Long Silence* (1983) 31.
14. Herbert Croly to Dorothy Straight, 10 February 1925.
15. Straight, *After Long Silence* (1983) 31.
16. Eduard Lindeman to Leonard Elmhirst, 9 February 1925.
17. Eduard Lindeman to Charles Shaw, January 1925.
18. Louise Croly to Dorothy Straight, 4 February 1925; Dorothy Straight to Eduard Lindeman, 22 September [1924?]; Betty Leonard, conversation with author.
19. Betty Leonard, conversations with author.
20. Martha Anderson, interview with Miriam Stewart.
21. Martha Anderson, interview with Miriam Stewart.
22. Eduard Lindeman to Charles Shaw, 8 August 1925.
23. Betty Leonard, conversations with author.
24. Eduard Lindeman to Dorothy and Leonard Elmhirst, 9 April 1925.
25. Eduard Lindeman to Dorothy and Leonard Elmhirst, 9 April 1925.
26. Eduard Lindeman to Charles Shaw, 8 April 1925.
27. Eduard Lindeman to Dorothy and Leonard Elmhirst, 9 April 1925.
28. Eduard Lindeman to Dorothy and Leonard Elmhirst, 9 April 1925.
29. Eduard Lindeman to Dorothy and Leonard Elmhirst, 9 April 1925.
30. Eduard Lindeman to Dorothy Elmhirst, 29 May 1925.
31. Eduard Lindeman to Dorothy Elmhirst, 29 May 1925.
32. Eduard Lindeman to Dorothy Elmhirst, 29 May 1925.
33. Eduard Lindeman to Charles Shaw, 17 May 1925.
34. Martha Anderson, interview with Miriam Stewart.
35. Martha Anderson, interview with Miriam Stewart.
36. Martha Anderson, interview with Miriam Stewart.
37. Eduard Lindeman to Dorothy Elmhirst, 22 June 1925.
38. Eduard Lindeman to Dorothy Elmhirst, 18 July 1925.
39. Eduard Lindeman to Dorothy Elmhirst, 22 June 1925.
40. Dorothy Elmhirst to Eduard Lindeman, 14 July 1925.
41. Eduard Lindeman to Dorothy Elmhirst, 18 July 1925.
42. Michael Straight, interview with author.
43. Eduard Lindeman to Dorothy Elmhirst, 11 July 1925.
44. Diggins, *Mussolini* (1972) 234.
45. Martha Anderson, interview with Miriam Stewart.
46. Eduard Lindeman to Charles Shaw, 8 August 1925.
47. Eduard Lindeman to Dorothy Elmhirst, 31 July 1925.
48. Eduard Lindeman to Dorothy Elmhirst, 12 August 1925.
49. Eduard Lindeman to Charles Shaw, 8 August 1925.
50. Eduard Lindeman to Dorothy Elmhirst, 12 August 1925.
51. Eduard Lindeman to Dorothy Elmhirst, 12 August 1925.
52. Eduard Lindeman to Dorothy Elmhirst, 12 August 1925.
53. Eduard Lindeman to Dorothy Elmhirst, 12 August 1925.
54. Eduard Lindeman to Dorothy Elmhirst, 12 August 1925.
55. Eduard Lindeman to Charles Shaw, 8 August 1925.
56. Eduard Lindeman to Dorothy Elmhirst, 12 August 1925.
57. Eduard Lindeman to Dorothy Elmhirst, 12 August 1925.
58. *Dictionary of Current Biography (1944)*, 514–515.

59. *Webster's Biographical Dictionary* (1976).
60. Dorothy Elmhirst to Eduard Lindeman, 9 June 1925.
61. Young, *The Elmhirsts* (1982) 104–105.
62. Young, *The Elmhirsts* (1982) 2–3.
63. John and Mathilda Hader, interview with author.
64. Betty Leonard, conversations with author.
65. Herbert Croly to Dorothy Elmhirst, 13 August 1925.
66. Herbert Croly to Dorothy Elmhirst, 13 August 1925.
67. Herbert Croly to Dorothy Elmhirst, 13 August 1925.
68. Herbert Croly to Dorothy Elmhirst, 13 August 1925.
69. Herbert Croly to Dorothy Elmhirst, 13 August 1925.
70. Herbert Croly to Dorothy Elmhirst, 13 August 1925.
71. Eduard Lindeman to Charles Shaw, 5 September 1925.
72. Eduard Lindeman to Dorothy Elmhirst, 10 September 1925.
73. Eduard Lindeman to Dorothy Elmhirst, 10 September 1925.
74. Eduard Lindeman to Dorothy Elmhirst, 10 September 1925.
75. Eduard Lindeman to Charles Shaw, 5 September 1925.
76. Eduard Lindeman to Dorothy Elmhirst, 10 September 1925.
77. Eduard Lindeman to Charles Shaw, 5 September 1925.
78. Eduard Lindeman to Charles Shaw, 5 September 1925.
79. Eduard Lindeman to Charles Shaw, 5 September 1925.
80. Eduard Lindeman to Dorothy Elmhirst, 10 September 1925.
81. Maxtone-Graham, *Only Way* (1972) 137.
82. Betty Leonard, conversations with author.
83. Eduard Lindeman to Charles Shaw, 8 August 1925.
84. Eduard Lindeman to Dorothy Elmhirst, 10 September 1925.
85. Chambers, *Seedtime of Reform* (1963) 235.
86. Chambers, *Seedtime of Reform* (1963) xi.

Chapter 7. The Meaning of Adult Education *in Its Time*

1. Eduard Lindeman to Charles Shaw, August 1926 and 21 October 1925.
2. Eduard Lindeman to Charles Shaw, August 1926.
3. Anna Bogue to Eduard Lindeman, 27 June 1926.
4. Small, review of *Social Discovery* (1924) 214.
5. Martin, *Liberal Education* (1926) 1–2.
6. Percy, "Education," in Stanley, *The Way Out* (1923) 67.
7. *1919 Report* (1980).
8. "Call for Preliminary Conference, 6 June 1924," Carnegie Corp. Archives.
9. Cartwright, *Ten Years* (1935) 1.
10. Rose, "Adult Education" (1979) 141.
11. Rose, "Adult Education" (1979) 142.
12. Rose, "Adult Education" (1979) 292.
13. Rose, "Adult Education" (1979) 149.
14. Rose, "Adult Education" (1979) 150.
15. Hart, *Adult Education* (1927) 190–191.
16. Hart, *Adult Education* (1927) 192.
17. Rose, "Adult Education" (1979) 186.
18. Cartwright, *Ten Years* (1935) 18.

19. Rose, "Adult Education" (1979) 314.
20. Eduard Lindeman to Leonard Elmhirst, 4 March 1926.
21. Morse Cartwright to Eduard Lindeman, 26 May 1926.
22. Eduard Lindeman to Leonard Elmhirst, 4 March 1926.
23. Herbert Hunsaker, interview with author.
24. Malcolm Knowles, interview with author.
25. Lindeman, "Goal" (1939) 571.
26. Malcolm Knowles, interview with author.
27. Malcolm Knowles, interview with author.
28. Buchholz, review of *The Meaning* (1927) 150–151.
29. Lindeman, "Adult Education" (1925) 8.
30. Martin, *Liberal Education* (1926) 309.
31. Martin, *Liberal Education* (1926) 312.
32. Martin, *Liberal Education* (1926) 313.
33. Martin, *Liberal Education* (1926) 317.
34. Martin, *Liberal Education* (1926) 315.
35. Martin, *Liberal Education* (1926) 314.
36. Martin, *Liberal Education* (1926) 311–312.
37. Rose Franco to Miriam Stewart, 23 October 1984.
38. Stubblefield, "Aims" in *Yearbook 1980-1981*, 18–19.
39. Hart, *Adult Education* (1927) 27.
40. Hart, *Adult Education* (1927) 313.
41. Hart, *Adult Education* (1927) 66.
42. Hart, *Adult Education* (1927) 116.
43. Hart, *Adult Education* (1927) 242.
44. Hart, *Adult Education* (1927) 257.
45. *Wisconsin State Journal*, 8 February 1930; Superior (Wisconsin) *Telegram*, 11 July 1938; Forrest Allen to Max Otto, 29 November 1938.
46. Stubblefield, "Aims" in *Yearbook 1980-1981*, 18.
47. Rose, "Adult Education" (1979) 118.
48. Learned, *Public Library* (1924) 6.
49. Learned, *Public Library* (1924) 7–8.
50. Learned, *Public Library* (1924) 8.
51. Learned, *Public Library* (1924) 13–17.
52. Learned, *Public Library* (1924) 7.
53. Yeaxlee, review of *Why Stop Learning* (1928) 200–201.
54. Lindeman, review of *Why Stop Learning* (1928) 526.
55. Cotton, *Adult Education* (1968) 8.
56. Clark, review of *The Meaning* (1927).
57. Clark, review of *The Meaning* (1927).
58. Clark, review of *The Meaning* (1927).
59. Clark, review of *The Meaning* (1927).
60. Fadiman, review of *The Meaning* (1927).
61. Fadiman, review of *The Meaning* (1927).
62. Mumford, review of *The Meaning* (1927) 139–141.
63. Hewes, review of *The Meaning* (1927) 654.
64. Hewes, review of *The Meaning* (1927). 654.
65. Kirkpatrick, review of *The Meaning* (1927).
66. Roger Baldwin to Eduard Lindeman, 28 December 1926.

67. Eduard Lindeman to Leonard Elmhirst, 7 January 1927.
68. Buchholz, review of *The Meaning* (1927) 124.
69. Buchholz, review of *The Meaning* (1927) 150–151.
70. Buchholz, review of *The Meaning* (1927) 150–151.
71. Lindeman, "Division" (1944) 784.
72. Bonaro Overstreet, interview with author.

Chapter 8. *What Adult Education Means: Discovering and Rediscovering the Concept of Andragogy*

1. Lindeman, *The Meaning* (1961) 4–7.
2. Lindeman, "Meaning of Adult Learning" (1929) 38.
3. Lindeman, *The Meaning* (1961) 3.
4. Lindeman, "Scrapbook 1946".
5. Lindeman, "Social Thinking" (1927) 9.
6. Lindeman, *The Meaning* (1961) 5.
7. Lindeman, "New Challenge" (1927) 681–682.
8. Lindeman, *The Meaning* (1961) 5.
9. "Manuscripts A–I," Box 12, ECL/RBML/CU, 47.
10. Lindeman, "Parent Education" (1930) 234.
11. Lindeman, *The Meaning* (1961) 5.
12. Lindeman, "Dynamics" (1948) 267.
13. Lindeman, *The Meaning* (1961) 35.
14. Lindeman, "Industrial Technique" (1923) 494.
15. Lindeman, "Scrapbook 1945," 103.
16. Lindeman, *The Meaning* (1961) 5.
17. Lindeman, "New Needs" (1944) 115.
18. Lindeman, *The Meaning* (1961) 6.
19. Lindeman, *The Meaning* (1961) 48.
20. Lindeman, "Meaning of Adult Learning" (1929) 38–39.
21. Lindeman, "Adult Education" (1937) 465.
22. Lindeman, *The Meaning* (1961) 112.
23. Lindeman, *Social Thinking* (1927) 9.
24. Lindeman, *Social Education* (1933) 173.
25. Lindeman, *The Meaning* (1961) 114.
26. Tough, *Adult's Learning Projects* (1979).
27. Smith, *Learning How to Learn* (1982).
28. Lindeman, *The Meaning* (1961) 7.
29. Lindeman, *The Meaning* (1961) xxviii.
30. Lindeman, *The Meaning* (1961) 6–7.
31. Lindeman, *The Meaning* (1961) 87.
32. Lindeman, "After Lyceums" (1927) 249.
33. Lindeman, "How Work" (1929) 340.
34. Lindeman, "*ANDRAGOGIK*" (1926) 38.
35. Anderson and Lindeman, *Education Through Experience* (1927) 2–3.
36. Martha Anderson, interview with Miriam Stewart.
37. Knowles, *Modern Practice* (1970) 38.
38. Lindeman, "Scrapbook 1937," 142.
39. Lindeman, "Recreation Worker" (1951) 533.
40. Lindeman, *The Meaning* (1961) 111.

41. Lindeman, *The Meaning* (1961) 19.

Chapter 9. *Danish Influence on America's Adult Education Movement*

1. Hall and Davis, *Europe Since Waterloo* (1947) 196.
2. *Encyclopaedia Britannica*, 11th ed.
3. Davies, *Education for Life* (1931) 102.
4. Knudsen, *Danish Rebel* (1955) 114.
5. Hall and Davis, *Europe Since Waterloo* (1947) 228–229.
6. *Encyclopaedia Britannica*, 11th ed.
7. *Encyclopaedia Britannica*, 11th ed.
8. Davies, *Education for Life* (1931) 13–14.
9. Dam, *N.S.F. Grundtvig* (1983) 24.
10. Slumstrup, "Factsheet Denmark" (1983) 1–8.
11. Dam, *N.S.F. Grundtvig* (1983) 35–36.
12. Slumstrup, "Factsheet Denmark" (1983) 7.
13. Slumstrup, "Factsheet Denmark" (1983) 7.
14. Skovmand, "Folk High School," in Thodberg and Thyssen, *N.S.F. Grundtvig* (1983) 322.
15. Dam, *N.S.F. Grundtvig* (1983) 43.
16. Knudsen, *Danish Rebel* (1955) 106.
17. Davies, *Education for Life* (1931) 70.
18. Knudsen, *Danish Rebel* (1955) 149.
19. Lindeman, "Community Organization," "E.C. Lindeman Manuscripts A–I," Box 12, ECL/RBML/CU, 57.
20. The author is indebted to Prof. K. E. Bugge at the Royal Danish School of Educational Studies for tracing the background of this statement which was often quoted by Lindeman. It has usually but incorrectly been attributed to Enrico Dalgas (1828–1894), a former military officer, who in the later part of his life devoted his energy to planting forests on the Danish moorlands. In the situation after war in 1864 this project actually served to "regain" an area of land corresponding to the area lost in the war. The actual source, however, is the poet H. P. Holst (1811–1893), who formulated the sentence as a motto for an industrial exhibition in 1872. The bibliographical references for this information are *Dansk Biografisk Leksikon* (Dictionary of Danish Biography) 3:542–544 (generally on Dalgas) and 6:499–500 (where Holst is explicitly named as the author of the sentence). (K.E. Bugge to author, 22 October 1984).
21. Lindeman, *The Meaning* (1961) xxix.
22. *Encyclopaedia Britannica*, 12th ed.
23. Howe, *Denmark* (1921) iii.
24. Howe, *Denmark* (1921) iv.
25. Howe, *Denmark* (1921) iv–vi.
26. Branson, *Farm Life Abroad* (1924) 84.
27. Branson, *Farm Life Abroad* (1924) 108.
28. Lindeman, "Community Organization for Leisure," "E. C. Lindeman Manuscripts A–I" Box 12, ECL/RBML/CU, 57.
29. Lindeman, "Denmark Rural Culture" (1922) 176.
30. Lindeman, "Denmark Rural Culture" (1922) 176.
31. Howe, *Denmark* (1921) iii–ix.

32. Bugge, "Grundtvig's Educational Ideas," in Thodberg and Thyssen, *N.S.F. Grundtvig* (1983) 211.
33. Knudsen, *Danish Rebel* (1955) v.
34. Grundtvig, *Selected Writings* (1976) 160.
35. Slumstrup, "Factsheet Denmark" (1983).
36. Slumstrup, "Factsheet Denmark" (1983).
37. Skovmand, "Folk High School," in Thodberg and Tyssen, *N.S.F. Grundtvig* (1983) 331.
38. Lindeman, "Adult Education" (1937) 464.
39. Howe, *Denmark* (1921) 89.
40. Howe, *Denmark* (1921) 90.
41. Lindeman, "Sociology" (1945) 4.
42. Howe, *Denmark* (1921) 91–92.
43. Howe, *Denmark* (1921) 91–92.
44. The author is especially indebted to Uffe Himmelstrup, Counselor in Charge of Cultural Relations, Royal Danish Embassy, Washington, D.C., for assistance in developing this interpretation of Danish culture in 1920.
45. Adams, *Seeds of Fire* (1975) 14.
46. Kulich, "Grundtvig's Idea" (1984) 12.
47. Davies, *Education for Life* (1931) 71.
48. Grundtvig, *Selected Writings* (1976) 147.
49. Grundtvig, *Selected Writings* (1976) 173.
50. Davies, *Education for Life* (1931) 82.
51. Lindeman, *The Meaning* (1961) 4.
52. Knudsen, *Danish Rebel* (1955) 158.
53. Davies, *Education for Life* (1931) 89.
54. Davies, *Education for Life* (1931) 89.
55. Grundtvig, *Selected Writings* (1976) 153.
56. Grundtvig, *Selected Writings* (1976) 153–154.
57. Hart, *Adult Education* (1927) 271.
58. Davies, *Education for Life* (1931) 90.
59. Davies, *Education for Life* (1931) 93.
60. Lindeman, "Scrapbook 1937," 187.
61. Lindeman, "Carol Kennicotts" (1925) 131.
62. Lindeman, *The Meaning* (1961) 6.
63. Bugge, "Grundtvig's Educational Ideas," in Thodberg and Thyssen, *N.S.F. Grundtvig* (1983) 218.
64. Bugge, "Grundtvig's Educational Ideas," in Thodberg and Thyssen, *N.S.F. Grundtvig* (1983) 218.
65. Bugge, "Grundtvig's Educational Ideas," in Thodberg and Thyssen, *N.S.F. Grundtvig* (1983) 219.
66. Davies, *Education for Life* (1931) 72–73.
67. Davies, *Education for Life* (1931) 72.
68. Lindeman, *The Meaning* (1961) 5.
69. Grundtvig, *Selected Writings* (1976) 173.
70. Davies, *Education for Life* (1931) 87.
71. Howe, *Denmark* (1921) 93.
72. Davies, *Education for Life* (1931) 85–86.
73. Knudsen, *Danish Rebel* (1955) 163–164.
74. Davies, *Education for Life* (1931) 91.

75. Grundtvig, *Selected Writings* (1976) 154.
76. Davies, *Education for Life* (1976) 157.
77. Lindeman, "Scrapbook 1933–1939," 60.
78. Lindeman, "Scrapbook 1941," 207.
79. Lindeman, *The Meaning* (1961) xvii.
80. Grundtvig, *Selected Writings* (1976).
81. Knudsen, *Danish Rebel* (1955) 151.
82. Thodberg and Thyssen, *N.S.F. Grundtvig* (1983) 51.
83. Bugge, "Grundtvig's Challenges," in *Education for Life* (Grundtvig Bicentenary Report, 1983) 19.
84. Lindeman, *College Characters* (1912) 95.
85. Lindeman, *College Characters* (1912) 53.
86. Eduard Lindeman to Dorothy Straight, "Sunday Afternoon" [1924?].
87. Lindeman, "Enjoying While Learning" (1928) 413; Also "E. C. Lindeman Manuscripts, A–I," Box 12, ECL/RBML/CU.

Chapter 10. *The Importance of Experience in Adult Learning*

1. Eduard Lindeman to Dorothy and Leonard Elmhirst, 31 January 1926.
2. Eduard Lindeman to Dorothy and Leonard Elmhirst, 31 January 1926.
3. Eduard Lindeman to Dorothy and Leonard Elmhirst, 31 January 1926.
4. Eduard Lindeman to Dorothy and Leonard Elmhirst, 31 January 1926.
5. "Annual Report AAAE" (1926–1927) 15.
6. Eduard Lindeman to Charles Shaw, 8 June 1926.
7. Eduard Lindeman to Charles Shaw, 22 August 1926.
8. Moore, *American Pragmatism* (1961) 262.
9. James, *Pragmatism* (1975) 97.
10. Smith, *Philosophy of Education* (1964) 89.
11. Durant, *Story of Philosophy* (1926) 558.
12. Dewey, *Democracy and Education* (1916) 63.
13. Durant, *Story of Philosophy* (1926) 2–3.
14. Dewey, *Democracy and Education* (1916) 63.
15. Dewey, *Democracy and Education* (1916) 61.
16. Elias and Merriam, *Philosophical Foundations* (1980) 55.
17. Dewey, *Democracy and Education* (1916) 59.
18. Power, "John Dewey" (1969) 356.
19. Lindeman, "Psychology" (1930) 365–366.
20. Lindeman, "Maturity and Culture" (1947) 88.
21. Eduard Lindeman to Max Otto, 9 August 1944.
22. Eduard Lindeman to Max Otto, 9 August 1944.
23. Lindeman, "Scrapbook, March 1950–January 1953," 144.
24. Lindeman, "Modern Student and Reform," (Unpaged in original but appears as pages 51–52 in Lindeman's "Scrapbook No. 1").
25. Dewey, *Democracy and Education* (1916) 92.
26. Lindeman, "Russell's Philosophy," (1944) in Schlipp, *Bertrand Russell* (1971) 566.
27. Lindeman, "Social Philosophy" (1952) 55.
28. Lindeman, "Social Philosophy" (1952) 62.
29. Lindeman, "Scrapbook, 1936–1937," 169.
30. Lindeman, "Parents' Dilemma" (1930) 356.
31. Lindeman, "A Re-affirmation" (1940) 17.

32. Lindeman, "John Dewey as Educator" (1940) 35.
33. Lindeman, "Six Questions" (1931) 171.
34. Lindeman, "Meaning of Adult Learning" (1929) 37.
35. Lindeman, "A Re-affirmation" (1940) 16.
36. Lindeman, "Education in War" (1943) 4.
37. Lindeman, "Contingency" (1943) 51.
38. Lindeman, "A Re-affirmation" (1940) 15.
39. Lindeman, "Education in War" (1943) 5.
40. Lindeman, "Education in War" (1943) 4–5.
41. Lindeman, "World Peace" (1945) 8.
42. Betty Leonard, conversations with author.
43. Marion Beers, interview with Betty Leonard; Eduard Lindeman to Max Otto, 13 June 1948.
44. John Dewey to Eduard Lindeman, 20 June 1938; Eduard Lindeman to John Dewey, 6 July 1938.
45. Eduard Lindeman to John Dewey, 9 June 1941.
46. Eduard Lindeman to Dorothy and Leonard Elmhirst, 19 January 1930.
47. Lindeman, "John Dewey" (1952) 9.
48. Lindeman, "John Dewey" (1952) 9.
49. Lindeman, "John Dewey as Educator" (1940) 37.
50. Elias and Merriam, *Philosophical Foundations* (1980) 51.
51. Lindeman, "Mary Parker Follett" (1934) 86.
52. For basic information about Mary Parker Follett, the author used these sources: Fox, "Mary Parker Follett" (1968) 520–529; Bird, *Enterprising Women* (1976) 176–181; and McHenry, *Liberty's Women* (1980) 136.
53. Lindeman, *Social Discovery* (1924) v.
54. Follett, *Creative Experience* (1924) 133.
55. Follett, *Creative Experience* (1924) 134.
56. Follett, "Community Is a Process" (1919) 586.
57. Fox, "Mary Parker Follett" (1968) 524.
58. Follett, *Creative Experience* (1924) 135.
59. Follett, *Creative Experience* (1924) 136.
60. Follett, *Creative Experience* (1924) 137.
61. Follett, *Creative Experience* (1924) 139.
62. Follett, *Creative Experience* (1924) 190.
63. Follett, *Creative Experience* (1924) 199–200.
64. Follett, *New State* (1965) 159.
65. Follett, *New State* (1965) 160.
66. Follett, *New State* (1965) 160–161.
67. Follett, *New State* (1965) 369.
68. Follett, *New State* (1965) 370.
69. Follett, *New State* (1965) 371.
70. Lindeman, "Mary Parker Follett" (1934) 86.
71. Eduard Lindeman to Charles Shaw [1924?].
72. Mary Parker Follett to Eduard Lindeman, 11 January 1923.
73. Alfred Dwight Sheffield to Eduard Lindeman, 31 December 1923.
74. Lindeman, *Social Discovery* (1924) 114, 115, 195.
75. Lindeman, *The Meaning* (1961) 38, 45.
76. Follett, *Creative Experience* (1924) xviii–xix.
77. "Manuscript 101," MOP/WSHS.

78. Eduard Lindeman to Max Otto, 1 May 1945.

79. Max Otto to Eduard Lindeman, 6 November 1945.

80. Max Otto to Eduard Lindeman, 30 December 1945.

81. Lindeman, "Scrapbook 1946 Autumn–1947 Winter," 171.

82. Lindeman, "Scrapbook 1946–1947," 46–47.

83. Bonham Carter and Curry, *Dartington Hall* (1970) 45–46.

84. Leonard Elmhirst to Eduard Lindeman, 11 August 1926.

85. Dorothy Elmhirst to Eduard Lindeman, 12 September 1926.

86. Straight, *After Long Silence* (1983) 37.

87. "Report of Meeting to Discuss Plans," 11 September 1926 DHT.

88. Letters reflecting the aftermath of this episode though not fully descriptive of the triggering events include these: Dorothy Elmhirst to Eduard Lindeman, 16 May 1927; Leonard Elmhirst to Eduard Lindeman, 6 May 1927; Wyatt Rawson to Eduard Lindeman, 16 May 1927 and July 1927; ECL/RBML/CU.

89. Eduard Lindeman to Dorothy Elmhirst, 30 September 1926.

90. Eduard Lindeman to Dorothy Elmhirst, 30 September 1926.

91. Ruth Morgan to Dorothy Elmhirst, 11 January 1927.

92. Eduard Lindeman to Leonard Elmhirst, 28 April 1929.

93. Eduard Lindeman to Leonard Elmhirst, 28 April 1929.

94. Eduard Lindeman to Dorothy Elmhirst, 15 December 1929.

95. Eduard Lindeman to Dorothy Elmhirst, 15 December 1929.

Chapter 11. *Adult Educators as Facilitators of Learning: Operationalizing Pragmatism*

1. Lindeman, "Industrial Technique" (1923) 507.

2. Eduard Lindeman to Dorothy Straight, 9 August 1924.

3. Eduard Lindeman to Dorothy Straight, 9 August 1924.

4. Eduard Lindeman to Dorothy Straight, 9 August 1924.

5. Bernstein, *New York School* (1942) 63.

6. Malcolm Knowles, interview with author.

7. Demorest, "He Saw the Mountain" (1953) 18–19.

8. Alice Collins, interview with Betty Leonard; confirmed in interview with Philip Klein.

9. Lindeman, "Adult Education" (1937) 465.

10. Susan Pettis, interview with Betty Leonard.

11. Lindeman, "Dum Placem Peream" (1942) 158.

12. John Hader, interview with author.

13. Alice Collins, interview with Betty Leonard.

14. Lindeman, "Creative Opportunity" (1925) 445.

15. Lindeman, "Scrapbook 1936," from an outline of a Social Philosophy course as taught by Lindeman, unpaged.

16. Letter to author 26 April 1981 (writer requested confidentiality).

17. Letter to author 26 April 1981 (writer requested confidentiality).

18. Eleanor McConnell to Julia Follansbee, 2 December [1924?].

19. Lucille Astin, interview with Betty Leonard.

20. Eduard Lindeman to "Miss Dunn," 25 November 1946.

21. Eduard Lindeman to "Miss Dunn," 25 November 1946.

22. Eduard Lindeman to "Miss Dunn," 25 November 1946.

23. Jerold Apps to author, 14 August 1985.

24. Eduard Lindeman to "Miss Dunn," 25 November 1946.

25. Eduard Lindeman to "Miss Dunn," 25 November 1946.
26. Eduard Lindeman to "Miss Dunn," 25 November 1946.
27. Eduard Lindeman to "Miss Dunn," 25 November 1946.
28. Anderson and Lindeman, *Education Through Experience* (1927) 22–23.
29. Anderson and Lindeman, *Education Through Experience* (1927) 23.
30. Lindeman, *The Meaning* (1961) 113.
31. Lindeman, "Prepared Leaders" [1937?] 5–6 [unpublished].
32. Lindeman, "Prepared Leaders" [1937?] 5–6 [unpublished].
33. Lindeman to Michigan Council, 11 November 1947.
34. Lindeman, "What is Adult Education?" (1925) [unpublished].
35. Lindeman, "Place of Discussion" (1935) 349.
36. Lindeman, "Prepared Leaders" [1937?] 6 [unpublished].
37. Lindeman, "Prepared Leaders" [1937?] 6 [unpublished].
38. Lindeman, "Goals" (1932) 125.
39. Lindeman, *The Meaning* (1961) 83. [The interior quotes are from Charles H. Cooley, *Social Process* (New York: Scribner's, 1918) 382].
40. Lindeman, "Scrapbook 1935," 80.
41. Lindeman, *The Meaning* (1961) 85–86.
42. Eduard Lindeman to Max Otto, 21 October 1944.
43. Lindeman, *The Meaning* (1961) 84.
44. Lindeman, "The Social Worker and Community" (1924) 84.
45. Lindeman, "Scrapbook 1932–1933," 131.
46. Hutchins, *The Learning Society* (1968).
47. Lindeman, *The Meaning* (1961) 119.
48. Lindeman, "Adult Education" (1937) 465.
49. Notes from Lindeman speech, 30 April 1948, "Manuscripts 1946–1948," ECL/RBML/CU.
50. "Alfred Dwight Sheffield," "Letters to and from Dewey and Others," Box 2, ECL/RBML/CU.
51. Hulda Knowles, conversation with author.
52. Lindeman, "Social Methods" (1933) 254.
53. Lindeman, "Place of Discussion" (1935) 349.
54. Lindeman, "After Lyceums" (1927) 249–250.
55. Lindeman, speech at City Club, Portland, Oregon, June 1952.
56. Lindeman, speech at City Club of Portland, Oregon, June 1952.
57. Lindeman, "Place of Discussion" (1935) 350.
58. Lindeman, "Place of Discussion" (1935) 350.
59. Eduard Lindeman to Michigan Council, 11 November 1947.
60. Lindeman, "Concurring People" (1951) 134–135.
61. Lindeman, "Concurring People" (1951) 135.
62. Lindeman, speech, 30 April 1948, ECL/RBML/CU.
63. Lindeman, "Social Methods" (1933) 254.
64. Lindeman, *The Meaning* (1961) 120.
65. Lindeman, *The Meaning* (1961) 120.
66. Lindeman, "Social Methods" (1933) 255.
67. Lindeman, "Social Methods" (1933) 255.
68. Lindeman, "Social Methods" (1933) 255.
69. Lindeman, *The Meaning* (1961) 119–120.
70. Nathan Cohen, interview with Betty Leonard.
71. Flora Thurston Allen, interview with Betty Leonard.

72. Byron Mock, interview with Betty Leonard.
73. Lindeman, "Public Ownership" (1927) 2.
74. Lindeman, *The Meaning* (1961) 121.
75. Lindeman, "Limitations of Discussion" (1926) 7.
76. Lindeman, "Limitations of Discussion" (1926) 7.
77. Lindeman, speech at City Club of Portland, Oregon, June 1952.
78. Lindeman, "Self-Education" (1924) 192.
79. Lindeman, "Self-Education" (1924) 192–193.
80. Lindeman, "Conference and Compromise" (1929) 364.
81. Lindeman, "Self-Education" (1924) 193.
82. Lindeman, "Scrapbook October 1951 To March 1953," 161.
83. Lindeman, speech at City Club of Portland, Oregon, June 1952.
84. Lindeman, "After Lyceums" (1927) 143.
85. Lindeman, "After Lyceums" (1927) 143.
86. Lindeman, "After Lyceums" (1927) 144.
87. Lindeman, "After Lyceums" (1927) 144.
88. Lindeman, "After Lyceums" (1927) 144.
89. [Lindeman?] "Ramparts" (1939) 22.
90. Eduard Lindeman to Michigan Council, 11 November 1947.
91. Lindeman, speech "What is Propaganda Doing to Us?" 9 January 1940, "1940 Articles," Box 7, ECL/RBML/CU.
92. Lindeman, "Psychology" (1930) 369–370.
93. Lindeman, *Church in Community* (1929) 3.
94. [Lindeman?] "Ramparts" (1939) 24.
95. Eduard Lindeman to Bernard Geis, 22 October 1941.
96. Lindeman, "Recreation and Morale" (1941) 396.
97. Eduard Lindeman to Bernard Geis, 22 October 1941.
98. "Recent Developments in the Field of Social Welfare in the U.S.", "Manuscripts and Printed, Undated, J–Z and Miscellaneous," Box 13, ECL/RBML/CU.
99. Lindeman, text of radio broadcast to Germany, 6 June 1944, "Manuscripts, etc., 1944," Box 9, ECL/RBML/CU.

Chapter 12. *Adult Education as the Lifeblood of Democracy*

1. Lindeman, "Dum Placem Peream" (1942) 159.
2. Lindeman, "A Fantasy" (1952) 3–4.
3. Lindeman, "Scrapbook 1939," 40–41.
4. Lindeman, "Scrapbook 1939," 40–41.
5. Gessner, *Democratic Man* (1956) 239.
6. Lindeman, second speech at City Club of Portland, Oregon, June 1952.
7. Mussolini, "*A Noi*" (1927) 694.
8. Salvemini, "Reign of the Bludgeon" (1927) 695.
9. Eduard Lindeman to "Miss Waite," 26 January 1926.
10. Eduard Lindeman to "Miss Waite," 26 January 1926.
11. Lindeman, "New Challenge" (1927) 680.
12. Lindeman, review of *An Introduction to Pareto* (1934) 363.
13. Lindeman, review of *The Mind and Society* (1935) 453.
14. Lindeman, undated manuscript fragment, "Letters to John Dewey and Others," Box 2, ECL/RBML/CU.
15. Lindeman, "Group Living" (1936) 5.

16. Lindeman, "Group Living" (1936) 5.
17. Lindeman, "Crisis" (1938) 129.
18. Roger Baldwin, interview with Betty Leonard.
19. Bird, *Invisible Scar* (1966) 141.
20. Lindeman, *The Meaning* (1961) 97.
21. Rosen, review of *The Meaning* (1961).
22. *Philadelphia Record* (1 June 1934).
23. Gessner, *Democratic Man* (1956) 28.
24. Lindeman, "Russian Trip," Box 4, ECL/RBML/CU.
25. Lindeman, "Human Nature" (1933) 97.
26. Lindeman, "Human Nature" (1933) 97–98.
27. Lindeman, "Human Nature" (1933) 98.
28. Lindeman, "Individual" (1951) 16.
29. Lindeman, "Democratic Era" (1949) 80.
30. Lindeman, "Democratic Era" (1949) 80.
31. Lindeman, "Democratic Era" (1949) 80–81.
32. "Left-Wing Communism An Infantile Disorder," International Publishers, 1934, 38 [as quoted by Lindeman, "Concurring People" (1951) 129].
33. Lindeman, "Group" (1951) 130.
34. Lindeman, "Group" (1951) 130.
35. Eduard Lindeman to John Dewey, 24 June 1949.
36. Eduard Lindeman to Max Otto, 30 June 1949.
37. Lindeman, "Group," in Lieberman, *New Trends* (1938) 281; Nathan Cohen, interview with Betty Leonard.
38. Lindeman, "Recreation" (1920) v.
39. Lindeman, "Industrial Technique" (1923) 494.
40. Lindeman, "Carol Kennicotts" (1925) 132.
41. Lindeman, "New Psychology" (1923) 211.
42. Lindeman, "Consumers" (1926) 6–9.
43. Lindeman, "Social Perspectives" (1932) 12.
44. Lindeman, "The Labor Movement," in "1938 A.A.S.W. Lectures," Box 6, ECL/RBML/CU.
45. Lindeman, "People's War and Peace," radio talk over WQXR (31 May 1942) "Manuscripts and Printed, Undated J–Z and Misc.," Box 13, ECL/RBML/CU, 14.
46. Lindeman, "Scrapbook 1945," 102.
47. Lindeman, "Scrapbook March 1950–January 1953," 218.
48. Lindeman, "Scrapbook March 1950–January 1953," 218.
49. Lindeman, "1931 Articles," Box 4, ECL/RBML/CU.
50. Lindeman, "1931 Articles," Box 4, ECL/RBML/CU.
51. Eduard Lindeman to Max Otto, 1 December 1952.
52. Lindeman, "1931 Articles," Box 4, ECL/RBML/CU.
53. Lindeman, "Scrapbook 1932–1933," 242.
54. Lindeman, "Pragmatic Mood" (1947) 62.
55. Lindeman, "Pragmatic Mood" (1947) 62.
56. Lindeman, "Scrapbook 1933–1939," (Insert in front).
57. "Dr. Eduard C. Lindeman, NCSW President—1952–1953," (1953) 33.
58. Lindeman, "The Educational Discipline," in "Emerson," (unnumbered file) ECL/SWHA/UM, 31.
59. Lindeman, "The Educational Discipline," in "Emerson" (unnumbered file) ECL/SWHA/UM, 31.

60. Lindeman, *Basic Selections* (1954) 198.
61. Lindeman, *Basic Selections* (1954) 213.
62. Lindeman, *Basic Selections* (1954) 179.
63. Lindeman, *Basic Selections* (1954) 408.
64. Lindeman, *Basic Selections* (1954) 176.
65. Lindeman, *Basic Selections* (1954) 161.
66. Lindeman, *Basic Selections* (1954) 172–173.
67. Lindeman, *Basic Selections* (1954) 194.
68. Lindeman, "Enduring Goal" (1947) 637.
69. Lindeman, "Functional Democracy" (1952) 27–28.
70. Lindeman, "Functional Democracy" (1952) 29.
71. Lindeman, "Egoism" (circa 1925) 58 [unpublished].
72. Lindeman, "Functional Democracy" (1952) 33.
73. Lindeman, "Functional Democracy" (1952) 28–29.
74. Lindeman, speech at City Club, Portland, Oregon (June 1952).
75. Smith and Lindeman, *Democratic Way* (1951) 123.
76. Lindeman, "Maturity" (1947) 89.
77. Lindeman, second speech at City Club of Portland, Oregon (June 1952).
78. Lindeman, "Maturity" (1947) 89.
79. Lindeman, "More Discipline" (1947) 36.
80. Lindeman, second speech at City Club of Portland, Oregon (June 1952).
81. Lindeman, "Birth Control" (1939) 27.
82. Lindeman, "New Patterns" (1937) 318.
83. Lindeman, "Prophetic" (1945) 380–381.

Chapter 13. *Bursting Institutional Boundaries: Reaching Out to Adult Learners*

1. Lindeman, "Manuscripts, A–I," Box 12, ECL/RBML/CU, 10–11.
2. Lindeman, "People Are Ready" (1943) 6.
3. Lindeman, "Education and Crisis" (1938) 129.
4. Lindeman, "Adult Education" (1944) 115.
5. Lindeman, "Professional School" (1928) 4.
6. Lindeman, "Scrapbook 1946 Autumn–1947 Winter," 127.
7. Lindeman, "After Lyceums" (1927) 248.
8. Eduard Lindeman to Max Otto, 21 October 1944.
9. Lindeman, "Grassroots" (1944) 282.
10. Eduard Lindeman to Frank King, 31 January 1947, in "Manuscripts, etc., 1946–1948," Box 10, ECL/RBML/CU.
11. Lindeman, "After Lyceums" (1927) 250.
12. Lindeman, "Rural Culture" (1924) 330.
13. Lindeman, "Preaching" (1926) 28.
14. Lindeman, "Preaching" (1926) 29.
15. Lindeman, "Preaching" (1926) 30.
16. Lindeman, "Preaching" (1926) 30.
17. Lindeman, "Preaching" (1926) 30.
18. Lindeman, "Preaching" (1926) 31.
19. "Editor," *Homiletic Review* (August 1926) 112.
20. Lindeman, "Rural Culture" (1924) 331.
21. Lindeman, "Scrapbook 1936," 69.
22. Lindeman, "Scrapbook 1936," 69.

23. Lindeman, "Why the American Labor," undated text, "Manuscripts A–I," Box 12, ECL/RBML/CU.
24. Lindeman, "Newer Currents" (1927) 174.
25. Lindeman and Thurston, *Parent Educators* (1929) 21.
26. Lindeman, "Bringing Father Back" (1932) 160–161.
27. Obituary, *Child Study* (1953) 2.
28. Davis, *Two-Bit Culture* (1984) 178.
29. Davis, *Two-Bit Culture* (1984) 113.
30. Davis, *Two-Bit Culture* (1984) 279–280.
31. Davis, *Two-Bit Culture* (1984) 337.
32. Konopka, *Eduard C. Lindeman* (1958).
33. Lindeman, "Basic Unities" (1934) 511.
34. Lindeman, "Basic Unities" (1934) 511.
35. Lindeman, "Basic Unities" (1934) 511.
36. Cohen, "Meaning of Lindeman for Social Work" (1953) [unpublished].
37. Lindeman, "Social Worker" (1924) 369.

Chapter 14. *Adult Education and National Crisis*

1. Lamson, *Roger Baldwin* (1976) 159–160.
2. Eduard Lindeman to Dorothy and Leonard Elmhirst, 19 February 1928.
3. John Hader, interview with author.
4. Eduard Lindeman to Dorothy Elmhirst, fall 1929.
5. *World Almanac 1932*.
6. John Hader, interview with author.
7. Wrege and Sakae, "Before Bales" (1984) 1, 15.
8. Eduard Lindeman to Leonard Elmhirst, 22 January 1932.
9. Eduard Lindeman to Leonard Elmhirst, 22 January 1932.
10. "The World of Today," "1935 Articles," Box 5, ECL/RBML/CU.
11. Eduard Lindeman to Dorothy Elmhirst, 2 January 1933.
12. Malcolm Knowles, interview with author.
13. e.g., Lindeman, "Scrapbook 1947–1948," 218.
14. Lindeman, "1928," Box 4, ECL/RBML/CU.
15. Lindeman, "Scrapbook 1947–1948," 94.
16. Lindeman, "Scrapbook 1937," 75.
17. Lindeman, "Scrapbook 1941–1942," 60–62.
18. Lindeman, "Undated, J–Z and Miscellaneous," Box 13, ECL/RBML/CU.
19. Lindeman, "1924 Articles," Box 4, ECL/RBML/CU.
20. Lindeman, "Scrapbook January 1951–October 1951," 228.
21. D.W.E., U.S. Office, "Bogue, No. 7, 1935–1936," DHT.
22. D.W.E., U.S. Office, "October 29, 1935 Report," DHT.
23. Eduard Lindeman to Dorothy Elmhirst, 14 March 1929.
24. Eduard Lindeman to Dorothy Elmhirst, 14 March 1929.
25. Eduard Lindeman to Dorothy Elmhirst, 14 March 1929.
26. Eduard Lindeman to Dorothy and Leonard Elmhirst, 19 January 1930.
27. Lindeman, *Social Education* (1933).
28. Eduard Lindeman to Charles Shaw, 12 January 1936.
29. e.g., Beard, *Saturday Review of Literature* (1936) 20, and Bricknell, *Review of Reviews* (1936) 14–21.
30. John Hader, interview with author.

31. Martha Anderson, interview with Miriam Stewart; Sally Ringe Goldmark, interview with Betty Leonard; John Hader, interview with author.
32. Max Otto to Eduard Lindeman, 13 October 1944.
33. e.g., Louise Croly to Dorothy Elmhirst, 3 June [1934?].
34. D.W.E., Gen. 2, "Croly Correspondence at Dartington," E. A. Stettner interview with Leonard Elmhirst, 7 June 1973, DHT.
35. Anne Reed Brenner to Eduard Lindeman, 2 December 1941, "Letters to and from John Dewey and Others," Box 2, ECL/RBML/CU.
36. Eduard Lindeman to Dorothy Elmhirst, 2 January 1933.
37. Gessner, *Democratic Man* (1956) 28.
38. Eduard Lindeman to Dorothy and Leonard Elmhirst, 14 July 1936.
39. Eduard Lindeman to Dorothy and Leonard Elmhirst, 3 January 1939.
40. Eduard Lindeman to Charles Shaw, 21 April 1936.
41. Eduard Lindeman to Max Otto, 13 June 1948.
42. Malcolm Knowles to author, 16 August 1985.
43. Lindeman, "Community Organization for Leisure," "Manuscripts, A–I," Box 12, ECL/RBML/CU.
44. Lindeman, "Community Organization for Leisure," "Manuscripts, A–I," Box 12, ECL/RBML/CU.
45. Lindeman, "Community Organization for Leisure," "Manuscripts, A–I," Box 12, ECL/RBML/CU.
46. Eduard Lindeman to Leonard Elmhirst, 3 November 1935.
47. Nathan Cohen, interview with Betty Leonard.
48. Eduard Lindeman to Charles Shaw, 12 January 1936.
49. Eduard Lindeman to Marion Beers, [1938?].
50. Marion Beers, interview with Betty Leonard.
51. Eduard Lindeman to Marion Beers, "Monday morning" [1939?].
52. Eduard Lindeman to Hazel Lindeman, August 1926.
53. Lindeman, "International Aspects" (1932–1933) 7.
54. Lindeman, "World Order" (1943) 26.
55. Lindeman, "World Order" (1943) 26.
56. Lindeman, "World Order" (1943) 26.
57. Lindeman, "World Order" (1943) 27.
58. Lindeman, "World Order" (1943) 27.
59. Eduard Lindeman to Dorothy and Leonard Elmhirst, 31 May 1940.
60. Eduard Lindeman to Dorothy and Leonard Elmhirst, 31 May 1940.
61. Eduard Lindeman to Leonard Elmhirst, 3 November 1935.
62. Straight, *After Long Silence* (1983).
63. Straight, *After Long Silence* (1983) 146.
64. Bruce Bliven to Eduard Lindeman, 13 August 1941.
65. Eduard Lindeman to Bruce Bliven, undated.
66. Lindeman, *Mental Hygiene* (1952) 14.
67. Lindeman, "Scrapbook 1941," 75.
68. Lindeman, "Pennsylvania League" (1930) 13.
69. Lindeman, *The Meaning* (1961) 49.

Chapter 15. *How Firm a Foundation? Adult Education for a Postwar World*

1. Lindeman, "Scrapbook 27 May 1948–October 29, 1948," 184.
2. Lindeman, "Scrapbook 1945," 166.

3. Lindeman, "Scrapbook 1945," 194.
4. Lindeman, "What Must We Do" (1946) 8.
5. Lindeman, "What Must We Do" (1946) 8.
6. Lindeman, "What Must We Do" (1946) 8.
7. Lindeman, "What Must We Do" (1946) 8.
8. Lindeman, "Death" (1945) 705.
9. Lindeman, "Death" (1945) 705.
10. Lindeman, "Death" (1945) 706.
11. Lindeman, "German Mind" (1945) 6.
12. Eduard Lindeman to Dorothy and Leonard Elmhirst, 15 June 1949.
13. Leonard Elmhirst to Eduard Lindeman, 23 June 1949.
14. Eduard Lindeman to Max Otto, 15 October 1949.
15. Eduard Lindeman to Max Otto, 15 October 1949.
16. Eduard Lindeman, "Scrapbook June 1949–December 1949," 185.
17. Eduard Lindeman to Max Otto, 28 July 1950.
18. Betty Leonard, conversation with author.
19. Hazel Lindeman to Leonard Elmhirst, 3 August [1953?].
20. Eduard Lindeman to Charles Shaw, 11 May 1950.
21. Eduard Lindeman to Charles Shaw, 31 May 1950.
22. Lindeman, "Scrapbook 1946–Autumn to 1947–Winter," 0.
23. "Personalities" (1950) 459.
24. Betty Leonard, conversation with author.
25. Lindeman, manuscript beginning with the words "professional circles," "E.C. Lindeman Manuscripts," Box 12, ECL/RBML/CU, 18–19.
26. Lindeman, manuscript beginning with the words "professional circles," "E.C. Lindeman Manuscripts," Box 12, ECL/RBML/CU, 18–19.
27. Lindeman, manuscript beginning with the words "professional circles," "E.C. Lindeman Manuscripts," Box 12, ECL/RBML/CU, 18–19.
28. Eduard Lindeman to Max Otto, 22 February 1951.
29. Eduard Lindeman to Charles Shaw, 26 November 1950.
30. Eduard Lindeman to Charles Shaw, 26 November 1950.
31. Eduard Lindeman to Charles Shaw, 2 February 1951.
32. Gessner, *Democratic Man* (1956) 32.
33. Knowles, *Adult Education Movement* (1962) 176.
34. Valerie Keating, interview with Betty Leonard.
35. Robert Sutherland to Eduard Lindeman, 21 September 1951.
36. Robert Sutherland to members of the TSTA general session program, 26 October 1951.
37. William Dalton to school superintendents and newspapers, apparently undated [Recipients mentioned in Gessner, *Democratic Man* (1956) 33].
38. William Dalton letter to school superintendents and newspapers, apparently undated.
39. William Dalton letter to school superintendents and newspapers, apparently undated.
40. William Dalton letter to school superintendents and newspapers, apparently undated.
41. Mortimer Brown to Eduard Lindeman, 6 November 1951.
42. *Dallas Morning News*, 8 November 1951.
43. Elmer Scott to Mortimer Brown, 8 November 1951.

44. Notes on statements in William H. Dalton letter for general circulation. "E.C. Lindeman Manuscripts, etc., 1949–1953," Box 11, ECL/RBML/CU.

45. Eduard Lindeman to Joe Hoffer, 16 February 1953.

46. Eduard Lindeman to Max Otto, 3 August 1952.

47. "Adult Education," ECL/SWHA/UM.

48. Gessner, *Democratic Man* (1956) 36.

49. Gessner, *Democratic Man* (1956) 36.

Chapter 16. *Eduard Lindeman's Agenda for Lifelong Education in America*

1. Eduard Lindeman to Dorothy Elmhirst, 14 March 1929.

2. Eduard Lindeman to Dorothy Elmhirst, 14 March 1929.

3. Naisbitt, *Megatrends* (1982) 93–94.

4. Toffler, *Third Wave* (1980) 384.

5. Toffler, *Third Wave* (1980) 346–347.

6. Toffler, *Third Wave* (1980) 353.

7. Toffler, *Third Wave* (1980) 130.

8. Lindeman, "Meaning of Adult Learning" (1929) 36.

9. Toffler, *Third Wave* (1980) 377.

10. Lindeman, "New Needs" (1944) 121–122.

11. Smith and Lindeman, *Democratic Way* (1951) 136.

12. Smith and Lindeman, *Democratic Way* (1951) 136.

13. Lindeman, *Social Education* (1933) 18.

14. Demorest, "He Saw the Mountain" (1953) 19.

15. Lindeman, *The Meaning* (1961) xxiii.

16. Lindeman, *The Meaning* (1961) xiv.

17. Tead, "About Eduard C. Lindeman" (1953) 55.

18. Knowles, *Andragogy* (1984) 9–12.

19. Lindeman, "Adult Education in Post War America" (undated) "Manuscripts, etc., 1946–1948," Box 10, ECL/RBML/CU.

20. Lindeman, "Adult Education in Post War America" (undated) "Manuscripts, etc., 1946–1948," Box 10, ECL/RBML/CU.

21. Lindeman, "American Education" (1939) 574.

22. Lindeman, *Workers' Education* (1926) 10.

23. Lindeman, "John Dewey" (1940) 7.

24. Lindeman, *The Meaning* (1961) 39.

25. Lindeman, "New Needs" (1944) 118.

26. Lindeman, "Social Thinking" (1927) 9.

27. Lindeman, "Trouble" (1944) 282.

28. Knowles, "New Way" (publication pending 1986) 5.

29. Lindeman, "Sociology" (1945) 8.

30. Lindeman, "Sociology" (1945) 8.

31. Eduard Lindeman to Michigan Council, 11 November 1947.

32. Lindeman, "After Lyceums" (1927) 247.

33. Lindeman, audio-tape of speech, 30 April 1948.

34. Lindeman, "Evaluating" (1953) 18–19.

35. Eduard Lindeman to Michigan Council, 11 November 1947.

36. Lindeman, "Broadcast—American Labor Party," 1 November 1942, "1942–1943 Manuscripts," Box 8, ECL/RBML/CU.

37. Lindeman, "Workers and Libraries" (1926) 16.
38. Lindeman, "After Lyceums" (1927) 250.
39. Eduard Lindeman to Michigan Council, 11 November 1947.
40. Eduard Lindeman to Michigan Council, 11 November 1947.
41. Lindeman, "How Work" (1929) 339; "How Shall Our Schools Educate To Eliminate the Menace of Extensive Social Upheavals," (undated) in "Manuscripts, etc., A–I," Box 12, ECL/RBML/CU, 10–11.
42. Lindeman, "Evaluating" (1953) 18.
43. Lindeman, "World Peace" (1945) 23.
44. Lindeman, "Next Steps" (1944) 413.
45. Lindeman, review of *Progress to Freedom* (1942) 835.
46. Lindeman, "Democratic Era" (1949) 65.
47. Lindeman, "Scrapbook 1945," 107.
48. Lindeman, "Group" (1938) 50.
49. Lindeman, "Scrapbook 1947–1948," 5.
50. Lindeman, *Dum Placem Peream"* (1942) 159.
51. Lindeman, "Introduction" (1937) 6.
52. Lindeman, "Introduction" (1937) 6.
53. *Chronicle of Higher Education*, 4 May 1981.
54. Eide, "Changing Realities" in Himmelstrup, Robinson, and Fielden (eds.) *Strategies* (1981) 42–43.
55. Lindeman, "Social Philosophy" (1952) 52.

Select Bibliography

This bibliographic listing is not an exhaustive accounting of sources. Rather, it is a selected recording of primary sources, secondary sources, and unpublished references that were found to be most useful in the construction of this book about the work and life of Eduard Lindeman.

CITED OR RELEVANT WORKS OF EDUARD LINDEMAN IN CHRONOLOGICAL ORDER

1912, *College Characters: Essays and Verse*. Port Huron, Mich.: Riverside Printing Co.

15 May 1915, "Legislature That Did No Harm." *Survey* 34: 163.

1919, *Boys' and Girls' Clubs; A Course of Study in Boys' and Girls' Club Leadership for County Normal Training Classes*, Bulletin No. 26. Lansing, Mich.: Dept. of Public Instruction.

April 1920, *Recreation and Rural Health*, Teachers' Leaflet No. 7 (Washington: U.S. Bureau of Education, Government Printing Office).

August 1921, "Feeding the Spirit of Childhood." *American Child* 3: 164–170.

1921, *The Community: An Introduction to the Study of Community Leadership and Organization*. New York: Association Press.

15 June 1922, "Professor Lindeman and the Klan." Letter to the editor and editor's reply. *Survey* 48: 417–418.

July 1922, "Peoples' Colleges for the New Europe." *Review of Reviews* (American) 66: 84–85.

Summer 1922, "Denmark: A Rural Culture." *World Agriculture* 2: 176, 179.

6 September 1922, "Cooperation in Tobacco." *New Republic* 32: 44–45.

1922, "Place of the Local Community in Organized Society. *National Conference of Social Work Proceedings* (Providence, R. I.) 67–77.

July 1923, "Recreation and the New Psychology." *Playground* 17: 211–212, 246–248.

1 August 1923, "Industrial Technique and Social Ethics." *Survey Graphic* 50: 492–494.

28 November 1923, "The Collapse of the Fishing Industry." *New Republic* 37: 17.

16 January 1924, "Self-Education for Scientists." *New Republic* 37: 192–193.

April 1924, "The Modern Student and Social Reform." *The Broadcaster* (Bulletin of Undergraduate Section, Intercollegiate Community Service Association, Poughkeepsie, N. Y.) I.

15 April 1924, "The Social Worker and His Community." *Survey* 52: 83–85.

15 April 1924, "The Social Worker as Prophet." *Survey* 52: 346, 369, 371.

30 July 1924, "The Farmer-Capitalist Myth." *New Republic* 39: 263–265.

19 November 1924, "Emerging American Philosophy." *New Republic* 40: 290–291.

15 December 1924, "Religion and Rural Culture." *Survey* 53: 329–331.

1924, *Social Discovery: An Approach to the Study of Functional Groups*. New York: Republic Publishing Co.

15 May 1925, "Adult Education: A Creative Opportunity." *Library Journal* 50: 445–447.

25 November 1925, "Adult Education." *New Republic* 54:7–8.

23 December 1925, "Integrating the Carol Kennicotts." *New Republic* 45: 130–132.

January 1926, "The Place of Producers and Consumers in a Co-operative Program from the Point of View of a Social Scientist." *Co-operation* 12: 6–9.

15 February 1926, "To Discover the Meaning of Experience." *Survey* 55: 545–546.

9 June 1926, reviews of *Spiritual Values in Adult Education*, by Basil A. Yeaxlee; and *The Way Out*, by Hon. Oliver Stanley, ed. *New Republic* 47: 96.

July 1926, "Is Preaching a Valid Method?" *Homiletic Review* 92: 27–31.

4 September 1926, reviews of *Regional Sociology*, by Radhamal Mukerjee; *History of Human Society*, by Frank W. Blackmar; and *Historical Materialism*, by Nikolai Bukharin. *Saturday Review of Literature* 3: 89.

October 1926, "Limitations of Discussion Methods." *Rural America* 4:7.

November 1926, "*Andragogik*: The Method of Teaching Adults." *Workers' Education* 4: 38.

8 December 1926, reviews of *The Folk High Schools of Denmark and the Development of a Farming Community*, by Holger Begtrup, Hans Lund, and Peter Manniche; *A Short Survey of Agriculture in Denmark*, by H. Hurtel (and three other books). *New Republic* 48: 84–85.

1926, *The Meaning of Adult Education*. New York: New Republic, Inc. (Reissued in 1961. Montreal: Harvest House, Ltd. Unless otherwise indicated, all citations are to the 1961 edition).

1926, *Workers' Education and the Public Libraries*, Workers Education Pamphlet Series, No. 7. New York: Workers' Education Bureau of America.

22 January 1927, "What Is Social Thinking?" *Scholastic* 8–9, 18.

1 March 1927, "A New Challenge to the Spirit of 1776." *Survey* 57: 679–82.

1 March 1927, (editor of special section), "An American Look at Fascism." *Survey* 57: 678–765.

1 March 1927, "A New Challenge to the Spirit of 1776." *Survey* 57: 679–682.

May 1927, "After Lyceums and Chautauquas, What?" *Bookman* 65: 246–250.

6 July 1927, "Newer Currents of Thought on Parent Education." *New Republic* 51: 172–174.

August 1927, "Private Life of Mary Haugen." *World Tomorrow* 10: 325–328.

1927, "Public Ownership," Bulletin No. 2. New York Federation of Progressive Women.

1927, (with Martha Anderson) *Education Through Experience: An Interpretation of the Methods of the Academy of Labor, Frankfurt-am-Main, Germany*, Workers' Education Research Series, Monograph No. 1. New York: Workers' Education Bureau Press, Inc.

15 January 1928, review of *Why Stop Learning*, by Dorothy Canfield Fisher. *Survey* 59: 526.

22 February 1928, "Adult Education: A New Means for Liberals." *New Republic* 54: 26–29.

7 March 1928, reviews of *What the Employer Thinks*, by J. David Houser; and *The Americanization of Labor*, by Robert W. Dunn. *New Republic* 54: 104–105.

April 1928, "Enjoying While Learning." *Trained Nurse* 413.

July 1928, "What May a Professional School of Social Work Reasonably Expect of Its Graduates?" *Bulletin of the New York School of Social Work* 21: 3–6.

1928, (with Nels Anderson) *Urban Sociology: An Introduction to the Study of Urban Communities*. New York: Alfred A. Knopf.

January–February–March 1929, "Meaning of Adult Learning." *Progressive Education* 6: 35–39.

April 1929, "Conference Method: A Plea for Interchange of Experience on a New Basis." *Journal of Adult Education* 1: 142–144.

June 1929, "Adult Learning and the University Woman." *American Association of University Women Journal* 22: 176–178.

August 1929, "How Work for a New Society?" *World Tomorrow* 12: 337–340.

September–October 1929, "Inquiry Principles." *Inquiry* 101–103.

28 October–9 November 1929, "Conference Method in Employee Representation Plans and Procedures," in *Conference as an Agency of Industrial Progress*. Preliminary papers prepared for the Third General Session of the Institute of Pacific Relations. American Council, Institute of Pacific Relations, 16: 35–48.

20 November 1929, "Conference and Compromise." *New Republic* 60: 364–365.

November 1929, "Adult Education Becomes a World Movement." *Fraternity* 2: 7.

1929, (editor with Flora Thurston) *Problems for Parent Educators: Outlines of Problems Discussed at the Annual Meeting of the National Council of Parent Education*. Outline of problems discussed at the annual meeting of the National Council of Parent Educators, Atlantic City, N.J., 14–17, November, 1928, and at The Home Problems Conference, the Merrill-Palmer School, Detroit, 18–20 April 1927. New York: National Council of Parent Education.

1929, (with John Hader) "The Authorities, Functions, and Limitations of Committees," in *Committees, Their Purposes, Functions and Administration*, General Management Series, No. 96. New York: American Management Association.

1929, (with John Hader) *What Do Workers Study?* Workers' Education Research Series, Monograph No. 2, Workers' Education Bureau Press.

1929, *Church in the Changing Community*, Community Religion Series No. 4, New York: Community Church of New York.

February 1930, "Parents' Dilemma," in *The Child's Emotions*. Proceedings of the Mid-West Conference on Character Development. Chicago Association for Child Study and Parent Education: 352–359.

April 1930, "Parent Education as a Social Movement," in *Parent Education: The First Yearbook*. Washington: National Congress of Parents and Teachers, 1: 10–16.

May 1930, "Parent Education as Adjustment to the Modern World." *Child Study* 7: 234–235.

16 July 1930, "A Man of Wisdom." [Herbert Croly] *New Republic* 63: 263–265.

October 1930, "Pennsylvania League of Women Voters." *Bulletin*, Pennsylvania League of Women Voters.

1930, "Community," in *Encyclopedia of the Social Sciences*. New York: Macmillan. 4: 102–105.

1930, "Psychology of Social Change," in *A New Economic Order*, ed. Kirby Page. New York: Harcourt, Brace and Co., 357–371.

February 1931, "Six Questions for Parent Education." *Child Study* 8: 171–172.

February 1931, "The Conditions of Creative Thought." *Progressive Education* 8: 112–115.

1931, (ed. jointly with Flora Thurston) *Problems for Parent Educators*. New York: National Council of Parent Education (Vol. 2).

February 1932, "Bringing Father Back into the Family." *Child Study* 9: 159–162.

July 1932, "Social Perspectives for Social Planning." *Bulletin*, New York School of Social Work 25: 11–14.

October 1932, "Education and the World Crisis." *Bulletin*, Temple University Teachers College, Conference on Secondary Education.

November 1932, "Goals and Methods." *International Quarterly of Adult Education* *1: 121–126.*

June 1932–1933, "Some International Aspects of Adult Education." *International Quarterly of Adult Education.* London: The World Association for Adult Education. 1: 6–13.

8 March 1933, "Is Human Nature Changing in Russia?" *New Republic* 74: 95–98.

May 1933, "Social Methods for Social Problems: A Note on the Function of the Discussion Leader in Educational Conferences." *Progressive Education* *10: 253–255.*

1933, (with John Hader) *Dynamic Social Research.* New York: Harcourt, Brace, and Co.

1933, *Social Education: An Interpretation of the Principles and Methods Developed by The Inquiry During the Years 1923–1933.* New York: New Republic, Inc.

February 1934, "Mary Parker Follett." *Survey Graphic* 23: 86.

November 1934, reviews of *An Introduction to Pareto: His Sociology*, by George C. Homans and Charles P. Curtis, Jr. *Survey Graphic* 70: 363–364.

1934, "Basic Unities in Social Work," in *Proceedings*, National Conference of Social Work.

15 February 1935, "Implications of Contemporary Social Trends for Education in Family Life and Parenthood." *Parent Education* 1: 6–10, 42.

June–July 1935, "The Place of Discussion in the Learning Process." *Journal of Home Economics* 27: 348–350.

September 1935, review of *The Mind and Society*, by Vilfredo Pareto. *Survey Graphic* 24: 453–454.

December 1935, review of *Rotary and Its Brothers: An Analysis and Interpretation of the Men's Service Club*, by Charles F. Marden. *Survey* 71: 378.

April 1936, "Democracy and Group Living." *School and Home* 17: 3–6.

April 1936, "Index of American Morale." *Survey Graphic* 25: 211–213.

1936, *Wealth and Culture.* New York: Harcourt, Brace and Co.

April 1937, "Farewell to Bohemia." *Survey Graphic* 26: 207–208.

23–29 May 1937, "New Patterns of Community Organization." *National Conference of Social Work Proceedings*, 64th Annual Session, Indianapolis, 317–323.

30 October 1937, "What Democracy Means to Me." *Scholastic* 31: 10.

1937, "Adult Education," in *Encyclopedia of the Social Sciences.* New York: Columbia University Press. 1: 463–466.

1937, "Introduction," in *Adult Education for Social Change: A Handbook for Leaders and Members of Discussion Groups, Forums, and Adult Classes*, ed. Thomas K. Brown, Jr. (Swarthmore Seminar, Philadelphia) 4–6.

1937, "Introduction," in *Adult Education for Social Change: A Handbook for Leaders and Members of Discussion Groups, Forums, and Adult Classes*, ed. Thomas K. Brown, Jr. (Prepared for Swarthmore Seminar, Philadelphia).

1937, "Economic Planning and the Culture Complex," in *Planner Society*, ed. Findlay MacKenzie. New York: Prentice-Hall. 613–628.

1937, "The Crisis of Maturity: Personal and Cultural," in *Educational Planning for the Future.* Columbus: American Education Press. 21–28.

November 1938, "Education and the Crisis of Democracy." *Michigan Education Journal* 16: 129.

1938, "Group and Democracy," in *New Trends in Group Work*, ed. Joshua Lieberman (New York: Association Press) 47–53.

July 1939, "The Responsibilities of Birth Control." *Atlantic Monthly* 164: 22–28.

October 1939, "The Goal of American Education." *Survey Graphic* 28: 570–571.

November 1939, [Lindeman?] "The Ramparts of Truth." *National Parent-Teacher* 34: 21–24.

13 January 1940, "John Dewey As Educator." *School and Society* 51: 33–37.

Summer 1940, "Behold Our Home!" *Child Study* 17: 104–106.

15 October 1940, "In the Face of Darkness: A Re-Affirmation." *Frontiers of Democracy* 7: 15–17.

1940, *Group Reading: An Experiment and an Invitation* (Excerpt reprinted in *Twentieth Anniversary Yearbook*, New York Education Council).

May 1941, review of *Children Are People*, by Emily Post (and two other books). *Survey* 77: 163–164.

October 1941, "Personality and Social Pressures." *National Association of Deans of Women Journal* 5: 3–6.

November 1941, "Recreation and Morale." *American Journal of Sociology* 47: 394–405.

15 February 1942, "*Dum Placem Peream*." *Library Journal* 67: 157–159.

Winter 1942, "Emerson: Radical Democrat." *Common Ground* 2: 3–6.

15 May 1942, "Why I Believe in Education?" *Library Journal* 67: 457–459.

15 June 1942, reviews of *Progress to Freedom*, by Agnes Benedict; and *Development and Learning: The Psychology of Childhood and Youth in a Democratic Society*, by William F. Bruce and Frank J. Freeman. *New Republic* 106: 835.

15 October 1942, "The Supreme Aim of This War." *Frontiers of Democracy* 9: 5–8.

1942, *A People's War and a People's Peace*. New York: Society for Ethical Culture.

Winter 1943, "Contingency Plus Continuity: An Essay in Defense of Pluralism." *Christendom* 8: 51–60.

January 1943, "Education in a Total War." *Progressive Education Association* 20: 4–6.

April 1943, "Education for World Order." *Social Progress* 33: 26–28.

July 1943, "The People Are Ready," in *The People Are Ready To Discuss the Post-War World*. ed. Winifred Fisher. New York: Joint Committee Supervising the Experiment in Adult Education for Post-War Planning, New York Adult Education Council. 9–11.

January 1944, "New Needs for Adult Education," in *Annals of the American Academy of Political and Social Sciences*. 231: 115–122.

April 1944, "Vacations in a Free Land." *National Parent-Teacher* 38: 16–18.

12 June 1944, "Division in Education." *New Republic* 110: 783–784.

June 1944, "Trouble at the Grass Roots." *Survey Graphic* 33: 280–282.

Summer 1944, "Next Steps for Racial Understanding: A Philosophical Approach." *Journal of Negro Education* 13: 407–413.

1944, "Russell's Concise Social Philosophy," in *The Philosophy of Bertrand Russell*, ed. Paul Arthur Schlipp. Evanston, Ill.: Northwestern University Press. 559–577. (Reissued in *The Library of Living Philosophers*, 5. LaSalle, Ill.: The Open Court Publishing Co., 1971).

March 1945, "World Peace Through Adult Education." *Nation's Schools* 35: 23.

Spring 1945, "The Professionals." *Antioch Review* 5: 6–15.

Summer 1945, "Professors in Prophetic Mood." *American Scholar* 14: 380–381.

September 1945, "The Sociology of Adult Education." *Educational Sociology* 19: 4–13.

22 October 1945, "For an Annual Wage in the South." *New Republic* 113: 531.

26 November 1945, "Death of a German Generation." *New Republic* 113: 705–707.

15 December 1945, "Inside the German Mind." *Saturday Review of Literature* 28: 5–6.

1945, "Group Tensions in American Society," in *Civilization and Group Relationship*, ed. R. M. MacIver, Institute for Religious and Social Study. New York: Harper. 29–37.

1945, *Palestine: Test of Democracy*. New York: Christian Council on Palestine and American Palestine Committee.

3 January 1946, "What Must We Do To De-Nazify the German People?" *Town Meeting Bulletin* 11: 36.

27 July 1946, review of *Concept of the Corporation*, by Peter Drucker. *Saturday Review of Literature* 29(2): 17–18.

Winter 1947, "Emerson's Pragmatic Mood." *American Scholar* 16: 57–64.

January 1947, "Character and Citizenship Through Democratic Discipline." *Journal of Religious Education* 42: 224–228.

Summer 1947, "More Discipline for Liberals." *Humanist* 7: 36–37.

July 1947, "Adult Education and the Democratic Discipline." *Adult Education Journal* 6: 112–115.

November 1947, "The Enduring Goal." *Survey Graphic* 36: 637–640.

1947, "Maturity and Culture." *American Journal of Psychoanalysis* 7: 88–89.

1947, (editor), *Emerson, the Basic Writings of America's Sage*. New York: Penguin Books, Inc.

January 1948, "Dynamics of Recreational Theory." *Journal of Educational Sociology* 21: 263–269.

December 1948, "The American Democracy: A Commentary and an Interpretation." *Political Science Quarterly* 63: 599–601.

June 1949, review of *Human Relations in a Changing World*, by Alexander H. Leighton. *Survey* 85: 332–333.

1949, "Education for a New Democratic Era," in *Defense of Democracy*, ed. Thomas Herbert Johnson. New York: G. P. Putnam's Sons. 63–82.

January 1950, "Rulers of the New India." *The Progressive* 14: 13–14.

1950, (editor), *Plutarch's Lives: Life Stories of Men Who Shaped History*. New York: New American Library.

Winter 1951, "The Voice of the Concurring People: An Appeal on Behalf of Democratic Discussion." *The University of Kansas City Review* 18: 129–135.

March 1951, "Qualities of a Professional Recreation Worker." *Recreation* 44: 533.

December 1951, "The Group: Hero and Villain of the Future." *Christian Register* 130: 15.

1951, (with T.V. Smith as principal author), *The Democratic Way of Life*, Mentor Book published by the New American Library of World Literature, Inc.

1951, "Individual in a World of Conflict," in *Education During World Transition*, proceedings of the Illinois Summer Educational Conference, ed. Charles Moore Allen and J. Lloyd Trump. Urbana, Ill.: University of Illinois Press. 11–20.

October 1952, "John Dewey on the Doctrine of the Golden Mean." *Progressive Education* 30: 8–10.

1952, "Functional Democracy in Human Relations," in *Toward Better Human Relations*, ed. Lloyd Allen Cook. Detroit: Wayne University Press. 21–34.

1952, *Mental Hygiene and the Moral Crisis of Our Time*. Austin, Texas: The Hogg Foundation for Mental Health, The University of Texas.

1952, "Social Philosophy: Its Method and Purpose," in *Cleavage in Our Culture: Studies in Scientific Humanism in Honor of Max Otto*, ed. Frederick Henry Burkhardt. Boston: The Beacon Press. 51–66.

April 1953, (with the Issue Committee), "Evaluating Your Program (Tool Kit)." *Adult Leadership* 1: 13–20.

1952, "A Fantasy," foreword to *Volunteer Handbook for YWCA*, reprinted as special booklet. [Also printed in *Protestant Welfare News* (April 1950) 1:4].

May 1953, "Choosing Our Goals for Leadership: Our Readers' Goals." *Adult Leadership* 2: 25–26.

1954, (editor), *Basic Selections From Emerson: Essays, Poems and Apothegms*. New York: A Mentor Book, New American Library.

1961, *The Meaning of Adult Education*. Montreal: Harvest House. (Originally published by New Republic, Inc., New York, in 1926).

PUBLISHED SECONDARY SOURCES

Abrahams, Edward. Review of *Herbert Croly of the New Republic*, by David Levy. *Washington Post* (12 May 1985).

Adams, Frank (with Myles Horton). *Unearthing Seeds of Fire*. Winston-Salem, N.C.: John F. Blair, Publisher, 1975.

Adams, Henry. *The Education of Henry Adams*. Boston: Houghton Mifflin Co., 1961.

"An Addition to the College Faculty." *The Association College Bulletin* 13 (December 1918): 19.

Alford, Harold J. "The Evolution of an Idea: from Danish Folk High School to Residential Center for Continuing Education." University of Chicago, Continuing Education Report, No. 18, 1969.

"Annual Report of the Executive Director." Bulletin of the American Association for Adult Education. New York: 1926–1927.

Apps, Jerold W. *Improving Practice in Continuing Education*. San Francisco: Jossey-Bass, Publishers, 1985.

————. *Toward a Working Philosophy of Adult Education*. Syracuse, N.Y.: Syracuse Publications in Continuing Education and ERIC Clearinghouse on Adult Education, 1973.

Baunsbak-Jensen, Asger. "Danes Flock To Adult Education Classes." *Factsheet/Denmark*. Copenhagen: Press and Cultural Relations Department, Ministry of Foreign Affairs, undated.

Beal, W. J. *History of the Michigan Agricultural College and Biographical Sketches of Trustees and Professors*. East Lansing, Mich.: Michigan Agricultural College, 1915.

Beals, Ralph A., and Leon Brody. *The Literature of Adult Education*. New York: American Association for Adult Education, 1941.

Beard, Charles A. Review of *Wealth and Culture*, by Eduard Lindeman. *Saturday Review of Literature* 13 (14 March 1936): 20.

Bernstein, Saul, et al. *The New York School of Social Work 1898–1941*. New York: Institute of Welfare Research, Community Service Society of New York, 1942.

Bird, Caroline. *Enterprising Women*. New York: W. W. Norton and Co., Inc., 1976.

————. *The Invisible Scar*. New York: D. McKay, Co., 1966.

Bonham Carter, Victor, and W. B. Curry. *Dartington Hall*. London: Phoenix House, 1958, and Somerset: Exmoor Press, 1970.

Branson, Eugene C. *Farm Life Abroad: Field Letters from Germany, Denmark, and France*. Chapel Hill, N.C.: The University of North Carolina Press, 1924.

Brickell, Herschel. Review of *Wealth and Culture*, by Eduard Lindeman. *Review of Reviews* 93 (April 1936): 14–21.

Brookfield, Stephen. "The Contribution of Eduard Lindeman to the Development of Theory and Philosophy in Adult Education." *Adult Education Quarterly* 34 (Summer 1984): 185–196.

Buchholz, H.E. Review of *The Meaning of Adult Education*, by Eduard Lindeman. *The Nation* 124 (9 February 1927): 150–151.

Bugge, K.E. "Grundtvig's Challenge to Modern Educational Thought." *Education for Life*. International Conference on the Occasion of the Bicentenary of N.S.F. Grundtvig. Copenhagen: *Det Danske Selskab* (10–14 September 1983).

Bugge, K.E. "Grundtvig's Educational Ideas," in *N.S.F. Grundtvig, Tradition and Renewal*. Copenhagen: *DET Danske Selskab*; Philadelphia: Nordic Books Distributor, 1983.

Bugge, K.E. *Skolen for Livet: Studier over N.F.S. Grundtvigs Pædagogiske Tanker*. Copenhagen: *Institut for Dansk Kirkehistorie*, 1965. [Published in Danish but includes English language summary by Nöelle Davis, 361–369].

Bukharin, Nikolai. *Historical Materialism: A System of Sociology*. New York: International Publishers, 1925.

Carlson, Robert A. "Professionalization of Adult Education: An Historical-Philosophical Analysis." *Adult Education* 28 (Fall 1977): 53–63.

Cartwright, Morse A. *Ten Years of Adult Education*. New York: The Macmillan Co., 1935.

_____, ed. *Adult Education and Democracy*. New York: American Association for Adult Education, 1936.

Chambers, Clarke A. *Paul U. Kellogg and the Survey: Voices for Social Welfare and Social Justice*. Minneapolis: University of Minnesota Press, 1971.

_____. *Seedtime of Reform*. Minneapolis: University of Minnesota Press, 1963.

Clark, Evans. Review of *The Meaning of Adult Education*, by Eduard Lindeman, *New York Times*, 9 January 1927.

Cooley, Charles H. *Social Process*. New York: Charles Scribner's Sons, 1918.

Cotton, Webster E. *On Behalf of Adult Education*. Boston: Center for the Study of Liberal Education for Adults, 1968.

Croly, Herbert. *The Promise of American Life*. New York: Archon Books, Copyright 1909 by the Macmillan Co., reprinted 1963.

_____. *Willard Straight*. New York: The Macmillan Co., 1924.

Cross, K. Patricia. *Adults As Learners*. San Francisco: Jossey-Bass, Inc., 1981.

_____. "The Changing Role of Higher Education in the Learning Society." *Continuum* (Spring 1985): 101–110.

Dam, Poul. *N.S.F. Grundtvig*. Copenhagen: Royal Danish Ministry of Foreign Affairs, Press and Cultural Relations Department, 1983.

Dave, Ravindra H., ed. *Foundations of Lifelong Education*. Published for the UNESCO Institute for Education. Oxford: Pergamon Press, 1976.

_____. *Reflections on Lifelong Education and the School*. Published for UNESCO Institute for Education. Hamburg: 1975.

Davies, Nöelle. *Education for Life: A Danish Pioneer*. London: Williams and Norgate, 1931.

Davis, Kenneth C. *Two-Bit Culture: The Paperbacking of America*. Boston: Houghton Mifflin Co., 1984.

Demorest, Charlotte D. "He Saw the Mountain in the Molehill." *20th Anniversary Yearbook of Adult Education 1953*. New York: New York Adult Education Council, Inc., 1953. 18–20.

Dewey, John. *Democracy and Education.* New York: Macmillan, 1916.

————. *Experience and Nature.* New York: Dover Publications, Inc., 1958; original by Open Court in 1925.

————. *How We Think.* Boston: D. C. Heath and Co., Publishers, 1910.

————. *Human Nature and Conduct,* War Department Education Manual EM618. Published for the U.S. Armed Forces Institute. New York: Henry Holt and Co., Inc., 1944, original by Henry Holt and Co., 1922.

————. *John Dewey on Education.* ed. Reginald D. Archambault. New York: The Modern Library, Random House, Inc., 1964.

Diggins, John P. *Mussolini and Fascism: The View from America.* Princeton, N.J.: Princeton University Press, 1972.

"Dr. Eduard C. Lindeman, NCSW President—1952–53." *Conference Bulletin,* National Council of Social Work, Columbus, Ohio (Summer 1953): 5.

Durant, Will. *The Story of Philosophy.* New York: Simon and Schuster, Inc., 1926.

Education for Life. Report on an International Conference on the Occasion of the Bicentenary of N.S.F. Grundtvig. *Det Danske Selskat* (10–14 September 1983).

Eide, Kjell. "Changing Realities of Work, Leisure, Education," in *Strategies for Lifelong Learning,* edited by Per Himmelstrup, John Robinson, and Derrick Fielden. Esbjerg, Denmark: Published jointly by the University Centre of South Jutland, Denmark, and the Association for Recurrent Education, United Kingdom, 1981.

Elias, John, and Sharan Merriam. *Philosophical Foundations in Adult Education.* Melbourne, Fla.: Krieger Publishing Co., Inc. 1980.

Fadiman, Clifton. Review of *The Meaning of Adult Education,* by Eduard Lindeman. *New York Evening Post Literary Review* (15 January 1927).

"Farmers and Tradespeople Soon To Rule." *Toronto Globe,* 28 June 1924.

54th Annual Report of the Secretary of the State Board of Agriculture of the State of Michigan and 28th Annual Report of the Experiment Station, 1 July 1914–30 June 1915. Lansing, Mich.: 1 July 1915 (AHC/MSU).

55th Annual Report of the Secretary of the State Board of Agriculture of the State of Michigan and 29th Annual Report of the Experiment Stations, 1 July 1915–30 June 1916. Lansing, Mich.: 1916 (AHC/MSU).

56th Annual Report of the Secretary of the State Board of Agriculture of the State of Michigan and 30th Annual Report of the Experiment Station, 1 July 1916–30 June 1917. Lansing, Mich.: 1917 (AHC/MSU).

57th Annual Report of the Secretary of the State Board of Agriculture of the State of Michigan and the 31st Annual Report of the Experiment Station, 1 July 1917–30 June 1918. Lansing, Mich.: 1919 (AHC/MSU).

58th Annual Report of the Secretary of the State Board of Agriculture of the State of Michigan and 32nd Annual Report of the Experiment Station, 1 July 1918–30 June 1919. Lansing, Mich.: 1920 (AHC/MSU).

Fisher, Winifred, "Eduard C. Lindeman, 1885–1953." *Adult Education* 3 (May 1953): 133.

————, and Anthony Netboy. "An Experiment in Adult Education." *Dynamic America* 13 (November 1941): 15–16.

Follett, Mary P. "Community Is a Process." *Philosophical Review* 28 (November 1919): 576–588.

————. *Creative Experience.* New York: Longmans, Green and Co., 1924.

————. *The New State.* Gloucester, Mass.: Peter Smith, 1965, copyright, 1918.

Fox, Elliot M. "Mary Parker Follett: The Enduring Contribution." *Public Administration Review* 28 (November–December 1968): 520–528.

Gessner, Robert, ed. *The Democratic Man; Selected Writings.* Boston: Beacon Press, 1956.

Grundtvig, Nikolai. *Selected Writings / N.S.F. Grundtvig.* Edited and with an introduction by Johannes Knudsen. Philadelphia: Fortress Press, 1976.

Hall, Walter Phelps, and William Stearns Davis. *The Course of Europe Since Waterloo.* New York: D. Appleton-Century Co., Inc., 2nd ed. 1947.

Harrington, Avery. "Normal Physiology and Function of the Kidney," in *Proceedings of the Conference on the Dietetic Therapy of Renal Diseases.* Sponsored by The Wisconsin Regional Medical Program, The Kidney Foundation of Wisconson, and the Wisconsin Dietetic Association. Madison, Wis. (September 1971): 19–22.

Hart, Joseph K. *Adult Education.* New York: Thomas Y. Crowell Co., 1927.

———. "Education and the Folk-Ways." *The New Republic* 54 (22 February 1928): 41–44.

Hesburgh, Theodore M., Paul A. Miller, and Clifton R. Wharton, Jr. *Patterns for Lifelong Learning.* San Francisco: Jossey-Bass Publishers, 1973.

Hewes, Amy. Review of *The Meaning of Adult Education*, by Eduard C. Lindeman. *Survey* 57 (15 February 1927): 653–654.

Higher Education Act of 1965, Title I, Part B.

Hilton, Ronald J. "The Short Happy Life of a Learning Society: Adult Education in America, 1930–39." Ph.D. dissertation, Syracuse University, 1981.

Himmelstrup, Per; John Robinson and Derrick Fielden, eds. *Strategies for Lifelong Learning.* Esbjerg, Denmark: Published jointly by the University Centre of South Jutland, Denmark, and the Association for Recurrent Education, United Kingdom, 1981.

The Holcad (AHC/MSU).

Houle, Cyril O. *Patterns of Learning.* San Francisco: Jossey-Bass Publishers, 1984.

Howe, Frederic C. *Denmark A Cooperative Commonwealth.* New York: Harcourt, Brace, and Co., 1921.

Howick, William H. *Philosophies of Western Education.* Danville, Ill.: The Interstate Printers and Publishers, Inc., 1971.

Hutchins, Robert M. *The Learning Society.* New York: Praeger Publishers, 1968.

Isley, P. "The Relevance of the Future in Adult Education: a Phenomenological Analysis of Images of the Future." *Proceedings of the Adult Education Research Conference* (1983) 24:124–129.

James, William. *Pragmatism.* Cambridge, Mass.: Harvard University Press, 1975.

King, Evelyn M., comp. and ed. *Under the Mustard Tree.* Centennial 1864–1964, Plymouth Congregational Church, Lansing, Michigan.

Kirkpatrick, J. E. Review of *The Meaning of Adult Education*, by Eduard C. Lindeman. *New York World*, 16 January 1927.

Knowles, Malcolm S. *The Adult Education Movement in the United States.* New York: Holt, Rinehart and Winston, 1962.

———. *Andragogy in Action.* San Francisco: Jossey-Bass Publishers, 1984.

———. *The Modern Practice of Adult Education.* New York: Association Press, 1970.

———. "Toward a Model of Lifelong Education." in *Reflections on Lifelong Education and the School.* Edited by Ravindra H. Dave. UIE Monographs 3: 10–14. Hamburg: UNESCO Institute for Education, 1975.

Knox, Alan B. *Adult Development and Learning.* San Francisco: Jossey-Bass Publishers, 1977.

Knudsen, Johannes. *Danish Rebel: A Study of N.S.F. Grundtvig.* Philadelphia: Muhlenberg Press, 1955.

Konopka, Gisela. *Eduard C. Lindeman and Social Work Philosophy.* Minneapolis: University of Minnesota Press, 1958.

Kuhn, Madison. *Michigan State University: The First Hundred Years.* East Lansing, Mich.: State University Press, 1955.

Kulich, Jindra. "N.S.F. Grundtvig's Folk High School Idea and the Challenge of Our Times." *Lifelong Learning* 7 (January 1984): 10–13.

Lamson, Peggy. *Roger Baldwin.* Boston: Houghton Mifflin Co., 1976.

Landon, Fred. *Lake Huron.* Indianapolis: Bobbs-Merrill Co., 1944.

Laski, Harold J. "On the Prospects of Adult Education." *The New Republic* 54 (22 February 1928): 47–50.

Lawton, William Cranston. "An Extensionist's Apologia." *The Citizen* 1 (June 1895): 84–87.

Learned, William S. *The American Public Library and the Diffusion of Knowledge.* New York: Harcourt, Brace and World, Inc., 1924.

Levy, David W. *Herbert Croly of the New Republic.* Princeton, N.J.: Princeton University Press, 1985.

Lewis, Rosa B. "The Philosophical Roots of Lifelong Learning." Toledo, Ohio: Center for the Study of Higher Education, 1981.

"Lindeman, Mr. Edward [sic] C. (U.S.A.)—at Cambridge on Adult Education." *London Times*, 28 August 1929.

Livingston, Sir Richard. *On Education.* Cambridge: University Press, 1956.

Lord, Russell. *The Agrarian Revival.* New York: American Association for Adult Education, 1939.

Martin, Everett Dean. *The Meaning of a Liberal Education.* New York: W. W. Norton and Co., 1926.

Martin, Glen Otis. *N.F.G. Grundtvig: The Man and His Theology.* Ann Arbor, Mich.: University Microfilms, 1950.

Maxtone-Graham, John. *The Only Way To Go.* New York: The Macmillan Co.,1972.

McHenry, Robert, ed. *Liberty's Women.* Springfield, Mass.: G & C Merriam Co.,1980.

Merriam, Sharan B., ed. *Selected Writings on Philosophy and Adult Education.* Malabar, Fla.: Robert E. Krieger Publishing Co., 1984.

————. "Philosophical Perspectives on Adult Education: A Critical Review of the Literature." *Adult Education* 27 (No. 4, 1977): 195–208.

Mezirow, Jack. "Perspective Transformation." *Adult Education* 28 (No. 2, 1978): 100–110.

Moore, Edward C., *American Pragmatism: Peirce, James, and Dewey.* New York: Columbia University Press, 1961.

Mumford, Lewis. Review of *The Meaning of Adult Education*, by Eduard C. Lindeman. *Progressive Education* 4 (April-May-June 1927): 139–141.

Mussolini, Arnaldo. "*A Noi!*" *Survey* 57 (1 March 1927): 691–694.

Naisbitt, John. *Megatrends.* New York: Warner Books, 1982.

Nicholls, Charles W. deLyon. *The Ultra-Fashionable Peerage of America.* New York: G. Harjes, 1904.

The 1919 Report. The Final and Interim Reports of the Adult Education Committee of the Ministry of Reconstruction 1918–1919. Nottingham, England: Department of Adult Education, University of Nottingham, 1980.

"Obituary" [Eduard Lindeman]. *Child Study* 30 (Summer 1953): 2.

Overstreet, Harry A. *Influencing Human Behavior.* New York: The People's Institute Publishing Co., Inc., 1925.

———, and Bonaro W. Overstreet. *Leaders for Adult Education.* New York: American Association for Adult Education, undated.

Patten, Simon N. "The Place of University Extension." *University Extension* 3 (February 1894): 258–292.

Percy, Lord Eustice. "Education and National Politics," in *The Way Out.* ed. Oliver Stanley. London: Oxford University Press, 1923. 60–67.

"Personalities and Projects." [Eduard Lindeman] *Survey* 86 (October 1950): 459–460.

Power, Edward J. "John Dewey: Reform for Relevance." *Evolution of Educational Doctrine: Major Educational Theorists of the Western World.* New York: Appleton-Century Crofts, 1969.

"Professor Lindeman." *The Association College Bulletin* 14 (August 1919): 5.

"Professor Lindeman Resigns." *The Association College Bulletin* 14 (December 1919): 11.

"Program." 2nd Annual Meeting of the American Association for Adult Education. Cleveland Museum of Art, Cleveland, Ohio (16–18 May 1927).

Propaganda Analysis. Vol. 1 of the Publications of the Institute for Propaganda Analysis, Inc. (October 1937–October 1938).

Propaganda Analysis. Vol. 2 of the Publications of the Institute for Propaganda Analysis, Inc. (November 1938–September 1939).

Review of *The Meaning of Adult Education*, by Eduard C. Lindeman. *Boston Transcript*, 5 February 1927.

Review of *The Meaning of Adult Education*, by Eduard C. Lindeman. *Michigan Library Bulletin* (November 1927): 278.

Review of *The Meaning of Adult Education*, by Eduard C. Lindeman. *Saturday Review of Literature* 3 (January 1927): 551.

Review of *The Meaning of Adult Education*, by Eduard C. Lindeman. *Wisconsin Library Bulletin* 23 (October 1927): 222.

Robinson, James Harvey. *The Humanizing of Knowledge.* New York: George H. Doran Co., 1924.

Rose, Amy O. "Toward the Organization of Knowledge: Adult Education in the 1920's." Ph.D. dissertation, Teachers College, Columbia University, 1979.

Rosen, Vivian. Review of *The Meaning of Adult Education*, by Eduard C. Lindeman. *The Daily Worker* [Clipping in "1927 Manuscripts, etc.," Box 4, ECL/RBML/CU].

Salvemini, Gaetano. "The Reign of the Bludgeon." *Survey* 57 (1 March 1927): 595–598.

Sheats, Paul H. "The Bridge Between Schooling and Adult Education," in *Reflections on Lifelong Education and the School.* Edited by Ravindra H. Dave. UIE Monographs 3: 21–26. Hamburg: UNESCO Institute for Education, 1975.

Skovmand, Roar. "Grundtvig and the Folk High School," in *N.S.F. Grundtvig, Tradition and Renewal.* Copenhagen: *DET Danske Selskab*; Philadelphia: Nordic Books Distributor, 1983.

Slumstrup, Finn. *N.S.F. Grundtvig (Factsheet/Denmark).* Copenhagen: Royal Danish Ministry of Foreign Affairs, 1983.

Small, Albion W. Review of *Social Discovery*, by Eduard C. Lindeman. *American Journal of Sociology* 30 (September 1924): 214–216.

Smith, Philip G. *Philosophy of Education.* New York: Harper and Row, 1964.

Smith, Robert. *Learning How To Learn.* Chicago: Follett, 1982.

Smith, T.V., and Eduard C. Lindeman. *The Democratic Way of Life.* New York: New American Library, 1951.

Stanley, Oliver, ed. *The Way Out.* Essays on the Meaning and Purpose of Adult Education by Members of the British Institute of Adult Education. London: Oxford University Press, 1923.

Stewart, David W. "Eduard Lindeman and the Idea of Lifelong Learning in America," in *Proceedings, Lifelong Learning Research Conference.* University of Maryland, College Park (17–18 February 1983): 97–100.

––––––. "Nikolai Grundtvig: Eduard Lindeman's Denmark Connection," in *Proceedings, Lifelong Learning Research Conference.* University of Maryland, College Park (21–22 February 1985): 56–60.

Straight, Michael. *After Long Silence.* New York: W. W. Norton and Co., 1983.

Stubblefield, Harold W. "The Aims of the American Adult Education Movement in the 1920's," in *Yearbook of Adult and Continuing Education 1980–81,* 6th ed. Chicago: Marquis Academic Media, Marquis Who's Who Inc., 1980.

––––––. "From Chautauqua to Adult Education: The Evolution of an Idea, 1874–1924," in *Proceedings of the Adult Research Conference.* DeKalb, Ill. (1–3 April 1981): 218–223.

––––––. "Emerging Paradigms and Forms of Adult Education: A Classification Scheme," in *Proceedings, Lifelong Learning Research Conference.* The University of Maryland, College Park (21–22 February 1985): 61–64.

Swanberg, W. A. *Whitney Father, Whitney Heiress.* New York: Charles Scribner's Sons, 1980.

"The Tar of the Ku Klux Klan." [unsigned article] *Survey* 48 (20 May 1922): 267–268.

Taylor, Thurston. "Improving Techniques in Adult Education." *Booklist* 30 (April 1934): 239–240.

Tead, Ordway. "About Eduard C. Lindeman," in *20th Anniversary Yearbook of Adult Education 1953.* New York: New York Adult Education Council, Inc., 1953: 55.

Thodberg, Christian, and Anders P. Thyssen, eds. *N.S.F. Grundtvig, Tradition and Renewal.* Copenhagen: *DET Danske Selskab*; Philadelphia: Nordic Books Distributor, 1983.

Thoreau, Henry David. *Walden.* New York: Dodd, Mead and Co., 1946.

Toffler, Alvin. *Future Shock.* New York: Bantam Books, 1971.

––––––. *The Third Wave.* New York: Bantam Books, 1980.

Tough, Allen. *The Adult's Learning Projects.* Toronto: The Ontario Institute for Studies in Education, 1979.

Wells, Evelyn. *A Treasury of Names.* New York: Essential Books, Duell, Sloan, and Pearce, 1946.

The Wolverine (AHC/MSU).

Yeaxlee, Basil A. *Lifelong Education.* London: Cassell and Co., Ltd., 1929.

––––––. Reviews of *Why Stop Learning?* by Dorothy Canfield Fisher and *Inside Experience,* by Joseph K. Hart. *The Journal of Adult Education* 2 (April 1928): 199–203.

––––––. *Spiritual Values in Adult Education,* 2 vols. London: Oxford University Press, 1925.

Young, Michael. *The Elmhirsts of Dartington.* London: Rutledge and Kegan Paul,1982.

UNPUBLISHED REFERENCES

Scrapbooks

For almost all of his adult life, Eduard Lindeman kept scrapbooks, which are now held in the archives at Columbia University and the University of Minnesota.

The "Eduard C. Lindeman Papers" at Columbia University's Rare Book and

Manuscript Library include Lindeman scrapbooks bearing the following labels: "No. 1;" "1934–35, 1932–33, 1932–35;" "1935" [apparently also includes some materials from 1947]; "1939;" "1944 and Very Early 1945;" "1946;" "1946–Autumn—1947 Winter;" "1947–1948;" "May 27, 1948–October 29, 1948;" "November 1948–June 1949;" "June 1949–December 1949;" "June 1951–October 1951;" "October 1951–March 1953;" "March 1950–January 1953."

The "Eduard Christian Lindeman Papers" deposited at the Social Welfare History Archives Center of the University of Minnesota include sixteen scrapbooks with these labels: "1922–1927;" "1932–1933;" "No. 4—1934;" "No. 4, 1934–1934;" "No. 5, 1934 and 1935;" "No. 6, 1935;" "No. 7, 1936–1937;" "No. 8, 1936;" "No. 9, 1936;" "No. 10, 1937;" "No. 11, 1937;" "1933–1939;" "1936–1940;" "No. 12, 1940;" "No. 13, 1941;" No. 14, 1941–1942;" No. 15, 1944–1945;" "No. 16, 1945." Some of these scrapbooks are photocopies of originals held by Columbia University.

Letters

The "Eduard C. Lindeman Papers" at Columbia University, Rare Book and Manuscript Library, contain some of Lindeman's correspondence with the following persons: John Dewey, Aubrey Williams, Candace Stone, Leonard Elmhirst, Dorothy Straight Elmhirst, Anna Bogue, Wyatt Rawson, A. N. Gorton, John Wales, Mary Parker Follett, Isobel L. Briggs, Max Otto, Harriet McGraw, Kathleen Hendrie, Herbert Croly, and Harry Hopkins.

The "Betty Leonard Collection" at the Social Welfare History Archives Center includes certain of Lindeman's correspondence with Dorothy and Leonard Elmhirst, Marion Beers, Anna Bogue, John Dewey, Lewis Mumford, Max Otto, and Charles Shaw. (Some of these letters are photocopies of letters held in other repositories.) Letters sent to Lindeman at the time of the New York Adult Education Council's "Twentieth Anniversary Testimonial Dinner" are also in this archive in the "Eduard Christian Lindeman Collection."

The "Max Otto Papers" at the Wisconsin State Historical Society include some of Otto's correspondence with Eduard Lindeman and John Dewey.

The "Dorothy Whitney Straight Elmhirst Papers" at Cornell University include some of Dorothy Straight Elmhirst's correspondence with Leonard Elmhirst (before their marriage) and with Ruth Morgan.

In the archives of the Dartington Hall Trust is some of Dorothy Elmhirst's correspondence with Herbert Croly, Eduard and Hazel Lindeman and members of the Lindeman family, and Anna Bogue. Some of Leonard Elmhirst's correspondence with Eduard Lindeman and others is also maintained.

Certain of Eduard Lindeman's correspondence with John Hader is in the possession of John Hader, Silver Spring, Maryland.

The author retains his correspondence with persons who knew Lindeman, including those responding to his queries in the "Book Section" of the *New York Times* and the *Alumni Newsletter* of the Columbia University School of Social Work.

Interviews

Taped interviews done by the author with the following persons are in possession of the author: John and Mathilda Hader, Michael Straight, Bonaro Overstreet, Malcolm and Hulda Knowles, Stephen Gessner, Herbert Hunsaker, and Eleanor Von Erffa. Also possessed by the author are notes of his conversations with Fran Garlieb and the tape of Miriam Stewart's interview with Martha Anderson.

A taped interview with Wilbur Hallenbeck by Alexander Charters is in the Audio Collection at Syracuse University.

The "Betty Leonard Collection" at the Social Welfare History Archives Center,

University of Minnesota, includes transcripts of taped interviews done by Betty Leonard with the following individuals who knew Eduard Lindeman: Flora Thurston Allen, Lucille Astin, Roger Baldwin, Bradley Buell, Nathan Cohen, Alice Collins, Clara Kaizer, Frank Karelson, Philip Klein, Fern Lowrey, Leonard Mayo, Laura Pratt, Susan Pettis, and Hester Turner.

Unpublished Manuscripts and Papers

The following unpublished materials are those having particular significance in development of this volume. References to very short or less significant materials are stated in complete form at the point of reference in "Notes."

Cohen, Nathan E. "The Meaning of the Teachings and Philosophy of Eduard C. Lindeman for Social Work in the Present Scene." Paper read at National Conference of Social Work, Cleveland. 25 May 1953 (EC/RBML/CU).

Cross, K. Patricia. "Responding To Learning Needs in the 1980's." Paper presented to the National Council of Instructional Administrators, San Francisco, Calif. 1 April 1980. (ERIC No. ED 187 419).

Knowles, Malcolm S. "A New Way of Thinking about Education," in *Creating Lifelong Learning Connections* (Manuscript for chapter in book-publication pending).

Lindeman, Eduard C. "Adult Education in Post War America." "Manuscripts, etc. 1946–1948," Box 10 (ECL/RBML/CU).

———. Speech to City Club of Portland, Oregon, June 1952. (Two separate talks to same group) (ECL/RBML/CU).

———. "Community Organization for Leisure." "Undated A–C," Box 12 (EC/RBML/CU).

———. "Egoism, a Venture in Empirical Criticism." (circa 1925) (ECL/SWHA/UM).

———. "The Evolution of Inquiry Philosophy" (Exhibit IV). Inquiry Occasional Paper (New York Public Library).

———. Memo to Executive Committee, Michigan Council on Adult Education, 11 November 1947. "Manuscripts, etc., A–I," Box 12 (ECL/RBML/CU).

———. "How Shall Our Schools Educate To Eliminate the Menace of Extensive Social Upheavals?" "Manuscripts, etc. A–I," Box 12 (ECL/RBML/CU).

———. "The Need of Prepared Leaders in Adult Education." Speech at Pennsylvania State Association for Adult Education, 18–19 November [1937?] "E.C. Lindeman Articles, etc. 1937–1939," Box 6 (ECL/RBML/CU).

———. "Russian Trip," Box 4 (ECL/RBML/CU).

———. "What Is Adult Education?" "Russian Trip," Box 4 (ECL/RBML/CU) [probably misfiled].

———. "Why the American Labor." "Manuscripts A–I," Box 12 (ECL/RBML/CU).

Patterson, James K. Commencement Address, Michigan Agricultural College, June 1911 (Special Collections and Archives, University of Kentucky Libraries). "Tributes 1953" (ECL/RBML/CU).

Wrege, Charles D., and Sakae Hata. "Before Bales: Pioneer Studies in Analyzing Group Behavior: 1921–1930." Submitted to Management History Division of the Academy of Management for the 1984 Meeting in Boston.

INDEX

Page references followed by the letter "n" refer to footnotes. Page references followed by the letter "p" refer to photographs.

DATE DUE